4 application & tutorial

Advanced
WordPerfect
5.1

Jean Gonzalez & Ric Williams

D1710684

Mitchell McGRAW-HILL
New York St. Louis San Francisco Auckland Bogotá Caracas
Hamburg Lisbon London Madrid Mexico Milan Montreal
New Delhi Oklahoma City Paris San Juan São Paulo Singapore
Sydney Tokyo Toronto Watsonville

Mitchell **McGraw-Hill**
55 Penny Lane
Watsonville, CA 95076

Advanced WordPerfect 5.1

1 2 3 4 5 6 7 8 9 0 SEM SEM 9 0 9 8 7 6 5 4 3 2 1

P/N 046243-7

ORDER INFORMATION:
ISBN 0-07-909585-2   Text with 5¼-inch data disk
ISBN 0-07-909586-0   Text with 3½-inch data disk

Sponsoring editor: James Hill
Production manager: Betty Drury
Series concept and creation: Susan Nelle, BMR
Production services by BMR, Mill Valley, CA
    Copy edit by Linda Purrington
    Cover and text design by Paul Quin
    Desktop production by Curtis Philips
    Development management by Christine Hunsicker
    Project management by Geri McCauley
Printer: Semline, Inc.

Library of Congress Catalog Card No. 90-083391

Contents

CHAPTER 4

CHAPTER 7

Speech Outline

CHAPTER **8**

Preface

Beginning WordPerfect 5.1 addresses the need for a text/tutorial that can help students combine basic word processing skills with practical business applications. The methodology, design, and applications have been developed from our combined teaching and real-world experiences.

This WordPerfect 5.1 text/tutorial provides specific, step-by-step instructions for using WordPerfect 5.1 to create letters, memos, and reports similar to those that are created in business. We designed these documents to enhance your student's abilty to work with common business styles, understand word processing concepts, and use the beginning features of WordPerfect 5.1 to its full advantage.

Organization of the Text

WordPerfect 5.1 is a powerful word processing program with many features such as footnotes, macros, headers, spelling checker, thesaurus, automatic references, tables, search and replace, and mail merge. To blend these features into a single, basic course, *Beginning WordPerfect 5.1* presents ten chapters with ten business applications around which the tutorial is written. Each chapter introduces a complete business document and provides a tutorial that steps the student through the entire creation of the business document. Each chapter builds upon the preceding one, so that all of the commands and concepts are presented in a spiral approach.

To give the business documents a sense of purpose and continuity, we have developed a fictional business: **The Exhibit Place**, a company that coordinates exhibits and trade shows and develops marketing literature and programs for other companies. All of the applications and documents in this book reflect the correspondence, reports, memos, press releases, resumes, invoices, and articles to and from the employees of The Exhibit Place.

Chapter Organization

Each chapter contains numerous learning tools to enhance a students' ability to become a proficient user of the software. Ease of use and learning were our number one concerns as we designed and wrote these text/tutorials. To help the novice users, we created a format that would help instructors and students alike. Each book in the series has a distinctive chapter organization containing numerous learning tools and features.

Learning Tools and Features

A full document print-out that the student will create begins each chapter. We found that learning and comprehension is increased when the student can actually see what they will be creating.

Chapter Objectives list what the student will master at the completion of each chapter.

WordPerfect 5.1 commands list the specific commands that will be taught and used to create the application.

Overview of the concepts and commands in the tutorials are presented in a descriptive/narrative fashion to prepare the student for the full tutorial.

Tutorial with a Student Data Disk leads the student in numbered, step-by-step interactive fashion to create the document shown on the opening section of each chapter. Each tutorial is organized around six important steps required for creating a document:

1. *Setting up.* These instructions help students start WordPerfect and ensure that they have the lesson files they need to complete the tutorial.

2. *Formattting.* These instructions provide all the special formatting requirements for the document, such as margin settings, spacing instructions, and tab stops.

3. *Keyboarding.* These instructions list all the commands and keystrokes that students need in order to enter the text.

4. *Saving.* These instructions detail the steps for saving the document and stress proper methods for saving and naming documents so that they can be quickly found again.

5. *Printing.* These instructions provide printing details. Students will print every document they create, just as they would in real-world business situations.

6. *Exiting.* These instructions help students clear the screen to start another document or leave WordPerfect entirely.

Summary presents a review of all of the commands introduced in the tutorial.

Key Terms list the important words and commands in the chapter.

Review Questions tap the conceptual information and instructions about the software.

Applications for drill and practice reinforcement are the heart of this text series. Each chapter has four to six complete applications for the student to create, edit and or modify. Many of these applications are partially done on the Student Data Disk that accompanies each text.

Advanced Skills is an optional section at the end of each chapter that provides more challenge for students who are interested in greater mastery of the software. Advanced Skills carries its own set of Key Terms, Review questions, and Applications.

On Your Own, a composing-at-the-keyboard activity, gives the student an opportunity to respond in writing to a case situation related to The Exhibit Place.

By focusing on the Overview and Tutorial, beginning students can become competent using WordPerfect; for those somewhat familiar with word processing concepts, studying the Advanced Skills will help them master the program quickly.

Requirements

This book is designed to teach WordPerfect 5.1 on an IBM PC, XT, AT, PS/2 or compatible computer with a minimum of 512K memory. To make the applications appear exactly as shown in this book, students need access to a Hewlett-Packard LaserJet Series II printer. If students have access to a different printer, you can still successfully use this book—simply inform students that their documents will appear slightly, but not substantially, different from the ones shown in the book.

Instructor's Guide

To help your WordPerfect 5.1 class succeed, we provide an Instructor's Guide that contains suggestions for software installation, lecture outlines, additional applications, answers to chapter review questions, and a testbank.

Businesses rely so heavily on word processing systems to get the job done that people who understand how to use them are valuable in today's work world. To help students create career opportunities for themselves, we designed this book to simulate the actual work environment as much as possible, and we have provided competency-based tests to measure students' proficiency.

Complete Curriculum

Beginning WordPerfect 5.1 is designed as part of a comprehensive curriculum for using word processing in business:

> *Keyboarding with WordPerfect 5.1* focuses on keyboarding skills and elementary WordPerfect 5.1 commands.

- *Beginning WordPerfect 5.1* presents basic WordPerfect 5.1 commands and applications.
- *Advanced WordPerfect 5.1* covers commands and skills for completing complex business documents.
- *Desktop Publishing with WordPerfect 5.1* focuses on desktop publishing commands, skills, and applications.

Using these text/tutorials, you will have a complete curriculum from keyboarding to calculating invoices and designing attractive page layouts.

Acknowledgements

We are indebted to a large number of business people and teaching colleagues who assisted us in developing the content and format for this series. We especially appreciate the help received from reviewers Barbara Howard, Northern Virginia Community College; Lorraine Laby, Santa Rosa Junior College; Nelda Shelton, Tarrant County Junior College; Becky Briggs, Bunker Hill Community College; Gloria McKinnon, Butte College; Connie Pechak, software writer and trainer; Mick Winter, computer consultant; Harry Hoffman, Miami-Dade Community College; Mary Auvil, Ohlone College; Nora Wilson, Cabrillo College; Aileen Fugita, Cabrillo College; and Yoshiko Izumi; and from the students who classroom-tested drafts of this manuscript, and from the editors who did countless accuracy checks. We are also indebted to the editors and project managers at BMR: Susan Nelle, series concept development; Christine Hunsicker, Project Editor; Matthew Lusher, and Melanie Field, who worked tirelessly to review and develop the concept for this series.

J. G.

R. W.

SENSES SELL THE PRODUCT!

All good exhibits stimulate more than one sense at once. When working together, sight, sound, touch, smell, and taste are the best sales tools we have.

Sight

Simply because a product is small does not mean that it will "disappear" in an exhibit. You can focus attention upon small objects by placing them in enclosed spaces. For example, the Metropol displays its superb collection of gems and jewels in a large exhibition hall by placing them in a succession of sparkling and velvet-lined walk-through jewel boxes.

Lighting also plays an important part in highlighting small objects. Different light produces different effects:

1. **Fluorescent lighting** is suitable for many exhibits. It is soft, nearly shadowless light with a minimum of heat.
2. **Incandescent light** emphasizes an object. For example, you might want to use incandescent light to spotlight electronic circuits that have been placed against a velvety black background.
3. **Natural Light** can also be effective. View the product first in natural light to determine if natural lighting is sufficient.

Sound

Sound and light can set the stage for any presentation. Department stores use sound and light to influence customers. Organ music and/or special lighting may be used to create a mood to stimulate the sale of religious products. Carnival music and flashing lights can do the same for the sale of computer games.

Touch

Don't forget touch when planning an exhibit. Engineers and technicians love to touch equipment and examine parts minutely. Plan your exhibits using items that people can touch. How about a dial that they can turn or a magnifying glass through which they can look? Let the customer feel the parts of a product.

Smell

Take advantage of the power of association through the sense of smell. A scent of pine in a logging exhibit draws attention to the product. Identify the smell of an industry or product and use it. Who knows how many automobile owners are "sold" by the new car smell?

Taste

Can you develop a strategy to appeal to the taste buds? For example, a vendor selling a recipe database provided welcome stations dispensing free orange juice.

In this chapter you will create a document containing two "newspaper-style" columns of text.

1

Two Newspaper Columns

Chapter Objectives

After completing this chapter, you will be able to

1. Set "units of measurement" to "lines and columns."

2. Add a Document Summary to your file.

3. Create, scroll through, and edit two "newspaper" columns of text.

WordPerfect Commands

[Shift]-[F8], 3, 5	Create a Document Summary
[Alt]-[F7], 1, 3	Define a column
[Alt]-[F7], 1, 1	Turn columns on (toggle switch)
[Alt]-[F7], 1, 2	Turn columns off (toggle switch)
[Ctrl]-[Home]-[→]	Move cursor one column to the right
[Ctrl]-[Home]-[←]	Move cursor one column to the left
[Ctrl]-[Enter]	Create a new column
[Shift]-[F1], 3, 8	Set measurement units
[F5], [Enter], 5, 2	Show long display

Overview

WordPerfect can print more than one column of text on a page so that it looks like a newspaper page—the text "snakes" from the bottom of one column to the top of the next. When a page is filled, the text can flow onto following pages.

You create columns by using the Column key (Alt-F7) and following four basic steps: (1) define columns, (2) turn them on, (3) enter text, and (4) turn them off.

1. *Defining Columns.* To define columns, you use the Columns Definition screen shown in Figure 1.1. At this screen, you tell WordPerfect the number of columns you want and the number of spaces that should separate them. Based on your definition, WordPerfect calculates the left and right margins of each column and inserts a [Col Def] code into your document. WordPerfect's defaults are to place five spaces between each column and make each column the same size.

Just as when using any other formatting command, you should define your columns at the beginning of the document before you enter text. It is not necessary, though, to begin creating columns immediately after you define them. You can type titles or anything you like and the text will format regularly on the page. When you are ready to type text in column form, you then turn columns on.

2. *Turning columns on.* Use the Column On/Off option from the Columns key (Alt-F7) to turn your column on. Once columns are turned on, a column indicator appears on the status line to let you know which column the cursor is in. For example, if the cursor is in column 1, the status line will look something like the following:

    Col 1 Doc 1 Pg 1 Ln 1 Pos 10

    You can now enter your text as you normally would.

3. *Entering text.* When you type text in columns, your text will be formatted automatically to fit the left and right margins of the column. When the cursor reaches the bottom of the page, it jumps up to the next column at the top of the same page. When you finish entering text in columns, you must turn columns off.

4. *Turning Columns Off.* Note that Column On/Off is a toggle key. When you turned columns on, WordPerfect inserted a [Col On] code into your document. Once you have finished entering text, you use the Column On/Off option to turn columns off and WordPerfect

```
Text Column Definition

   1 - Type                                    Newspaper

   2 - Number of Columns                       2

   3 - Distance Between Columns

   4 - Margins

   Column    Left      Right      Column    Left      Right
     1:      1"        4"           13:
     2:      4.5"      7.5"         14:
     3:                             15:
     4:                             16:
     5:                             17:
     6:                             18:
     7:                             19:
     8:                             20:
     9:                             21:
    10:                             22:
    11:                             23:
    12:                             24:

Selection: 0
```

FIGURE I.1

The defaults on the Column Definition screen are automatically set for two newspaper style columns. If you change the number of columns that you want, WordPerfect calculates the new margins for you automatically. Your Column Definition screen may differ from the one shown here.

inserts a [Col Off] code at the end of the column. From this point, anything you type will be formatted within the original margins, not in columns.

How the Column Feature Works

When you start inserting or deleting text in columns, it is important that you understand how the column function works. In WordPerfect, each column is an independent page. As shown in Figure 1.2, when you reach the bottom of a column, WordPerfect inserts a Soft Page code [SPg] and moves the cursor to the next column. If you want the cursor to jump to the top of a new column before the cursor has reached the bottom of the page, you can press the Hard Page key ([Ctrl]-[Enter]) to insert a [HPg] code and create a new column.

FIGURE I.2

WordPerfect puts a soft return at the end of a column as you enter text and need to start a new column. If you press Hard Page [HPg], WordPerfect starts a new column.

Moving the Cursor

If you remember that WordPerfect considers each column a separate page, you will have little trouble moving the cursor. When you hold down the right or down arrow keys in a column, the cursor will move to the bottom of the first column and then jump up to the top of the next—just as though it were moving between pages of text.

If you want to move the cursor quickly into another column, you can jump horizontally between columns by using the Go To key ([Ctrl]-[Home]). When you press [Ctrl]-[Home], the following prompt appears in the lower left corner of the screen:

Go To

If you press the right arrow, the cursor moves to the next column on the right. If you press the left arrow, the cursor moves to the column on the left. For example, if the cursor is in column 1 and you want to move it to column 2, press [Ctrl]-[Home], [→].

A word of caution about moving the cursor between existing columns: Once your columns are filled with text, *do not use the Hard Page key ([Ctrl]-[Enter]) to move the cursor between columns.* As you recall, each time you press Hard Page, you create a new column. If you press Hard Page, you will add a new column and disrupt the column(s) that follow.

If you accidentally press Hard Page while editing your columns, the text following your cursor will jump into the next column. But don't worry—you can correct it by deleting the Hard Page [HPg] command that you just entered by using the [Del] key in Reveal Codes.

Using Reveal Codes to Edit Columns

Reveal Codes ([Alt]-[F3]) functions the same way with columns as it does in normal edit mode with one difference. Because WordPerfect considers each column to be a page, each column appears directly beneath the previous one in Reveal Codes. For example, Figure 1.3 shows how two columns appear as one long column in Reveal Codes. Note that while the word *exhibition* appears in the single column in the lower part of the screen, it appears at the beginning of the second column in the top part. Do you see the Hard Page code [HPg] just before *exhibition?* The Hard Page code starts the new column.

If you accidentally create a new column by pressing Hard Page, turn on Reveal Codes and delete [HPg]—the columns will quickly reformat themselves to the way they should be.

Inserting and Deleting Text

You insert and delete text in columns in the same way that you do in a regular edit screen—WordPerfect reformats the columns after each

```
All good exhibits stimulate                    exhibition hall by placi
more than one sense at once.                   in a succession of spark
When working together, sight,                  and velvet-lined walk-th
sound, touch, smell, and taste                 jewel boxes.
are the best sales tools we
have.                                          Lighting also plays an
                                               important in highlightin
Sight                                          objects.   Different ligh
Simply because a product is                    produces different effec
small does not mean that it                    Three basic kinds of lig
will "disappear" in an exhibit.                exist:
C:\WP50\WPBOOK\III\III-1                 Col 2 Doc 2 Pg 1 Ln 5 Pos 45
   {                               }       {
its superb collection of gems[SRt]
and jewels in a large[HPg]
Exhibition hall by placing them[SRt]
in a succession of sparkling[SRt]
and velvet[-]lined walk[-]through[SRt]
jewel boxes.   [HRt]
[HRt]
Lighting also plays an[SRt]
important in highlighting small[SRt]
objects.   Different light[SRt]

Press Reveal Codes to restore screen
```

FIGURE 1.3

Two on-screen columns appear as one long column in Reveal Codes. Each column is separated by a Hard Page code [HPg].

change that you make. You should be careful, though, not to move or delete a [HPg] code.

As you work with WordPerfect, you will be creating documents with more and more sophisticated formatting codes such as column definitions, margin changes, and so on. You can spend a lot of time studying how you created the document when you come back to it at a later time to make changes. To help you work with your growing number of documents, WordPerfect provides the Document Summary and Long Display options described in the next section.

Document Summary

As you probably are aware, it is difficult to squeeze into the eight characters of a DOS filename all the detail that you need to tell you what is in a file. The more documents you create with WordPerfect, the more of a challenge it is to keep track of each one.

To help you organize your files, WordPerfect provides the *Document Summary.* In the Document Summary, you can write a longer name for a file, including its author, typist, subject, creation date, and special information about the document, such as the account it may refer to or an abstract providing a synopsis of the document. This information is not printed with the document but appears whenever you use either the Look or Long Display options in the List Files menu.

Using the Look Option to see the Summary

After choosing the Look option, the Document Summary appears at the top of the document as shown in Figure 1.4.

You create a Document Summary by using the Document option in the Format menu (Shift - F8). We recommend that you include a Document Summary with each file you create, especially if you use a hard disk.

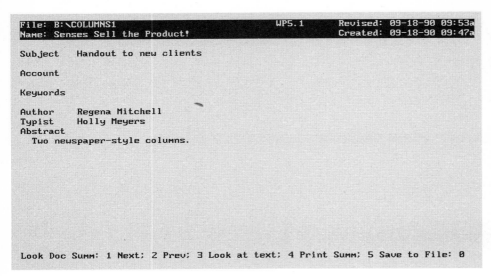

```
File: B:\COLUMNS1                          WP5.1        Revised: 09-18-90 09:53a
Name: Senses Sell the Product!                          Created: 09-18-90 09:47a

Subject    Handout to new clients

Account

Keywords

Author     Regena Mitchell
Typist     Holly Meyers
Abstract
   Two newspaper-style columns.




Look Doc Summ: 1 Next; 2 Prev; 3 Look at text; 4 Print Summ; 5 Save to File: 0
```

FIGURE 1.4

The Document Summary appears when you use the Look option in List Files. The summary shows you the date the file was made, as well as its name, purpose, who created it, and other information.

When used with the Long Display option, the Document Summary enables you to keep track of your files more easily.

Using Long Display to See the Document Name

To help you identify what is in a file, the Long Display option in List Files shows the long (30 characters) document name next to the DOS file name. For example, if you create a letter called MASTER4.DOC, you can identify it by entering a document name, such as "Mr. Master's Final Invoice," in the Summary. The Long Display option in List Files will then show the file as follows:

Mr. Master's Final Invoice MASTER4.DOC 7,456 1-10-91

WordPerfect provides another useful tool for working with documents; it can measure the position of the cursor on your page in two different ways, as discussed in the next section.

Measuring Cursor Position with Rows and Columns

As you may recall, when you start WordPerfect, the edit screen is blank except for a line of information in the lower right corner called the *status line*. The status line is WordPerfect's way of telling you where the *cursor* (the small blinking dash) is on the page. The cursor marks the position where the next character you type will appear. When you first start working on a document, the cursor is 6 lines or 1 inch from the top of the paper (Ln), and 10 spaces or 1 inch from the left edge of the page (Pos). (Pos tells you the position of the cursor on a line).

You can set WordPerfect to measure the position of the cursor on your page in two different ways:

1. With rows and columns (similar to the spaces and lines on a typewriter).

2. With inches.

In this book, we recommend that you position the cursor by measuring the number of lines down from the top of the page and the number of spaces across a line. You can set the way WordPerfect measures cursor position using the *Setup command* ([Shift]-[F1]).

Tutorial

Your supervisor, Regena Mitchell, wants to send the handout "Senses Sell Your Product!" to each new client. To help it stand out and provide it a newsworthy feel, you decide to create the document in two newspaper-style columns.

To make it appear more like a newspaper, you will justify the text in each column. You will call the document COLUMNS1.

Setting Up

To begin creating the two-column article, follow these steps:

1. Place the Student Data disk in drive B.

NOTE: If you do not have a drive B, place it in drive A and use A instead of B when naming or retrieving files. You will use this disk to store the file you create in this tutorial.

2. Start WordPerfect.

NOTE: If you do not know how to start WordPerfect and have a hard disk (a C drive) in your computer, see Appendix B for instructions. If your system contains floppy drives (A and B) and no hard disk, refer to Appendix A for instructions.

Setting Cursor Measurement

Look at the status line in the right-hand corner of the screen. If the line indicator (Ln) and position indicator (Pos) show 1", you need to change the way WordPerfect measures cursor position by following the steps below. Even if your system is set to measure cursor position in rows and columns, we suggest that you follow the steps below for practice.

To set WordPerfect's measurement default to rows and columns, follow these steps:

Set Rows and Columns
[Shift]-[F1], *3, 8*

1. Press the Setup command ([Shift]-[F1]).

RESULT: As shown in Figure 1.5, the Setup menu appears.

2. Type **3** to select the Environment option.

RESULT: The Environment menu appears.

3. Type **8** to select Units of Measurement.

```
Setup

    1 - Mouse

    2 - Display

    3 - Environment

    4 - Initial Settings

    5 - Keyboard Layout

    6 - Location of Files




Selection: 0
```

FIGURE 1.5
The Setup menu.

RESULT: As shown in Figure 1.6, the Units of Measure menu appears.

4. Type **1** to select the Display and Entry of Numbers option.
    RESULT: The cursor moves to the Display and Entry of Numbers selection area.

5. Type **u** to select Lines/Columns.
    RESULT: u appears in the selection area for option 1 and the cursor returns to the bottom of the screen.

6. Type **2** to select Status Line Display.
    RESULT: The cursor moves to the Status Line Display selection area.

7. Type **u** to select Lines/Columns.

```
Setup: Units of Measure

    1 - Display and Entry of Numbers            "
          for Margins, Tabs, etc.

    2 - Status Line Display                     "


Legend:

    " = inches
    i = inches
    c = centimeters
    p = points
    w = 1200ths of an inch
    u = WordPerfect 4.2 Units (Lines/Columns)






Selection: 0
```

FIGURE 1.6
*The Units of
Measure menu.*

```
Format: Document

    1 - Display Pitch - Automatic Yes
                        Width     1

    2 - Initial Codes

    3 - Initial Base Font          Courier 10cpi

    4 - Redline Method             Printer Dependent

    5 - Summary




 Selection: 0
```

FIGURE 1.7

The Document screen allows you to create a document summary for a file.

RESULT: u appears in the selection area for option 2, and the cursor returns to the bottom of the screen.

8. Press the Exit key (F7) once to return to the edit screen. WordPerfect is now set to show the cursor position in terms of rows (lines) and columns on the page (Ln1, Pos10).

Create a Document Summary
Shift - F8 , *3, 5*

You then decide that you want to create a Document for the new file you will create, COLUMNS1.

1. Press Format (Shift - F8).

2. Type **3** to select the Document option.
   RESULT: The Document menu appears on the screen as shown in Figure 1.7.

3. Type **5** to select the Summary option.
   RESULT: As shown in Figure 1.8, the Summary screen appears.

4. Type **2** to select Document Name and Type.
   RESULT: Note that the cursor jumps to the column next to Document Name.

5. Type **Senses Sell the Product!** and press Enter twice.
   NOTE: Entering the Document Type is optional.

6. Type **4** to select subject.

7. Type **Handout to new clients** and press Enter .

8. Type **3** to select the Author option.

9. Type **Regena Mitchell** and press Enter .
   RESULT: You are at the Typist option.

10. Type your name and press Enter .

```
Document Summary

          Revision Date

   1 - Creation Date   05-15-90 03:00p

   2 - Document Name
       Document Type

   3 - Author
       Typist

   4 - Subject

   5 - Account

   6 - Keywords

   7 - Abstract




Selection: 0                    (Retrieve to capture; Del to remove summary)
```

FIGURE 1.8

The Document Summary screen lets you enter information about the file, author, typist, subject, and any comments. WordPerfect enters the filename, if there is one, and the date for you.

11. Type 7 to select the Abstract option.

12. Type: **Two newspaper-style columns.**

13. Press Exit ([F7]) twice to return to the edit screen.
    NOTE: The Summary does not appear at the edit menu or when you print the document. It only appears when you use the Look option in List Files.

Looking at the Document Summary [F5], *6*

To see the Document Summary, follow these steps:

1. Save the document by pressing the Save key ([F10]) and typing **B:COLUMNS1** and pressing [Enter]

2. Press the List Files key ([F5]).

3. Type **B:** and press [Enter]
   RESULT: The files on the Student Data Disk appear on the screen.

4. Move the cursor bar to COLUMNS1.

5. Type **6** to select the Look option.
   RESULT: The subject, account, author, and other Document Summary information appear on the screen.

6. Press the Exit key ([F7]) twice to return to the edit menu.
   You can now format your document.

Formatting

To format two columns of newspaper-style text, follow these steps:

Define a Column [Alt]-[F7], *1, 3*

1. Press the Columns key ([Alt]-[F7]).
   RESULT: The following menu appears across the bottom of the screen:

   1 Columns; 2 Tables; 3 Math; 0

```
Text Column Definition

    1 - Type                              Newspaper

    2 - Number of Columns                 2

    3 - Distance Between Columns

    4 - Margins

    Column   Left     Right     Column   Left     Right
     1:       10       40        13:
     2:       45       75        14:
     3:                          15:
     4:                          16:
     5:                          17:
     6:                          18:
     7:                          19:
     8:                          20:
     9:                          21:
    10:                          22:
    11:                          23:
    12:                          24:

Selection: 0
```

FIGURE I.9
*The Column
Definition screen.*

2. Type **1** to select Columns.
   RESULT: The following prompt appears:

   Columns: 1 On; 2 Off; 3 Define; 0

3. Type **3** to choose the Define option.
   RESULT: The Column Definition screen shown in Figure 1.9 appears.

4. Press the Exit key ([F7]) twice to accept the default settings for the number of columns and the margin placement.

WordPerfect has now put a [Col Def] code at the beginning of your document. You are now ready to justify the text.

Justify Text
[Shift]-[F8], *1, 3, 4*

To line-justify the text, follow these steps:

1. Press the Format key ([Shift]-[F8]).
2. Type **1** to select the Line option.
3. Type **3** to select the Justification option.
4. Type **4** to select full justification.
5. Press Exit ([F7]) once to return to the edit screen.

Keyboarding

To create the two-column article, you first need to create the centered title.

Center Title
[Shift]-[F6]

1. Press the Center key ([Shift]-[F6]).
2. Type **SENSES SELL THE PRODUCT!** in boldface and press [Enter] three times.
   NOTE: Be sure to boldface the title by pressing the Bold key ([F6]) before you type the title and after you finish.

Turn Columns On
[Alt]-[F7], *1, 1*

You are now ready to turn columns on.

1. Press the Columns key ([Alt]-[F7]).
2. Type **1** to select Columns.
3. Type **1** to turn columns on.
   RESULT: Note that the status line now includes the Col 1 indicator to show you that the cursor is in the first column.

Enter Text

1. Type the following text, exactly as if you were in a normal edit screen. Press [Enter] three times before a heading and twice after it.
   NOTE: When entering the text, be sure to:
   a. Bold the heading by pressing the Bold key ([F6]) at the beginning and end of the heading.
   b. Bold the text as shown by pressing the Bold key ([F6]) at the beginning and end of the text to be bolded.
   c. Create the hanging indents on the paragraphs numbered 1, 2, and 3 by pressing the Indent key ([F4]). (*Hint:* Type the number of the paragraph, a period, press [F4], and then type the remainder of the paragraph.)

```
All good exhibits stimulate more than one sense at
once. When working together, sight, sound, touch,
smell, and taste are the best sales tools we have.


Sight

Simply because a product is small does not mean
that it will "disappear" in an exhibit. You can
focus attention upon small objects by placing them
in enclosed spaces. For example, the Metropol
displays its superb collection of gems and jewels
in a large exhibition hall by placing them in a
succession of sparkling and velvet-lined
walk-through jewel boxes.

Lighting also plays an important part in
highlighting small objects. Different light
produces different effects:

1.   Fluorescent lighting is suitable for many
     exhibits. It is soft, nearly shadowless light
     with a minimum of heat.

2.   Incandescent light emphasizes an object. For
     example, you might want to use incandescent
     light to spotlight electronic circuits that
     have been placed against a velvety black
     background.

3.   Natural light can also be effective. View the
     product first in natural light to determine if
     natural lighting is okay.
```

You are now ready to type the second column. Press ⌷Enter⌷ until your cursor is opposite the first line of column 1. As you do, note how the cursor wraps to the top of column 2 when you reach the end of column 1.

2. Save this file as B:COLUMNS1 using the Save key (⌷F10⌷).

3. Type the following text and then save again:

Sound

```
Sound and light can set the stage for any
presentation. Department stores use sound and light
to influence customers. Organ music and/or special
lighting may be used to create a mood to stimulate
the sale of religious products. Carnival music and
flashing lights can do the same for the sale of
computer games.
```

Touch

```
Don't forget touch when planning an exhibit.
Engineers and technicians love to touch equipment
and examine parts minutely. Plan your exhibits
using items that people can touch. How about a dial
that they can turn or a magnifying glass through
which they can look? Let the customer feel the
parts of a product.
```

Smell

```
Take advantage of the power of association through
the sense of smell. A scent of pine in a logging
exhibit draws attention to the product. Identify
the smell of an industry or product and use it. Who
knows how many automobile owners are "sold" by the
new car smell?
```

Taste

```
Can you develop a strategy to appeal to the taste
buds? For example, a vendor selling a recipe
database provided welcome stations dispensing free
orange juice.
```

STOP! HAVE YOU REMEMBERED TO SAVE YOUR FILE? IF NOT, SAVE IT AS B:COLUMNS1 USING THE SAVE KEY (⌷F10⌷).

Use Long Display
⌷F5⌷, ⌷Enter⌷, *5, 2*

Take a moment now to look at the file using the Long Display option in List Files.

1. Press the List Files key (⌷F5⌷).

2. Type **B:** and press ⌷Enter⌷.

3. Type **5** to select the Short/Long Display option.
    RESULT: The following prompt appears on the status line:

1 Short Display; 2 Long Display: 0

4. Type **2** to select Long Display and press Enter.
    RESULT: List Files displays the Long Display menu. Note the document name to the left of each DOS name.

5. Press the space bar once to return to the edit screen.
    Let's now take a look at how the document will look when you print it by using the View option.

View Columns
Shift -F7 , *6, 3, 1*

To view the document, follow these steps:

1. Press PgUp to move the cursor to the top of the document.

2. Press the Print key (Shift -F7).

3. Type **6** to view the document.

4. Type **3** to view the entire page.

5. Type **1** to view the document at normal size.

6. Press the Exit key (F7) to return to the edit screen.
    Let's now practice moving the cursor around this document.

Move Cursor to a New Column
Ctrl -Home , ← *or* → .

To move the cursor to the right-hand column, follow these steps:

1. Move the cursor to the first paragraph starting with "All good exhibits . . ."
    NOTE: The following words appear in the status line:

    Col 1

2. Press Ctrl -Home .
    RESULT: The following prompt appears on the screen:

    Go to

3. Press the right arrow (→).
    RESULT: The cursor jumps to column 2.

4. Press Ctrl -Home again and press the left arrow (←) to move the cursor back to column 1.

5. Press the up or down arrows (↑ or ↓) until the cursor is on the **S** of the bolded heading **Sight** in column 1.

Adding a Column with the Hard Page Code

A common mistake that people make when working with columns is to press Ctrl -Enter when they want the Hard Page to move the cursor to the next column—rather than move the cursor to a new column, they create an entirely new column! To correct this mistake, you need to delete the Hard Page code. Let's "accidentally" create a new column.

1. Press the up or down arrow (↑ or ↓) to move the cursor to the space after the phrase **jewels in a large** in the second paragraph.

```
All good exhibits stimulate        exhibition hall by placi
more than one sense at once.       in a succession of spark
When working together, sight,      and velvet-lined walk-th
sound, touch, smell, and taste     jewel boxes.
are the best sales tools we
have.                              Lighting also plays an
                                   important in highlightin
Sight                              objects.  Different ligh
Simply because a product is        produces different effec
small does not mean that it        Three basic kinds of lig
will "disappear" in an exhibit.    exist:
C:\WP50\WPBOOK\III\III-1             Col 2 Doc 2 Pg 1 Ln 5 Pos 45
{                                      }         {
its superb collection of gems[SRt]
and jewels in a large[HPg]
Exhibition hall by placing them[SRt]
in a succession of sparkling[SRt]
and velvet[-]lined walk[-]through[SRt]
jewel boxes.  [HRt]
[HRt]
Lighting also plays an[SRt]
important in highlighting small[SRt]
objects.  Different light[SRt]

Press Reveal Codes to restore screen
```

FIGURE 1.10
*Reveal Codes shows
the Hard Page code
[HPg] to delete.*

2. Press Ctrl - Enter .

   RESULT: You have just moved all the text below the cursor into the second column—you created a *new column.* The text in the original second column is now in the first column of page 2. To correct this problem, follow these steps.

Deleting [HPg]
Alt - F3 , Del

To delete the Hard Page [HPg] code, follow these steps:

1. Press the Reveal Codes key (Alt - F3).

   RESULT: The screen similar to the one in Figure 1.10 appears.

2. Move the cursor until it is on the [HPg] code that appears after the word *large.*

3. Press Del to delete the code.

   RESULT: The column automatically realigns, as it should.

4. Press the Reveal Codes key to turn it off.

Inserting Text

You now decide that you want to add a sentence to the end of the third paragraph.

1. Move to the period after the sentence that ends . . . different effects." Press Space twice.

2. Type **Three basic kinds of lighting exist:**

   NOTE: Note how the text in the second column moves as you insert text into the first column!

Deleting Text
Alt - F4 , Enter , Del , *Y*

You now decide that you want to delete the sentence you just inserted.

1. Place the cursor on the **T** at the beginning of the sentence that starts **Three basic kinds of. . . .**

2. Press the Block key ([Alt]-[F4]).

3. Press [Enter] to highlight the paragraph.

4. Press the [Del] key and type **Y** to delete the paragraph.

Spell-Check Columns
[Ctrl]-[F2], *3*

Before you save and print the file, you first want to spell-check the document. To spell-check COLUMNS1, follow these steps:

1. Press the Spell key ([Ctrl]-[F2]).
   RESULT: The following options appear on the screen:

   ```
   Check: 1 Word; 2 Page; 3 Document; 4 New Sup.
   Dictionary; 5 Look Up; 6 Count: 0
   ```

2. Type **3** to check the document's spelling.

3. Respond to any prompts that WordPerfect may provide to misspellings that you may have.
   When the spell check is completed, the following prompt appears at the bottom of the screen:

   ```
   Word count: Press any key to continue
   ```

4. Press any key and the edit screen appears.

Saving
[F10], [Enter], **Y**

Save the file again as B:COLUMNS1 by following these steps:

1. Press the Save key ([F10]).
   RESULT: The following prompt appears on the screen:

   ```
   Document to be saved: B:COLUMNS1
   ```

2. Press [Enter].
   RESULT: The following prompt appears on the screen:

   ```
   Replace B:COLUMNS1? No (Yes)
   ```

3. Type **Y** to replace the old version of B:COLUMNS1 with the new.

Printing
[Shift]-[F7], *1*

Print the document by following these steps:

1. Press the Print key ([Shift]-[F7]).

2. Type **1** to print the document.

Exiting
[F7], **Y, Y**

We have completed the tutorial on columns for now and are ready to leave WordPerfect. To do so, exit by following these steps:

1. Press the Exit key ([F7]).
   RESULT: The following prompt appears on the screen:

   ```
   Save document? Yes (No)
   ```

2. Type **Y** to save the changes you may have made since last saving the file.

NOTE: Even if you have not made any changes since last saving the file, it is a good idea to get in the habit of typing Y at this prompt—you can never be too cautious about saving documents.

RESULT: The following prompt appears on the status line:

`Document to be saved: B:\COLUMNS1`

3. Press [Enter].

RESULT: The following prompt appears on the screen.

`Replace B:\COLUMNS1? No (Yes)`

4. Type **Y** to save the changes you made to the file.

RESULT: The following prompt appears on the status line:

`Exit WP? No (Yes)`

5. Type **Y** if you want to leave WordPerfect. Type **N** if you want to continue working.

Summary

You defined a two-column document using the Column Definition option of the Column key ([Alt]-[F7]). You then turned the column on by using the Column On/Off option of the same key. When columns were turned on, a column number appeared in the status line and you entered the text in your columns. You moved the cursor between columns using the Go To option ([Ctrl]-[Home]) and pressing the right or left arrow keys. You deleted and added text as you would normally do in regular edit. You deleted an accidental Hard Page code by pressing Reveal Codes, moving the cursor to the [HPg] code, and deleting it.

When you finished working with columns, you turned them off using the Column On/Off option of the Column key.

You also created a Document Summary using the Document option under the Format option ([Shift]-[F8]).

Chapter Review

Key Terms

Column key
Columns Off
Columns On

Defining columns
Document Summary
Go To key

Review Questions

1. Briefly describe what happens when you are entering text in a two-column document and you continue entering text, even though the two columns are already full.

2. List and briefly describe the four steps required to create newspaper-style columns.

3. True or False: Once you define columns, you must immediately enter text in them. Explain your answer.

4. Briefly explain why columns shown in Reveal Codes appear as one long column on the screen. How can you tell where one column ends and the other starts in Reveal codes?

5. Describe a situation in a two-column document in which it is more convenient to use the Go To key to move the cursor than to use the arrow keys.

6. What code must you delete if you accidentally enter a Hard Page command in a document?

7. True or False: The Document Summary appears at the beginning of the document when you are in edit mode.

8. Briefly describe one advantage to using a Document Summary.

9. What commands do you need to use in order to see a Document Summary when searching for a file?

Applications

1. Create the two-column chart shown in Figure 1.11 by following these instructions:

   a. Use the column feature.

   b. Define two newspaper-style columns.

   c. Use the default tab settings.   DRILL 1-1.ADV

   d. Save the chart as B:DRILL1-1.

   e. Print the chart.

2. Create the document shown in Figure 1.12 by following these instructions:

   a. Enter the title in boldface.

   b. Use the double indent to enter the quotation below the title.

   c. Define two columns.   DRILL 1-2 .ADV

   d. Enter the text.

FIGURE I.II

EXHIBIT PLACE STAFF
UNITED WAY DONATIONS
Winter and Summer Quarter 19--

NAME	WINTER	SUMMER	NAME	WINTER	SUMMER
A Ackroyd	32.43	45.62	B Reiner	---	---
R Adams	23.65	19.43	A Remy	24.98	53.26
L Adent	19.22	25.00	B Reynolds	13.76	12.81
R Ardrey	11.231	4.56	R Ricardo	42.14	32.55
J Baldwin	---	---	C Robertson	---	---
A Basel	---	---	J Salinger	34.65	36.43
R Basel	12.32	35.69	J Schindler	21.43	56.32
J Birchman	56.83	12.43	L Seybold	43.54	43.21
R Blane	9.47	3.21	B Silver	34.21	---
D Bonet	---	---	N Silver	21.45	65.32
K Brown	56.89	62.43	P Smith	53.21	51.22
N Burns	23.78	98.22	P Staff	45.77	25.00
A Camus	25.85	56.93	M Stein	---	---
J Heverly	---	---	M Strongman	75.87	87.00
R Ho	76.89	59.92	K Tanaka	81.25	93.14
M Hull	76.82	87.89	L Walsky	12.07	9.14
L Hutton	34.25	67.37	M Washington	---	---
B Joad	32.45	35.00	W White	---	---
M Laursen	88.76	76.32	G Williams	43.56	76.42
S Lawler	23.43	25.26	D Wolf	2.83	---
D Lawton	---	---			
D Lestle	18.27	18.87			
M Lincoln	56.43	45.83			
I Malone	19.21	18.77			
I Marezzo	22.14	32.10			
P Martin	20.09	21.12			
D McIntosh	14.07	15.76			
R Merle	19.12	34.56			
Y Mishima	---	---			
R Mitchel	---	78.32			
E Murphey	18.98	19.04			
J Mutz	22.65	43.56			
E Nasus	88.76	74.21			
F Neckerbow	14.12	9.27			
L Nelle	32.45	56.72			
B Neuendorff	---	---			
J Oates	25.32	32.87			
S O'Conner	---	---			
R Olson	56.75	65.32			
M Perkins	54.23	45.32			
B Preston	---	---			
A Rand	---	---			

FIGURE I.I2

PRE-PROPOSAL
FOR
NEW WAVE TRADE SHOW EXHIBIT

Good design and interesting, attention-getting exhibits are more a matter of common sense, creativity, and ingenuity than of great amounts of money.

Ken Tanaka
President

WHY USE A PROFESSIONAL EXHIBIT CONTRACTOR?

Trade shows are vital to your company's marketing strategy. Trade shows provide a unique marketing tool to accelerate sales and save money. At a show, you can generate sales contacts less expensively than by making individual sales calls, and you can find many qualified sales prospects.

However, inexperience with trade shows can hurt a company's position. For example, many beginning participants demand a position close to the front door--only later to find out that they lost many potential visitors who rushed past to get into the main body of the show. At other times, beginning participants may decline to be in a show because it does not feature the kind of products they offer. However, it is a known fact that being the only exhibitor of a particular type of product can produce numerous sales leads.

Simply because you are involved in a trade show does not mean you are developing wise marketing strategies. Often, knowing best how to participate in trade shows is a profession of its own. Companies frequently waste money with mishandled exhibits that could be generating vital sales leads for them.

OUR SERVICES

The New Wave Trade Show is the largest microcomputer show in America--hosting 2,000 computer vendors from around the world. To prepare you for this show, we offer services that include market research, design development, and trade show consulting follow up. In our market research phase, our professional staff works with your public relations staff to find out your previous show experience. If possible, we like to meet with you several times before the event. We teach your staff about the show and the market it reaches. We provide you figures on the show published by the Trade Show Bureau and Trade Show Week.

e. Save the file as B:DRILL1-2.

f. Print the file.

3. Create the document shown in Figure 1.13 by following these instructions:

a. Define two columns.

b. Enter the title in boldface.

c. Boldface the title of each movie.

d. Put reviews for three movies in each column.

e. Enter the text.

f. Save the file as B:DRILL1-3.

g. Print the file.

FIGURE 1.13

MOVIE REVIEWS

Halloween XVIII. *
Watch fifteen teenagers discover the meaning of boredom as Michael, now aged eighty-two, chases them from a wheelchair.

It's a Wonderful Life. **
A man (James Stewart) facing ruin is sent help from a guardian angel. Has great warmth and humor. Get your Kleenexes.

Jules and Jim. **
A tantalizing woman challenges the art and friendship of two men. Lovely and lyrical.

Somewhere in Time. **
Is there a love so strong that you can travel back in time to discover it? With enough emotion, it seems, anything is possible. Charming.

Star Wars **
A dazzling science fiction film for all ages. Cheer the good guys (rebels) as they fight the wicked Empire.

War Games. **
Matthew Broderick saves the world from global holocaust, after nearly setting it off!

4. Create the chart shown in Figure 1.14 by following these instructions:

a. Define two columns.

b. Set the tabs so that there are three spaces after the abbreviations.

c. Use the default margins.

d. Create headings for each column.

e. Save the chart as B:DRILL1-4.

f. Print the chart.

FIGURE 1.14

STATES AND TERRITORIES
OF THE UNITED STATES

AB	STATE	AB	STATE
AL	Alabama	MO	Missouri
AK	Alaska	MT	Montana
AZ	Arizona	NE	Nebraska
AR	Arkansas	NV	Nevada
CA	California	NH	New Hampshire
CZ	Canal Zone	NJ	New Jersey
CO	Colorado	NM	New Mexico
CT	Connecticut	NY	New York
DE	Delaware	NC	North Carolina
DC	District of Columbia	ND	North Dakota
FL	Florida	OH	Ohio
GA	Georgia	OK	Oklahoma
GU	Guam	OR	Oregon
HI	Hawaii	PA	Pennsylvania
ID	Idaho	PR	Puerto Rico
IL	Illinois	RI	Rhode Island
IN	Indiana	SC	South Carolina
IA	Iowa	SD	South Dakota
KS	Kansas	TN	Tennessee
KY	Kentucky	TX	Texas
LA	Louisiana	UT	Utah
ME	Maine	VT	Vermont
MD	Maryland	VI	Virgin Islands
MA	Massachusetts	VA	Virginia
MI	Michigan	WA	Washington
MN	Minnesota	WV	West Virginia
MS	Mississippi	WI	Wisconsin
		WY	Wyoming

5. Create the memorandum shown in Figure 1.15 by following these instructions:

a. Define two columns.

b. Use the default margins.

c. Create headings for each column.

d. Save the chart as B:DRILL1-5.

e. Print the memorandum.

FIGURE 1.15

```
TO:       Michelle Strongman

FROM:     Holly Myers

DATE:     August 23, 19--

SUBJECT:  United Way Donations Compared to Previous Year

Below I have listed what employees in your department donated
compared with what they donated last year.

If you have any questions, be sure to let me know.
```

NAME	LAST	CURRENT	NAME	LAST	CURRENT
A. Ackroyd	32.43	45.62	A. Caron	12.56	12.43
R. Adams	23.65	19.43	H. Caulfield	19.22	54.32
L. Adent	19.22	25.00	K. Clark	0.00	0.00
R. Ardrey	11.23	14.56	D. Curtis	43.12	76.34
J. Baldwin	0.00	0.00	E. Dickerson	19.21	26.88
A. Basel	0.00	0.00	F. Ditterow	123.56	183.12
R. Basel	12.32	35.69	P. Dow	43.56	45.12
J. Birchman	56.83	12.43	R. Emilio	21.90	52.43
R. Blane	9.47	3.21	A. Florio	25.00	25.00
D. Bonet	0.00	0.00	L. Goldberg	31.14	42.87
K. Brown	56.89	62.43	A. Hamil	15.00	20.00
N. Burns	23.78	98.32	J. Heverly	0.00	0.00
A. Camus	112.32	45.67			

6. Create the memorandum shown in Figure 1.16 by following these instructions:

  a. Define two columns.

  b. Use the default margins.

  c. Create headings for each column.

  d. Save the chart as B:DRILL1-6.

  e. Print the memorandum.

FIGURE 1.16

```
TO:        Ken Tanaka

FROM:      Michelle Strongman

DATE:      August 23, 19--

SUBJECT:   New Wave Bookings to Date

Please examine the September booking statistics for exhibits at
the New Wave Trade Show. Note that the occupancy rate has
increased 12 percent since last month, but we are still below our
projections for September by 8 percent.
```

Aisle	Bookings	Rate		Aisle	Bookings	Rate
A1	36	36%		B1	67	67%
A2	32	43%		B2	01	01%
A3	51	51%		E2	21	26%
A4	59	59%		F1	43	39%
B1	67	67%		F2	12	15%
B2	01	01%		C1	64	84%
C1	64	84%		C2	63	32%
C2	63	32%		D1	42	25%
D1	42	25%		D2	31	31%
D2	31	31%		E1	33	20%
E1	33	20%		A1	36	36%
E2	21	26%		A2	32	43%
F1	43	39%		A3	51	51%
F2	12	15%		A4	59	59%
G1	29	34%		G1	29	34%
G2	12	11%		G2	12	11%

Advanced Skills

The Columns Definition screen shown in Figure 1.17 allows you to vary the format of your columns in several ways. You can change the amount of space between columns, the number of columns in a document, and the size of each column.

Changing the Number of Columns

The *Number of Columns* option lets you choose up to 24 columns in your document. When you choose a certain number of columns, WordPerfect assumes that you want all the columns to be the same size and then calculates their margins for you.

```
Text Column Definition

    1 - Type                              Newspaper

    2 - Number of Columns                 2

    3 - Distance Between Columns

    4 - Margins

    Column    Left      Right     Column    Left      Right
      1:      10        40          13:
      2:      45        75          14:
      3:                            15:
      4:                            16:
      5:                            17:
      6:                            18:
      7:                            19:
      8:                            20:
      9:                            21:
     10:                            22:
     11:                            23:
     12:                            24:

Selection: 0
```

FIGURE I.17
The Column Definition screen.

To move the cursor quickly to the first or last column in a document, you can press Ctrl-Home, Home followed by → or ←. If the cursor is in column 4, for example, you can press Ctrl-Home, Home, ← to move it into column 1.

Changing the Space Between Columns

WordPerfect's default is to put five spaces between each column. You can increase or decrease the number of these spaces by using the *Distance Between Columns* option in the Column Definition screen.

Changing the Size of Columns

If you do not want your columns to be all the same size, you can manually change their size by typing new margins in the *Margins* option of the Column Definition screen.

For example, the margins for the two columns in the preceding tutorial are set as follows:

Column	Left	Right
1:	10 (1")	40 (4")
2:	45 (4.5")	75 (7.5")

Each column is 30 spaces across. If you want the first column to be only 10 (1") spaces across and the second 50 (5") spaces across, you would set the margins as follows:

Column	Left	Right
1:	10 (1")	20 (2")
2:	25 (2.5")	75 (7.5")

By modifying the space between columns and their size, you can use WordPerfect to create many striking documents.

Advanced Key Terms	Columns Margin option Distance Between Columns option	Number of Columns option

Advanced Review Questions

1. You can have up to _____ columns in a document.
2. True or False: If you have more than two columns in a document, you need to calculate the margins manually.
3. List the keystrokes required to move the cursor to the far right column in a document containing five newspaper style columns.
4. WordPerfect automatically puts _____ spaces between columns.
5. True or False: To create columns of different widths, you must enter the margin settings for each column by hand.

Advanced Applications

1. Create the chart shown in Figure 1.18 by following these instructions:

   a. Define three columns.

   b. Use the default margins.

   c. Put two movies in each column.

   d. Separate each column by three spaces.

   e. Save the document as B:DRILL1-7.

   f. Print the document.

FIGURE 1.18

Halloween XVIII. *
Watch fifteen teenagers discover the meaning of boredom as Michael, now aged eighty-two, chases them from a wheelchair.

It's a Wonderful Life. ****
A man (James Stewart) facing ruin is sent help from a guardian angel. Has great warmth and humor. Get your Kleenexes.

Jules and Jim. ****
A tantalizing woman challenges the art and friendship of two men. Lovely and lyrical.

Somewhere in Time. **
Is there a love so strong that you can travel back in time to discover it? With enough emotion, it seems, anything is possible. Charming.

Star Wars ****
A dazzling science fiction film for all ages. Cheer the good guys (rebels) as they fight the wicked Empire.

War Games. ***
Matthew Broderick saves the world from global holocaust, after nearly setting it off!

2. Create the chart shown in Figure 1.19 by following these instructions:

   a. Define three columns.

   b. Set the tabs so that there are three spaces after the abbreviations.

   c. Use the default margins.

   d. Create headings for each column.

   e. Separate each column by three spaces.

   f. Save the document as B:DRILL1-8.

   g. Print the document.

FIGURE 1.19

AB	STATE	AB	STATE	AB	STATE
AL	Alabama	KS	Kansas	OH	Ohio
AK	Alaska	KY	Kentucky	OK	Oklahoma
AZ	Arizona	LA	Louisiana	OR	Oregon
AR	Arkansas	ME	Maine	PA	Pennsylvania
CA	California	MD	Maryland	PR	Puerto Rico
CZ	Canal Zone	MA	Massachusetts	RI	Rhode Island
CO	Colorado	MI	Michigan	SC	South Carolina
CT	Connecticut	MN	Minnesota	SD	South Dakota
DE	Delaware	MS	Mississippi	TN	Tennessee
DC	District of	MO	Missouri	TX	Texas
	Columbia	MT	Montana	UT	Utah
FL	Florida	NE	Nebraska	VT	Vermont
GA	Georgia	NV	Nevada	VI	Virgin Islands
GU	Guam	NH	New Hampshire	VA	Virginia
HI	Hawaii	NJ	New Jersey	WA	Washington
ID	Idaho	NM	New Mexico	WV	West Virginia
IL	Illinois	NY	New York	WI	Wisconsin
IN	Indiana	NC	North Carolina	WY	Wyoming
IA	Iowa	ND	North Dakota		

On Your Own

Create a one-page, two-column telephone list of 50 people that you know. Use the telephone book or any kind of directory that you have available. If you do not have telephone numbers for 50 people, use the names and numbers out of a directory.

Put the person's name in the left margin of the column, and the phone number flush to the right margin. Save the file as APP1. Print the file.

EXHIBITION METHODS FOR COMPLEX CONCEPTS

Subject	Display Items	Display Mode
SCIENCE		
Inventor	Scale model of invention, replica of inventor's work area, invention drawings, work notes	Bulletin boards and display cases
Laboratories and research	Lab equipment, photos of researchers, experiment model	Bulletin boards, display cases, display stage
BUSINESS		
Transportation/ communication infrastructure	Network diagrams, computers, distribution maps, models of satellites, ships, trains, airplanes	Large exhibit area, items hung from ceiling, pond for boats, bulletin boards, display cases
Manufacturing and service companies	Robots, state-of-the-art computers, product models, photographs of employees working with customers	Display stage, large exhibit area, bulletin boards, display cases
POLITICS		
Type of government	Copies of charters or constitution, photographs of leaders and capital	Bulletin boards
Political parties	Videotape of campaign advertisements, posters, flyers	Bulletin boards, kiosk for videotape
City management	Police car, fire engine, helicopter, handcuffs, badges	Large exhibit area, display stage and cases, bulletin boards

In this chapter, you will create a "landscape-style" table containing three columns and eight rows.

C H A P T E R

2

A Table in Landscape Mode

Overview

One of WordPerfect's most useful tools for placing information side by side is the table feature. In the previous chapter, you used newspaper columns to allow text to flow from one column to the next. In this chapter, you will use the Table command to neatly line up short blocks of text that you read across the page.

For example, you would use a table to create the following list:

NAME	ADDRESS	STATUS
John Sebastian	1412 Everton Tulsa, OK 62345 (302) 976-8105	Single
Alice Seymour	15 Glass Avenue Muncie, IN 43261 (214) 543-9686	Married

The table above has three columns consisting of "name," "address," and "status" information and three rows consisting of titles for the columns and two entries. Note that each entry is in a box, called a *cell*.

The advantage of using a table is that you can edit any cell and WordPerfect will use word wrap to maintain the right format. For instance, if you add two lines of text beneath John Sebastian's phone number, WordPerfect will automatically wrap the text properly in the cell margins and also make the cell larger.

NAME	ADDRESS	STATUS
John Sebastian	1412 Everton Tulsa, OK 62345 (302) 976-8105 Danced in the civic light opera	Single
Alice Seymour	15 Glass Avenue Muncie, IN 43261 (214) 543-9686	Married

When you complete the final entry of a column (such as the word *Single* in the example above) and press the right arrow key ($\rightarrow$), Word-Perfect automatically moves the cursor to the proper place in the first cell of the next row for another entry (Alice Seymour). In other words, WordPerfect maintains the table format for you; all you need to do is enter text in each cell.

Creating a Table

You create tables with the *Column/Table command* ($\boxed{\text{Alt}}$-$\boxed{\text{F7}}$). Creating a table involves three steps: (1) creating the table, (2) editing the table, and (3) entering text.

FIGURE 2.I
The Table Edit screen lets you adjust the width of columns and many other characteristics of the table.

```
Table Edit:  Press Exit when done         Cell A1 Doc 2 Pg 1 Ln 1.84 Pos 11.23
Ctrl-Arrows Column Widths; Ins Insert; Del Delete; Move Move/Copy;
1 Size; 2 Format; 3 Lines; 4 Header; 5 Math; 6 Options; 7 Join; 8 Split: 0
```

1. *Creating a table.* To create a table, you start by using the Columns/Table command ([Alt]-[F7]) and tell WordPerfect that you want to create a table. WordPerfect then prompts you how many rows and columns you want. For example, to create the table shown above, we told WordPerfect to define a table with 3 columns and 3 rows.

    WordPerfect then calculates the size of each column based on the left and right margins of your document. It also inserts a [Tbl Def] code with your specifications into the document and displays the Table Edit menu as shown in Figure 2.1.

2. *Editing the table.* Once the table appears on the screen, you are in *Table Edit mode* and can change any of its characteristics, such as the number of rows or columns it has, the width of each column, the appearance of text in cells, and so on. Once you have modified the table (if necessary), you can enter text.

3. *Entering text.* When typing text in cells, the text will wrap automatically to fit the left and right margins of the cell. When you reach the bottom of an entry in a cell and want to move to the next cell, press the arrow key in the direction of the cell you want to edit. The cursor then moves to the top of the next cell.

    A major advantage of the table feature is that you are not "locked in" to the table's format once you create it.

Editing Cells and Tables

After you work on a document, you will often need to change the format or content of a table. Changing the text in a cell is called *editing a cell*. Changing the layout of a table is called *editing a table*. Let's look at both of these operations more closely.

Editing a Cell

Editing a cell is straightforward. Simply move the cursor into the cell you want to edit using the cursor arrow keys (⌷↑⌷, ⌷↓⌷, ⌷→⌷, ⌷←⌷) and use the regular edit keys to make the changes you want.

You should be aware that all paired formatting commands (such as *underline* and *boldface)* in a cell are only effective in that cell. This means that if you want all the text in a row to be underlined, you need to underline the text in each cell individually.

To make editing cells easier, WordPerfect provides special commands for moving the cursor to the end or beginning of a table. If you want to move the cursor to the first or last cell in a column, press ⌷Ctrl⌷-⌷Home⌷ ⌷Home⌷ ⌷↑⌷ or ⌷↓⌷. If you want to move the cursor to the first or last cell in a row, press ⌷Ctrl⌷ ⌷Home⌷ ⌷Home⌷ ⌷←⌷ or ⌷→⌷.

One final word about moving the cursor: if you use paired format codes in a cell, you need to press the arrow key twice to move to the next cell: once to move past the format code, and once to move to the new cell.

Editing an Existing Table

In addition to editing text, you will sometimes need to change the layout or size of an existing table. Changing the layout of a table requires three steps:

1.   Move the cursor to a cell you want to change.
2.   Select the Table command (⌷Alt⌷-⌷F7⌷).
3.   Make the change using the Table Edit menu.

Perhaps the most commonly used edit command (and the most fun) is changing the width of a column.

Adjusting Column Width

Often, when you first create a column you will not know exactly how wide each column should be. If you later decide that a column is too wide or narrow, WordPerfect makes it simple to change its width. Simply move the cursor to a cell in the column you want to change and press ⌷Ctrl⌷-⌷→⌷ to widen the column or ⌷Ctrl⌷-⌷←⌷ to make it narrower. That's all there is to it. As you press the ⌷Ctrl⌷-⌷→⌷ or ⌷←⌷ key, WordPerfect automatically reformats the text in the column.

You should note, though, that if you want to change the width of a cell, you need to change the width of *all* the cells in the column. You will get a lot of practice changing the width of columns in this chapter.

Changing the Size of Paper and Layout Mode

Often when you are using tables you may find that you want to print on paper that is larger or smaller than normal. You may also want to change the layout mode from *portrait* to *landscape,* as shown in Figure 2.2.

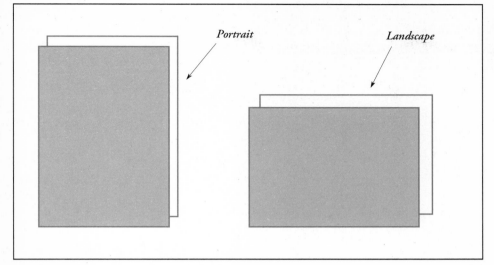

FIGURE 2.2
WordPerfect can print a document with either a portrait or landscape layout.

WordPerfect can print on any size paper that your printer is capable of handling.

To change the size of the paper and layout mode of your document, you can use the *Paper Size/Type* option on the Format Page menu. As shown in Figure 2.3, the Format: Paper Size menu lets you print on almost any size paper in either portrait or landscape mode.

When you choose a paper size and type from this menu, WordPerfect inserts a form change code into your document, similar to this example:

```
[Paper Sz/Typ:110 x 51, Standard]
```

In the preceding example, WordPerfect will print the file on paper that is 110 (11") columns wide and 51 (9.33") lines long (landscape mode)—if your printer is capable of doing so.

Changing the Document Summary Default

In the previous chapter, you created a Document Summary for your document. To help you keep track of your files, we recommend that you use WordPerfect's Setup command (Shift - F1) followed by options 3 and 4 to make it mandatory that you create a Document Summary for every file that you create. By making the Document Summary screen mandatory, it will appear automatically when you save the file for the first time. The advantage to you is that you'll never forget to make a Document Summary for your files.

```
Format: Paper Size/Type

                                                      Font   Double
Paper type and Orientation     Paper Size   Prompt Loc    Type   Sided   Labels

Envelope - Wide                95 × 24      No     Manual  Land   No
Legal                          85 × 84      No     Contin  Port   No
Legal - Wide                   140 × 51     No     Contin  Land   No
Standard                       85 × 66      No     Contin  Port   No
Standard - Wide                110 × 51     No     Contin  Land   No
[ALL OTHERS]                   Width ≤ 85   Yes    Manual         No




1 Select; 2 Add; 3 Copy; 4 Delete; 5 Edit; N Name Search: 1
```

FIGURE 2.3
The Format: Paper Size menu lets you work with many different sizes of documents.

Tutorial

Regena Mitchell wants you to create a one-page handout to help customer representatives come up with exhibit ideas. Because the handout consists of three columns, each headed—Subject, Display Items, and Display Mode—you decide to create a table in landscape layout mode.

As you begin the handout, you are not sure exactly what size each of the columns should be, so you are prepared to change them after you enter the text. In addition, you decide to change the left margin to 15 (1.5"). You will call the handout EXHIMETH.

Before you begin, you want to make creating a Document Summary mandatory.

Setting Up

To begin creating the three-column article, follow these steps:

1. Put the Student Data disk in drive B.
2. Start WordPerfect.

Make Document Summary Mandatory
Shift - F1, *3, 4, 1*

You then decide that you want to make creating a Document Summary mandatory for every file that you make.

1. Press the Setup command (Shift - F1).
2. Type **3** to select Environment.
3. Type **4** to select Document Management/Summary.
   RESULT: The Document Summary option menu appears on the screen as shown in Figure 2.4.
4. Type **1** to select Create Summary on Save/Exit.
   RESULT: The cursor jumps to the column next to option 1.
5. Type **Y**.

```
Setup: Document Management/Summary

    1 - Create Summary on Save/Exit        No

    2 - Subject Search Text                RE:

    3 - Long Document Names                No

    4 - Default Document Type

Selection: 0
```

6. Press the Exit key ([F7]).
   RESULT: The edit screen appears again. From now on, when you save a file, WordPerfect will prompt you to make a Document Summary for every document you create.

Formatting

To format the handout, you must change the layout mode of the paper to landscape and define your parallel columns.

Change to Landscape
[Shift]-[F8], *2, 7, 1*

To change paper layout mode, follow these steps:

1. Press the Format command ([Shift]-[F8]).

2. Type **2** to select the Page option.

3. Type **7** to select Paper Size/Type.
   RESULT: The Format: Paper Size/Type menu appears on the screen, as shown in Figure 2.5.

4. Press the down arrow ([↓]) until the Standard-Wide option is highlighted.

5. Type **1** to select Standard-Wide.
   RESULT: The Format: Page menu reappears on the screen.

6. Press Exit ([F7]) to return to the edit screen.
   WordPerfect has now put a [Paper Sz/Typ] code at the beginning of your document for landscape paper. Let's go to Reveal Codes to see it.

7. Press Reveal Codes ([Alt]-[F3]).
   RESULT: The Reveal Codes screen appears with the Paper Sz/Typ code visible.

8. Press Reveal Codes ([Alt]-[F3]) again.
   RESULT: The Reveal Codes screen disappears.

```
Format: Paper Size/Type
                                                    Font  Double
Paper type and Orientation    Paper Size  Prompt Loc  Type  Sided  Labels

Envelope - Wide               95 × 24      No   Manual  Land  No
Legal                         85 × 84      No   Contin  Port  No
Legal - Wide                  140 × 51     No   Contin  Land  No
Standard                      85 × 66      No   Contin  Port  No
Standard - Wide               110 × 51     No   Contin  Land  No
[ALL OTHERS]                  Width ≤ 85   Yes  Manual        No




1 Select; 2 Add; 3 Copy; 4 Delete; 5 Edit; N Name Search: 1
```

FIGURE 2.5

The Format: Paper Size menu appears on the screen.

Set Left Margin
[Shift]-[F8], *1, 7*

To change the left margin to 15 (1.5"), follow these steps:

1. Press the Format command ([Shift]-[F8]).

2. Type **1** to select the Line option.

3. Type **7** to select Margins.

4. Type **15** and press [Enter] twice.
    RESULT: Left margin is changed to 15 (1.5").

5. Press Exit ([F7]) to return to the edit screen.

Keyboarding

To create the handout, follow these steps:

Enter Title

1. Press [CapsLock].

2. Enter and center the following title by pressing the Center command ([Shift]-[F6]); also, boldface the title by using the Bold key ([F6]):

    `Exhibition Methods for Complex Concepts`

3. Press [F6] to turn Bold off.

4. Press [CapsLock] again to turn off caps. Press [Enter] four times to move the cursor to line 5 (1.67").
    You are now ready to create the table.

Creating a Table
[Alt]-[F7], *2, 1*

To create a table, follow these steps:

1. Press the Columns/Table command ([Alt]-[F7]).

2. Type **2** to choose the Tables option.
    RESULT: The following prompt appears on the status line:

    Table: 1 Create; 2 Edit: 0

FIGURE 2.6

```
Table Edit:  Press Exit when done          Cell A1 Doc 2 Pg 1 Ln 1.84 Pos 11.23

Ctrl-Arrows Column Widths; Ins Insert; Del Delete; Move Move/Copy;
1 Size; 2 Format; 3 Lines; 4 Header; 5 Math; 6 Options; 7 Join; 8 Split: 0
```

3. Type **1** to select the Create option.
   RESULT: The following prompt appears on the status line:

   Number of Columns: 3

4. Press [Enter] to accept the default of three columns.
   RESULT: The following prompt appears on the status line:

   Number of Rows: 1

5. Type **8** to create eight rows and press [Enter].
   RESULT: The table appears on the screen in edit mode, as shown in Figure 2.6.

   Looking at the table, you now decide that the cells in the first column are too wide.

Change Column Width
[Ctrl]-[←]

To change column width, follow these steps:

1. Press [Ctrl]-[←] five times.
   NOTE: Hold down the [Ctrl] key and press the left arrow ([←]) five times.
   RESULT: Each time you press the left arrow ([←]), the highlighted cell gets smaller by one space.

2. Press the Exit key ([F7]) once to accept the Table settings.
   WordPerfect has now put a [Tbl Def] code at the beginning of the table and created a table on the screen for you to work with. You are ready to enter text.

Enter Table

You will start by formatting text and then entering the heading for the first column.

1. Move cursor to the first cell, if not there already. Press the Underline key ([F8]).

2. Press the Center command ([Shift]-[F6]).

3. Type **Subject**
    RESULT: The heading "Subject" is centered and underlined in the first cell.

4. Press the right arrow ([→]) twice to move to the second cell in the first row.
    NOTE: You need to press [→] twice to move the cursor past the closing Underline code and into the next cell.
    RESULT: The cursor is now in the second cell of the first row.

5. Press the Underline key ([F8]).

6. Press the Center command ([Shift]-[F6]) and type **Display Items**

7. Press the right arrow ([→]) twice to move to the third cell.
    RESULT: The edit screen moves the display the entire third column.

8. Press the Underline key ([F8]).

9. Press the Center command ([Shift]-[F6]) and type **Display Mode**

10. Press the right arrow key ([→]) twice to move to the first cell of the second row.
    You can now enter the first entry of the table.

Enter Text in a Row

To create the entry in the second row, follow these steps:

1. Press the Bold key ([F6]) and [CapsLock], then type SCIENCE. Be sure to turn the Bold key off by pressing [F6] again.

2. Press [Enter] to move to the next line in the cell.
    NOTE: All the cells in the row become one line longer.

3. Press [CapsLock] to turn it off and type **Inventor**

4. Press the right arrow key ([→]) to move to the second cell in the second row.

5. Press [Enter] to move to the second line in the cell.
    NOTE: Moving down to the next line aligns text in the second cell with the text "Inventor" in the first cell of the row.

6. Type **Scale model of invention, replica of inventor's work area, invention drawings, work notes**

7. Press the right arrow key ([→]) to move to the last cell in the row.

8. Press [Enter] to move to the next line in the cell.
    NOTE: Moving down to the next line aligns text in the third cell with the text in the first and second cells in the row.

FIGURE 2.7

SUBJECT	DISPLAY ITEMS
SCIENCE Inventor	Scale-model of invention, replica of inventor's work area, invention drawings, work notes

Cell A3 Doc 2 Pg 2 Ln 11.2 Pos 11.23

9. Type **Bulletin boards and display cases**

10. Press the right arrow key (⟶) to move the cursor to the first cell of the next row.

    RESULT: Your table should now look like Figure 2.7.

11. Type the text shown below.

    NOTE: Remember, press the right arrow key (⟶) when you finish entering text in a cell and want to move to the next cell.

Laboratories and research	Lab equipment, photos of researchers, experiment model	Bulletin boards, display cases, display stage
BUSINESS Transportation/ communication infrastructure	Network diagrams, computers, distribution maps, models of satellites, ships, trains, airplanes	Large exhibit area, items hung from ceiling, pond for boats, bulletin boards, display cases
Manufacturing and service companies	Robots, state-of-the-art computers, product models, photographs of employees working with customers	Display stage, large exhibit area, bulletin boards, display cases
POLITICS Type of government	Copies of charters or constitution, photographs of leaders and capital	Bulletin boards
Political parties	Videotape of campaign advertisements, posters, flyers	Bulletin boards, kiosk for videotape
City management	Police car, fire engine, helicopter, handcuffs, badges	Large exhibit area, display stage and cases, bulletin boards

Saving

1. Press the Save key ([F10]) to save the document.
   RESULT: The Document Summary menu will appear on the screen.

Filling out a Document Summary Form
[F10], *2*, [Enter], *3, 4, 7,* [F7]

To fill out the summary menu, follow these steps:

1. Type **2** to select Document Name/Document Type.
2. Type **Exhibition Methods for Complex Concepts** and press [Enter] twice.
   NOTE: Entry of the Document Type is optional.
3. Type **3** to select the Author/Typist option.
4. Type **Regena Mitchell** and press [Enter].
5. Type your name in the Typist section and press [Enter].
6. Type **4** to select Subject.
7. Type **Exhibit Ideas for Different Topics** and press [Enter].
8. Type **7** to select the Abstract option.
9. Type **Landscape mode. Table with 3 columns and 8 rows.**
10. Press Exit ([F7]) twice.
    RESULT: The following prompt appears on the status line:

    `Document to be saved: EXHIMETH.`

    NOTE: WordPerfect has "guessed" that your filename will be the first four characters of the first two words of the document name. That name is fine, but without a drive name, the file will save on the WordPerfect disk or directory.
11. Type B:EXHIMETH and press [Enter].

View Columns
[Shift]-[F7], *6, 3, 1*

Let's now take a look at the document with the View option to see what you have created.

1. Press [PgUp] to move the cursor to the top of the page.
2. Press the Print command ([Shift]-[F7]).
3. Type **6** to view the document.
4. Type **3** to view the entire page.
5. Type **1** to view the document at normal size.
6. Press the Exit key ([F7]) to return to the edit screen.

Revising

You now decide that you need to make column 1 even smaller and column 2 larger.

```
┌─────────────────────────────────────────────────────────────────────────┐
│        SUBJECT          ▓▓▓▓│          DISPLAY ITEMS                      │
├──────────────────────────────┼──────────────────────────────────────────┤
│SCIENCE                        │                                          │
│Inventor                       │Scale-model of invention,                 │
│                               │replica of inventor's work                │
│                               │area, invention drawings,                 │
│                               │work notes                                │
├──────────────────────────────┼──────────────────────────────────────────┤
│Laboratories and               │Lab equipment, photos of                  │
│research                       │researchers, experiment model             │
├──────────────────────────────┼──────────────────────────────────────────┤
│BUSINESS                       │                                          │
│Transportation/                │Network diagrams, computers,              │
│communication                  │distribution maps, models of              │
│infrastructure                 │satellites, ships, trains,                │
│                               │airplanes                                 │
├──────────────────────────────┼──────────────────────────────────────────┤
│Manufacturing and              │Robots, state-of-the-art                  │
│service companies              │computers, product models,                │
│                               │photographs of employees                  │
│                               │working with customers.                   │
│Table Edit:   Press Exit when done        Cell A1 Doc 1 Pg 1 Ln 7.84 POS 11.23 │
└─────────────────────────────────────────────────────────────────────────┘
Ctrl-Arrows Column Widths; Ins Insert; Del Delete; Move Move/Copy;
1 Size; 2 Format; 3 Lines; 4 Header; 5 Math; 6 Options; 7 Join; 8 Split: 0
```

FIGURE 2.8

*Edit a Table and
Change Cell Width*
Alt - F7

To edit a table, follow these steps:

1. Move the cursor to the first cell in the first row (it should contain the heading "Subject").

2. Press the Columns/Tables command (Alt-F7).
   RESULT: As shown in Figure 2.8, the first cell of the table is highlighted and WordPerfect is in Table Edit mode.

3. Press Ctrl-← twice to reduce the size of the first column two more spaces.

4. Press the right arrow (→) once to move to the second cell of the first row.

5. Press Ctrl-→ three times to increase the size of the middle column 3 spaces.
   NOTE: Watch the text in the middle column reformat to the new cell size.

6. Press the Exit key (F7) once.
   RESULT: You are back in normal edit mode.
   View the document again using option 6 of the Print menu (Shift-F7) to see how the changes look.

Saving

Save your changes using the Save key (F10).

Printing

If your printer can handle a landscape layout, print the document using the Print command (Shift-F7) and selecting Full Document.

Exiting
F7, Y, Y

Exit the document by following these steps:

1. Press the Exit key (F7).

2. Type **Y** to save the changes you may have made since last saving the file.
   NOTE: Even if you saved just prior to printing and have not made any changes since, it is a good idea to get in the habit of typing Y at this prompt—you can never be too cautious about saving documents.

3. Press Enter .

4. Type **Y** to save the changes you made to the file.

5. Type **Y** if you want to leave WordPerfect. Type N if you want to continue working.

Summary

You created a landscape oriented document by selecting the Page Size/Type option of the Format: Page menu. You then created a table using the Tables option of the Column/Table command (Alt - F7). Each time you moved to a new cell, you pressed the arrow key that pointed in the direction of the cell. You also changed the width of cell columns, using the Ctrl - → and Ctrl - ← commands.

In addition, you made creating a Document Summary mandatory by choosing the Document Management/Summary option under Environment in the Setup Menu (Shift - F1).

Chapter Review

Key Terms

Cell
Column/Table command
Column width
Landscape mode

Paper Size/Type option
Portrait mode
Table Edit mode

Review Questions

1. Given your experience with the Table feature, briefly describe its main advantage.

2. What key(s) do you press to move the cursor between cells?

3. Why do you sometimes need to press an arrow key twice to move to a new cell?

4. What key(s) do you press to go to the last row in a table?

5. List the commands required to make the second column of an existing table four spaces wider.

6. Briefly describe why it is important to put the cursor inside the table before you press the Table command. What do you think would happen if you put the cursor outside of the table before pressing the Table command?

7. Two common printing layout modes are _____ and _____.

8. Do you think that it should be mandatory to enter a Document Summary? Briefly explain your answer.

Applications

Start WordPerfect and do the following exercises.

1. Create the document shown in Figure 2.9 by following these instructions:

   a. Set to landscape orientation.

   b. Create a table with four columns and rows.

   c. Save the document as B:DRILL2-1.

   d. Fill out the Document Summary.

   e. Print the document.

2. Create the document shown in Figure 2.10 by following these instructions.

   a. Set to landscape orientation.

   b. Create a table with three columns and 12 rows.

   d. Save the document as B:DRILL2-2.

   e. Fill out the Document Summary.

   f. Print the document.

3. Retrieve the document called BOOKINGS from the Student Data Disk and follow the instructions shown in Figure 2.11. Save the document as B:DRILL2-3. Print the document.

FIGURE 2.9

MULTIPLE LISTING SERVICE
COMPUTER CITY
(Homes Above $280,000)
June 1, 19—

Address	Features	Contact/Comments	Price
534 Hawarden Ct.	3 bedrooms 2 bath Pool	Sam Armstrong Realty 229-0409 Panoramic view and French gazebo	$280,500
2134 S. Bay Ave.	4 bedrooms 2 acres 3-car garage newly carpeted 12 years old	Walker Realty Alice Noteboom 329-4116 On golf course. Security system.	$498,200 Negotiable, Owner Anxious
5262 King St.	8 bedrooms tudor 13,000 sq. ft. Stables 9 acres	Lois Lauer Real Estate Pat Seymour 229-6100 Vaulted ceilins--art alcoves and built-in satellite-sound system. Stunning view. Call for appointment.	$1,405,000
12 Knoll Dr.	4 bedrooms 3,000 sq. ft. vacant	Lois Lauer Real Estate Carol Samuals 229-6100 Pool, jacuzzi, spa, stained glass	$365,000

FIGURE 2.10

Lot Number	Vendor	Contact/Comments
	NEW WAVE TRADE SHOW BOOKING GUIDE	
	Aisle B2	
1	Show Registration Committee	Jack Van Paddenberg
2	Empty	
3	MicroBound Publishing Company	Noel Laursen/Confirmed
4	Northwest Mail Order	Lisa Reyes/Independent
5	Empty	
6	Graphics Extravaganza	Todd Lincoln/Pending
7	Computer Interface Specialists	Mary Oshiro and Sandy Dennis/Confirmed
8	Empty	
9	Reginald Software Games and Innovations	Horace Reginald/Confirmed
10	Security Systems of America	Jan Heverly/Independent
11	Empty	

FIGURE 2.11

NEW WAVE TRADE SHOW BOOKING GUIDE
Aisle B2

Lot Number	Vendor	Contact/Comments
1	Show Registration Committee	Jack Van Paddenberg
2	Empty	
3	MicroBound Publishing Company	Noel Laursen/Confirmed
4	Northwest Mail Order	Lisa Reyes/Independent
5	Empty	
6	Graphics Extravaganza	Todd Lincoln/Pending
7	Computer Interface Specizlists	Mary Oshiro and Sandy Dennis/Confirmed
8	Empty	
9	Reginald Software Games and Innovations	Horace Reginald/Confirmed
10	Security systems of America	Jan Heverly/Independent
11	Empty	

Increase width by 5 spaces.

Decrease width by 8 spaces.

4. Retrieve the document called LISTINGS from the Student Data Disk, and follow the instructions shown in Figure 2.12. Save the document as B:DRILL2-4. Print the document.

FIGURE 2.12

MULTIPLE LISTING SERVICE
COMPUTER CITY
(Homes Above $280,000)
June 1, 19--

Decrease width by 5 spaces. →

Increase width by 5 spaces. →

Address	Features	Contact/Comments	Price
534 Hawarden Ct.	3 bedrooms 2 bath Pool	Sam Armstrong Realty 229-0409 Panoramic view and French gazebo	$280,500
2134 S. Bay Ave.	4 bedrooms 2 acres 3 car garage newly carpeted 12 years old	Walker Realty Alice Noteboom 329-4116 On golf course. Security system.	$498,200 Negotiable, Owner Anxious
5262 King St.	8 bedrooms tudor 13,000 sq. ft. Stables 9 acres	Lois Lauer Real Estate Pat Seymour 229-6100 Vaulted ceilings—art alcoves and built-in satellite-sound system. Stunning view. Call for appointment.	$1,405,000
12 Knoll Dr.	4 bedrooms 3,000 sq. ft. vacant	Lois Lauer Real Estate Carol Samuals 229-6100 Pool, jacuzzi, spa, stained glass	$365,000

5. Create the document shown in Figure 2.13 by following these instructions:

   a. Create a table with 3 columns and 6 rows.

   b. Create underlined headings for each column.

   c. Save the document as B:DRILL2-5.

   d. Fill out the Document Summary.

   e. Print the document.

FIGURE 2.13

TRADE SHOW SCHEDULES

Salesperson	Week Ending	City
R. Ho	January 12	Las Vegas
	January 19	Las Vegas
	January 26	Atlantic City
M. Lincoln	January 12	Atlantic City
	January 19	Atlantic City
	January 26	Computer City
L. Seybold	January 12	New York
	January 19	Las Vegas
	January 26	Pasadena
R. Basel	January 12	Las Vegas
	January 19	Los Angeles
	January 26	Los Angeles
F. Neckerbow	January 12	New York
	January 19	New York
	January 26	New York

6. Retrieve the document called SHOWS from the Student Data Disk and follow the instructions shown in Figure 2–14. Save the document as B:DRILL2-6. Print the document.

FIGURE 2.14

TRADE SHOW SCHEDULES

Salesperson	Week Ending	City
R. Ho	January 12	Las Vegas
	January 19	Las Vegas
	January 26	Atlantic City
M. Lincoln	January 12	Atlantic City
	January 19	Atlantic City
	January 26	Computer City
L. Seybold	January 12	New York
	January 19	Las Vegas
	January 26	Pasadena
R. Basel	January 12	Las Vegas
	January 19	Los Angeles
	January 26	Los Angeles
F. Neckerbow	January 12	New York
	January 19	New York
	January 26	New York

Decrease width by 7 spaces.   *Decrease width by 6 spaces.*

Advanced Skills

WordPerfect provides many tools to help you customize a table to your exact needs. For example, you can add or delete rows and columns anywhere in a table. Also, if you decide that you would prefer WordPerfect not to print lines around cells, or want to change the lines, you can edit them. Let's look at each of these options more closely.

Adding a Row or Column

If you find that you need to *insert a row or column* in your table, follow these steps:

1. Move the cursor to the place in the table where you want to insert a row or column.

2. Press the Column/Table command ([Alt]-[F7]).

3. Press the [Ins] key.

   WordPerfect will then ask you if you want to insert a row or a column. If you select a row, WordPerfect will insert a row at the cursor and move the remaining rows down. If you select a column, WordPerfect will insert a column at the cursor and move the remaining columns to the right. If the table is the width of the page and there is no more room to the right, WordPerfect will split the current column in two.

Deleting a Row a Column

You *delete a row or* column in almost the same way that you insert them; except that you press the [Del] key. To delete a row or column requires these steps:

1. Move the cursor to the row or column that you want to delete.

2. Press the Column/Table command ([Alt]-[F7]).

3. Press the [Del] key.

   WordPerfect will then ask you if you want to delete a row or column. As always, if you delete a row or column that you don't intend to, you can use the Undelete key ([F1]) to get it back.

   In addition to adding and deleting rows and columns, you can also change the lines around the cells.

Changing the Lines Around Cells

WordPerfect lets you change the format of lines around each cell, or group of cells, using the *Line option* in the Table Edit menu. For example, follow these steps to eliminate the line above the first cell in the following table:

1.   Move the cursor to the first cell.

2.   Press the Column/Table command ($\boxed{\text{Alt}}$-$\boxed{\text{F7}}$).

3.   Type **3** to select the Lines option.

RESULT: The following prompt appears on the status line:

```
Lines: 1 Left; 2 Right; 3 Top; 4 Bottom; 5 Inside;
6 Outside; 7 All; 8 Shade: 0
```

4.   Type **3** to select Top.

RESULT: The following prompt appears on the status line:

```
1 None; 2 Single; 3 Double; 4 Dashed; 5 Dotted; 6
Thick; 7 Extra Thick: 0
```

5.   Type **1** to select the None option.

RESULT: The Table then appears like this:

To change the appearance of lines for a group of cells, you need to highlight the cells you want to change with the Block command ($\boxed{\text{Ctrl}}$-$\boxed{\text{F4}}$). For example, to eliminate the top line in every cell of the preceding example, you would follow these steps:

1.   Move the cursor to the first cell.

2.   Press the Column/Table command ($\boxed{\text{Alt}}$-$\boxed{\text{F7}}$).

3.   Press the Block command ($\boxed{\text{Ctrl}}$-$\boxed{\text{F4}}$).

4.   Move the cursor to the last cell.

5.   Type **3** to select the Lines option.

6.   Type **3** to select Top.

7.   Type **1** to select the None option.

The table would then look like this:

Note that the top line in the bottom two cells still appears, even though you selected "None." This is because table lines are relative; one cell's top is another cell's bottom. To eliminate the top lines of the cells in the last row, you would need to highlight the bottom row and repeat the process again.

As you can see, the table feature provides several tools for creating a table that meets your exact needs.

Advanced Key Terms	Insert a row or column	Table Line option
	Delete a row or column	

Advanced Review Questions

1. If you are inserting a column and there is not enough room on the page to contain another column, what does WordPerfect do?

2. If you use the Top None command to eliminate the top lines to a group of eight cells in four rows, only the top lines in the first row are eliminated. Briefly explain why.

3. Look over the options in the Line menu. What command do you think would eliminate all the lines around a cell or group of cells?

Advanced Applications

1. Retrieve the document called LISTINGS from the Student Data Disk and follow these instructions:

   a. Add the following row of data after the row containing the Hawarden Court information:

3563 Echo Road	3 bedrooms; 2,300 sq. ft.	Sam Armstrong Realty 229-0409	$280,000

   b. Delete the row containing the Knoll Drive information.

   c. Eliminate all the lines in the table.

   d. Save the document as B:DRILL2-7.

   e. Fill out the Document Summary.

   f. Print the document.

2. Retrieve the document called BOOKINGS from the Student Data Disk and follow these instructions.

   a. Delete each row that contains the information "Empty" in the Vendor column.

   b. Add the following two rows of data after the row containing information for Northwest Mail Order: 14

14	Instant Communications Specialists, Inc.	Gil Hadley/Confirmed PC Magazine winner of Innovation Award
15	Olson Computer Company	Rick Olson/Confirmed

    c.   Eliminate the single lines around each cell.

    d.   Save the document as DRILL2-8.

    e.   Fill out the Document Summary.

    f.   Print the document.

On Your Own   Create a one-page, 4-column list of eight classes from your school directory that you have taken or would like to take. The list should have columns showing the class name, number, instructor, hours, prerequisites, and description about the class. Save the file as 3APP2. Print the file.

To reiterate our discussion Thursday, we do not think that "talking computers" and other such high-tech aides will help your sales. In general, we suggest that you should spend about 60 percent of your trade show budget on booth design and construction. Since you have only three seconds to grab a visitor for every 10 feet of exhibit, your display must command immediate attention.

RECOMMENDED STRATEGY

We find that product demonstration is the most effective way of keeping someone's attention and, in the long run, of generating leads. We are going to concentrate on methods for showing the superiority of your product.
My staff has several suggestions for your show.

1. Consider using 150 square feet of sales space. You will need this space to accommodate all the people you are trying to reach. We calculate that about fifty square feet per salesperson is about right.

2. Avoid games and raffles. Games attract the wrong kind of crowd. The serious prospect is not interested in a 10-cent ruler or rolling the dice to win a 50-cent prize.

3. Include equipment and parts that people can touch. Plan your exhibit so they can turn dials, look through a magnifying glass, feel the parts, and so on.

We will meet on September 30 in your office to lay out sketches for your exhibit. Remember, these are all ...inary ideas! At your request, I've included a list of ...ture on trade shows.

Schindler
Design Analyst

READING LIST

...us, "Trade Shows: Building Image on a Budget," ...rketing Communications, Vol. 13, Issue 7, July 1988; ...p. 40-45.
...ll, P., "Best from the Shows/Taking an Early Stand," ...rketing, Vol. 25, Issue 11, June 12, 1986; pp. 47-53.
...ll, R., "How to Tap Markets with Trade Shows," Public ...elations Journal, Vol. 41, Issue 9, September 1985; ...p. 34-35.
...sco, R., "Selling at Trade Shows: Avoid the Herd ...nstinct," Management Review, April 1986; pp. 46-47.

PRELIMINARY MARKET RESEARCH REPORT
Exhibit Place
Computer City, CA 94584
(404) 555-8105

INTRODUCTION

Based on our meetings last Thursday, my staff is currently compiling your Stage A marketing analysis. Before we get too far, however, I want to pass on to you our preliminary findings to prepare you in advance.

FINDINGS

Our current studies show that your sales people have not contacted 84 percent of all visitors at national trade shows and 92 percent at regional trade shows.[1] This means that your exhibit will be the first place that most people will encounter your product. Considering that it costs $254 to close a trade show lead as compared to $1,229 to close an industrial sale--your exhibit can be extremely cost effective.[2]

PRELIMINARY RECOMMENDATIONS

Bearing these facts in mind, you need to do the following:

1. Set specific sales objectives for the show. Without specific numbers and goals, it is almost impossible to evaluate whether the show has been a success. Do you want to sell three new systems, sign up 12 deals, or have 240 people agree to a sales call at a later date? These numbers help you determine exactly which shows to attend.

2. Focus on who your main audience at the New Wave Trade Show will be. Are you contacting technicians, engineers, high-level executives, or purchasing agents? New Wave is so large that you will be able to contact the audience you prefer.

---

[1]Hughes, M., "Trade Shows: America's Most Misunderstood Marketing Tool," Business Digest, May 1985.

[2]Hughes.= 1985.

In this chapter, you will create a style sheet to help you format documents quickly and easily. You will also create footnotes.

3

Marketing Research Report

Chapter Objectives	After completing this chapter, you will be able to

1. Create a style sheet and use it to develop a marketing research report.
2. Create footnotes.
3. Use the margin release.

WordPerfect Commands	Alt - F8 , 3, 2, 1	Create a paired style
	Alt - F8 , 1	Turn a style on
	Alt - F8 , 3, 2, 2	Create an open style
	Alt - F8 , 4	Edit a style sheet
	Ctrl - F7 , 1, 1	Create footnotes
	Alt - F8	Save a style
	Alt - F8 , 7	Retrieve a style

Overview

The key to creating professional-looking documents is being able to use WordPerfect's formatting tools to give documents a distinctive appearance. As you know, because different kinds of documents need different kinds of formats, formatting your documents requires a certain amount of time and thought; for example, (1) reports may need a specific heading to create a professional "look," (2) memos may require special margins to fit on various sizes of paper, and (3) business letters may require standard headings and closings. You can shorten the amount of time spent on formatting documents by using a WordPerfect feature called a style sheet.

What Is a Style Sheet?

A *style sheet* is a special file that contains a group of preset formatting codes created for a particular document or documents. Each time you start a document, rather than manually insert all your formatting commands, you can set up a style sheet to format the document for you. For example, you can set up one style sheet to format the margins, line spacing, and tab settings for internal memorandums and then use another style sheet to format the justification and headings of important marketing letters. You may recall that you can use macros to format your documents as well. The difference between style sheets and macros is that style sheets allow you to change the appearance of several documents at once, not just one document at a time. Macros insert a series of formatting commands and text into your documents; style sheets insert special preset formatting codes that are independent of your document.

For example, say that you used a style sheet to create one hundred memoranda with 2-inch top margins. Then, just before you mail the memos, your manager decides that she wants all memoranda to have 3-inch top margins. Rather than change the top margin in all hundred memos one by one, you can change the margin code in the style, so that the top margins in all hundred memos change!

Let's look in more detail at how the style sheet works.

Using Style Sheets   Say that you frequently send the following kind of statement to customers:

```
                        BALANCE DUE
     ITEM
            Fifteen thousand feet of copper wire and

            twelve thousand feet of 10-gauge tubing.

                                          $5,321


     LABOR
            Nine laborers (3 days), two electricians

            (1-1/2 days), inspector (1/2 day), and

            foreperson (3 days)

                                          $6,456
```

To create this statement, you needed to use several WordPerfect formatting features:

1. The title is centered ([Shift]-[F6]).
2. The heading is flush left.
3. The notations have double margins of 25 and 65 ([Shift]-[F4]).
4. The price is flush-right ([Alt]-[F6]). By using a style sheet, you can create this invoice without using any format commands. Instead, you would enter

```
Fifteen thousand feet of copper wire and twelve
thousand feet of 10-gauge tubing.

$5,321

LABOR

Nine laborers (3 days), two electricians (1-1/2
days), inspector (1/2 day), and foreperson (3 days)

$6,456
```

To begin formatting with a style sheet, you would move the cursor to where you want the heading to start and then press the Style key ([Alt]-[F8]). A screen similar to Figure 3.1 appears. *(Note:* The screen shown in Figure 3.1 is preset to format the previous balance due statement.) To use it, highlight the style sheet named HEADING, and type 1 to turn it on. "BALANCE DUE" and "ITEM" then appear on the screen.

You then highlight the sentence beginning "Fifteen thousand feet..." Using the Style key, turn on the style, ITEM DESC, and WordPerfect will double-indent the text for you.

```
Styles

   Name         Type       Description

   Bibliogrphy  Paired     Bibliography
   Doc Init     Paired     Initialize Document Style
   Document     Outline    Document Style
   Pleading     Open       Header for numbered pleading paper
   Right Par    Outline    Right-Aligned Paragraph Numbers
   Tech Init    Open       Initialize Technical Style
   Technical    Outline    Technical Document Style


















 1 On; 2 Off; 3 Create; 4 Edit; 5 Delete; 6 Save; 7 Retrieve; 8 Update: 1
```

FIGURE 3.1
A Style menu set for formatting a BALANCE DUE statement sheet.

The Style command is useful for giving all your documents a uniform look. If a team of people is creating hundreds of documents at different word processing machines, you can use style sheets to ensure that all documents appear exactly the same.

Creating a Style Sheet

When you first press the Style key ([Alt]-[F8]), you will see the styles screen shown in Figure 3.2. Note that there are three headings for a style: Name, Type, and Description.

Name

A *style name* quickly identifies what it does. For example, HEADING enters and centers the capitalized text "BALANCE DUE."

```
   Styles

      Name         Type       Description
```

```
 1 On; 2 Off; 3 Create; 4 Edit; 5 Delete; 6 Save; 7 Retrieve; 8 Update: 1
```

FIGURE 3.2
The style screen is blank when you begin, ready for you to create styles for your document.

```
Styles: Edit

    1 - Name

    2 - Type          Paired

    3 - Description

    4 - Codes

    5 - Enter         HRt
```

FIGURE 3.3

The edit screen for styles lets you give each style a name, type, description, and specific format codes.

```
Selection: 0
```

Type

Two kinds of styles exist: paired and open. You use a *paired style* with format commands that you can turn on and off, like Bold, Underline, Center, and so on. Paired styles have a definite beginning and end.

You use an *open style* with format commands that do not have an end, such as Double-space, Margin changes, Line justification, and so on. Each time you use an open style, it affects the rest of the document.

Description

The *style description* is helpful for describing exactly what a particular style does. By carefully describing your styles, you enable someone else to use your styles with a minimum of trouble.

Editing Style Sheets

One of the reasons people like using style sheets is that they are simple to create and change. You create or edit a style sheet with the styles edit screen shown in Figure 3.3. At this screen, you tell WordPerfect the name, type, description, and codes in a style sheet. When you enter codes, you work in one of two possible edit screens depending upon whether your style is open or paired: Figure 3.4 shows an edit screen for an open style and Figure 3.5 shows an edit screen for a paired style. Like the Reveal Codes screen, the bottom half of each screen shows all the codes that you enter. However, you use the open style and paired styles screens slightly differently.

Using an Open-Style Edit Screen

To enter commands for an open style, you simply press the commands that you want in the style. For example, if you want to create a style that double-spaces a document, you would follow these steps:

1. Press the Format command ([Shift]-[F8]).

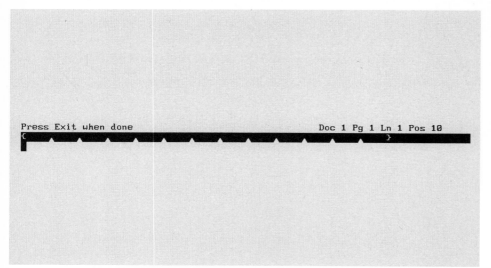

Press Exit when done   Doc 1 Pg 1 Ln 1 Pos 10

FIGURE 3.4

The edit screen for an open style works the same way as Reveal Codes. Every command you enter appears in the bottom half.

2. Type **1** to select the Line option.

3. Type **6** to select the Line-spacing option.

4. Type **2** and press ⌨Enter.

5. Press the Exit key (⌨F7) to leave the Format menu.

    The line-spacing code [Ln Spacing:2] then appears in the lower half of the edit screen.

Using a Paired Style Edit Screen

To enter commands for a paired style, you must remember that every command that you start must be ended. To end a command, press the right arrow key (⌨→) once so that the cursor appears after the comment box, and then close the command.

```
┌──────────────────────────────────────────────────────────────────┐
│  Place Style On Codes above, and Style Off Codes below.            │
└──────────────────────────────────────────────────────────────────┘




Style:   Press Exit when done                    Doc 1 Pg 1 Ln 1 Pos 10
[→Indent][←Mar Rel][Comment][HRt]
[HRt]
```

FIGURE 3.5

The edit screen for a paired style contains a [Comment] box. Enter the start codes before the [Comment] box, press the right arrow key (→) and enter the end codes after the [Comment] box.

FIGURE 3.6
This is a completed paired style that bolds text.

For example, if you want to create a style that bolds text, you would follow these three steps:

1. Press the Bold key ([F6]). The Start Bold code [Bold] will appear in the lower half of the screen.

2. Press the right arrow key ([→]) so that the cursor moves after the Comment Box code [Comment].

3. Press the Bold key again ([F6]) to end the Bold command. The End Bold code appears [bold].

Figure 3.6 shows what the completed style for bolding text looks like. If you make a mistake, you can delete an entry with the [Del] key.

If you later decide to edit an existing style, every document that you created with that style will change automatically. For example, if you use an open style to double-space text in ten documents, and then edit the style so that instead of double-spacing text, it triple-spaces it—all ten documents will be triple-spaced!

Style sheets provide a powerful way to make all your documents look professionally uniform. Another powerful formatting tool that Word-Perfect provides is the footnote feature.

Footnotes

Sometimes in documents such as books, articles, and research reports, you want to place *footnotes* at the bottom of a page. As you may know, footnotes can be quite challenging to type on a typewriter—you need to leave the right amount of space at the bottom of the page and offset them with the correct numbers. Using the Footnote key ([Ctrl]-[F7]), you can use WordPerfect to format, number, and place footnotes at the bottom of a page for you.

If there is enough room, WordPerfect places all footnotes on the same pages to which they refer. It separates the footnotes from the text with a blank line, a two-inch line, and a second blank line. As with automatic page numbers and headers, you cannot see footnotes on the edit screen. To see how they appear in your document, you need to use the View option under the Print key (Shift-F7).

Using Margin Release

Another helpful format tool is the *Margin Release* key (Shift-Tab). Each time you press Margin Release, the cursor moves to the first tab stop left of the left margin. For example, if your left margin is set at position 10 (1") and you have tab stops set at every five spaces, pressing Margin Release once moves the cursor to position 5 (.5"). Pressing it again moves the cursor to position 0 (0").

Because the Margin Release affects only the line where it is implemented, it is useful for creating *hanging indents.* As you know, if you press the Indent key (F4), the left margin of a paragraph moves to the next tab stop. By pressing Margin Release (Shift-Tab), the first line moves to the left five spaces and WordPerfect reformats the paragraph.

This is an example of using Margin Release to create a hanging indent. This paragraph was created by (1) pressing the Indent key (F4), (2) pressing the Margin Release key, and (3) typing text. The Indent key moved the left margin to the right five spaces. The Margin Release key moved the first line to the left five spaces.

Tutorial

Because of the impending New Wave Trade Show, Ellen Nasus is sending far more marketing reports to potential clients than ever before. She has hired two more word processing specialists to help create the documents. She wants all market reports to look the same so she has asked you to create a style sheet for them. Specific formatting instructions are as follows:

1. The title should be bolded and centered.
2. All reports should have a 15-space (1.5") left margin for future binding, if necessary.
3. Reports should be double-spaced, with tabs set every five spaces.
4. Each report requires four boldface headings: Introduction, Findings, Preliminary Recommendations, and Recommended Strategy.

```
Styles

  Name           Type       Description

                 Paired
  Bibliogrphy    Paired     Bibliography
  Doc Init       Paired     Initialize Document Style
  Document       Outline    Document Style
  Pleading       Open       Header for numbered pleading paper
  Right Par      Outline    Right-Aligned Paragraph Numbers
  Tech Init      Open       Initialize Technical Style
  Technical      Outline    Technical Document Style
  test           Open




 1 On; 2 Off; 3 Create; 4 Edit; 5 Delete; 6 Save; 7 Retrieve; 8 Update: 1
```

FIGURE 3.7
The Styles screen.

5. All numbered lists and magazine citations should be hanging indents.

6. Footnotes should appear at the bottom of each page where the reference appears.

   Ellen has given you a file called DRAFT3 that contains the rough text for the report. You need to create a style sheet for all reports, and then format DRAFT3 with it. You will then save the document as FINAL3.

Setting Up

To begin creating the style sheet, follow these steps:

1. Put the Student Data Disk in drive B.

2. Start WordPerfect.

3. Retrieve the file called DRAFT3 from the Student Data Disk by using the List Files key (F5), highlighting DRAFT3, and typing 1 to retrieve the document.

Keyboarding

Scroll through the document to become familiar with it.

Create a Paired Style
Alt -F8, *3, 1, 2*

First, you need to create a style sheet to title the market analysis reports.

1. Press the Style key (Alt-F8).
   RESULT: The styles screen shown in Figure 3.7 appears.

2. Type 3 to create a new style.
   RESULT: The Styles Edit screen shown in Figure 3.8 appears.

3. Type 1 to select the name option.

4. Type **Title** and press Enter.

5. Type 2 to select the Type option.

```
Styles: Edit

    1 - Name

    2 - Type          Paired

    3 - Description

    4 - Codes

    5 - Enter          HRt




Selection: 0
```

FIGURE 3.8
The Styles: Edit screen.

RESULT: The following prompt appears on the screen:

Type: 1 Paired; 2 Open; 3 Outline: 0

6. Type **1** to select the Paired option.
7. Type **3** to select the Description option.
8. Type **Bold and Center Title** and press Enter.
9. Type 4 to select Codes.
    RESULT: The paired codes screen appears on the screen with the cursor above the comment box as shown in Figure 3.9.
10. Press the Bold key (F6).
    RESULT: The Bold code [Bold] appears in the bottom half of the screen.

```
┌─────────────────────────────────────────────────────────────────┐
│ Place Style On Codes above, and Style Off Codes below.          │
└─────────────────────────────────────────────────────────────────┘




Style:  Press Exit when done                    Doc 1 Pg 1 Ln 1 Pos 10
{      ▲      ▲      ▲      ▲      ▲      ▲      ▲      ▲      ▲      }      ▲      ▲
[Comment]
```

FIGURE 3.9
The paired codes screen places the cursor above the Comment box.

FIGURE 3.10

11. Press the Center key ([Shift]-[F6]).
RESULT: The center code [Center] appears.

12. Type **PRELIMINARY MARKET RESEARCH REPORT** and press [Enter] to move the cursor to the next line.

13. Repeat step 11 to enter the three lines of address:
Exhibit Place
Computer City, CA 94584
(404) 555-8105

14. Press the right arrow key ([→]) once to move the arrow to the right of the [Comment] code.

15. Press the Bold key ([F6]) once to turn off boldface.
RESULT: Your screen should appear as shown in Figure 3.10.

16. Press Exit ([F7]) three times to return to the edit screen.

Apply the Style
[Alt]-[F8], *1*

You are now ready to apply the style to the document.

1. Press [PgUp] to move the cursor to the top of the document if it is not already there.

2. Press the Style key ([Alt]-[F8]).

3. Highlight the style called Title. (It may be the only style on the screen and is already highlighted.)

4. Type **1** to turn the style on.
RESULT: The edit screen appears with the phone number next to "Based on our meetings . . ."

5. Press ⎡Enter⎤ twice to separate the new title from "Based on our meetings" and scroll up to the top of the document. The title is now on the screen.

6. Press Reveal Codes (⎡Alt⎤-⎡F3⎤) to see that the title is not text—it is a style code.

7. Press Reveal Codes (⎡Alt⎤-⎡F3⎤) again to turn it off.

Create a Style
⎡Alt⎤-⎡F8⎤, *3, 1*

You now need to create a style that centers and bolds existing text.

1. Press the Style key (⎡Alt⎤-⎡F8⎤).

2. Type **3** to create a new style.

3. Type **1** to select the name option.

4. Type **B&C** and press ⎡Enter⎤.

5. Type **3** to select the Description option.

6. Type **Bolds and Center Text** and press ⎡Enter⎤.

7. Type **4** to select Codes.

8. Press the Bold key (⎡F6⎤) and the Center key (⎡Shift⎤-⎡F6⎤).

9. Press the right arrow key (⎡→⎤) once to move the arrow to the right of the [Comment] code.

10. Press the Bold key (⎡F6⎤) once to turn off boldface.

11. Press Exit (⎡F7⎤) twice to return to the Styles menu.

Create Open Style
⎡Alt⎤-⎡F8⎤, *3, 1, 2, 2*

You must now create a style that sets the format for the basic text of the document.

1. Type **3** to create a new style.

2. Type **1** and type **Normal Text**. Press ⎡Enter⎤.

3. Type **2** to select the Type option.
   RESULT: The following options appear at the bottom of the screen:
   `Type: 1 Paired; 2 Open; 3 Outline: 0`

4. Type **2** to select Open.

5. Type **3** to select Description and type **Sets tabs, left margin 15, and double-spaces text.** Press ⎡Enter⎤.

6. Type **4** to select Codes.

7. Insert the formatting codes for margins by pressing ⎡Shift⎤-⎡F8⎤, 1, 7, 15, ⎡Enter⎤, 10, ⎡Enter⎤, ⎡Enter⎤, ⎡Enter⎤.

8. Insert the formatting codes for line spacing by pressing ⎡Shift⎤-⎡F8⎤, 1, 6, 2, ⎡Enter⎤, ⎡Enter⎤, ⎡Enter⎤.

FIGURE 3.11

```
Style:   Press Exit when done                    Doc 1 Pg 1 Ln 1 Pos 15
    ▲   [      ▲        ▲      ▲      ▲      ▲  ▲    }▲    ▲     ▲     ▲
 [L/R Mar:15,10][Ln Spacing:2][Tab Set:Rel: -10,-5,+5,+10,+15,+20,+25,+30,+35,+40
 ,+45,+50,+55,+60]
```

9. Insert the formatting codes for setting new tabs by pressing [Shift]-[F8], 1, 8, T, 1, 0, [Enter], [Ctrl]-[End], 5, 5, [Enter], [F7], [F7]. Set tabs manually if you are working in inches.
   RESULT: The screen should now appear similar to Figure 3.11.

10. Press Exit ([F7]) twice to return to the Styles menu.

Create Heading Style
[Alt]-[F8], *3, 4*

You now need to create styles for the four headings.

1. Type **3** to create a new style.

2. Name the style Intro.

3. Describe the style as Enters Introduction in boldface.

4. Type 4 to select Codes.

5. Press [Enter] twice, two [HRt] codes, press the Bold key ([F6]), type **INTRODUCTION**.

6. Press the right arrow key ([→]) once to move the arrow to the right of the [Comment] code.

7. Press the Bold key ([F6]) once to turn off boldface.

8. Press [Enter] twice to insert two [HRt] codes.
   NOTE: The second [HRt] separates the heading from the text.
   RESULT: Your screen should now look like Figure 3.12.

9. Press Exit ([F7]) twice to return to the Styles menu.

10. Repeat steps 1 through 9 three times to enter styles for "FINDINGS," "PRELIMINARY RECOMMENDATIONS," and "RECOMMENDED STRATEGY." For steps 2, 3, and 5, enter the following information for each heading:

FIGURE 3.12

```
INTRODUCTION

┌─────────────────────────────────────────────────────────────────┐
│ Place Style On Codes above, and Style Off Codes below.          │
└─────────────────────────────────────────────────────────────────┘




Style:   Press Exit when done                    Doc 1 Pg 1 Ln 4 POS 10
{                                              }
[HRt]
[BOLD]INTRODUCTION[Comment][bold][HRt]
[HRt]
```

NAMES	DESCRIPTION	STYLE CODE
FINDINGS	Enters "FINDINGS" in boldface.	Enter , Enter , F6 , FINDINGS
PRELIMINARY	Enters "PRELIMINARY RECOMMENDATIONS" in boldface.	Enter , Enter , F6 , PRELIMINARY RECOMMENDATIONS
RECOMMENDED	Enters "RECOMMENDED STRATEGY" in boldface.	Enter , Enter , F6 , RECOMMENDED STRATEGY

Create Indent Style
Alt - F8 , *3*

You are now ready to create a style for numbered instructions.

1. Type **3** to create a new style.
2. Name the style **Indent.**
3. Describe the style as **Creates hanging indents.**
4. Type **4** to select Codes.
5. Press the Indent key (F4).
6. Press the Margin Release key (Shift - Tab).
   RESULT: Your screen should now look like Figure 3.13.
7. Press Exit (F7) three times to return to the Edit screen.

Apply Normal Text Style
Alt - F8 , *1*

Let's now apply these styles to the document.

1. Move the cursor to the beginning of the first paragraph.
2. Press the Style key (Alt - F8).
3. Highlight Normal Text and turn it on by pressing 1.

Apply Intro Style
Alt - F8 , *1*

1. Press the Style key (Alt - F8).
2. Highlight Intro and turn it on.
3. Move the cursor to the beginning of the second paragraph.

FIGURE 3.13

```
╔═══════════════════════════════════════════════════════╗
║ Place Style On Codes above, and Style Off Codes below. ║
╚═══════════════════════════════════════════════════════╝




Style:   Press Exit when done                   Doc 1 Pg 1 Ln 1 Pos 10
{         ▲     ▲    ▲     ▲     ▲     ▲     ▲    }    ▲     ▲
[→Indent][←Mar Rel][Comment]
```

4. Press the Style key ([Alt]-[F8]) and turn on the Findings style.

5. Move the cursor to the beginning of the paragraph starting "Bearing these facts . . ."

6. Press the Style key ([Alt]-[F8]) and turn on the Preliminary style.

7. Move the cursor to the beginning of the paragraph that begins "We find that . . ."

8. Press the Style key ([Alt]-[F8]) and turn on the Recommended style.

STOP! HAVE YOU REMEMBERED TO SAVE YOUR FILE? IF NOT, SAVE IT AS B:FINAL3 USING THE SAVE KEY ([F10]).

NOTE: If the Document Summary screen appears, enter this information:

Description	Preliminary Market Research Report
Subject/Acct	Frank Poole
Author	Ellen Nasus
Typist	Holly Myers
Comments	Contains a reading list.

Apply Indent Style

[Alt] - [F8]

You are now ready to apply the indent style to the document.

1. Move the cursor to the "1" in the first numbered item on Page 1 starting "Set specific sales objectives . . ."

2. Press the Style key ([Alt]-[F8]) and turn on the Indent style.

3. Move the cursor to the S in Set and press the [Tab] key to indent the first line with the rest of the paragraph.

4. Repeat steps 2 and 3 with each numbered list in the file. There are five in all.

```
 1




Press Exit when done                    Doc 1 Pg 1 Ln 4 Pos 15.53
```

FIGURE 3.14
*The footnote screen
lets you enter a
footnote of any length.*

Apply Style
[Alt]-[F8] , [Alt]-[F4]

You are almost done.

1. Highlight READING LIST using [Alt]-[F4] and [Enter].
2. Press the Style key ([Alt]-[F8]) and turn on B&C.
3. Highlight the first magazine reference by pressing the Block key
   ([Alt]-[F4]) and pressing [Enter].
4. Press the Style key ([Alt]-[F8]) and turn on the **Indent** style.
5. Repeat steps 3 and 4 on each of the remaining magazine references.

Saving

Press the Save key ([F10]) to save the document as B:FINAL3. When the
Document Summary screen appears, enter appropriate information.

Revising

On reviewing the document, your boss decides that the file should be
single-spaced. To single-space the document, you must edit the style.

Edit a Style
[Alt]-[F8] , *4*

1. Press the Style key ([Alt]-[F8]).
2. Highlight the **Normal Text** style.
3. Type 4 to edit the style.
4. Change the description to read **Set tabs and set left margin at 15**
   and press [Enter].
5. Type 4 to select Codes.
6. Delete the [**Ln Spacing:2**] code by highlighting and using [Del] key.
7. Press Exit ([F7]) three times to return to the edit screen.
   RESULT: The document is now single-spaced.

Create Two Footnotes
[Ctrl]-[F7] , *1, 1*

To give the document more authority, your supervisor would like to enter
two footnotes.

1. Move the cursor to the end of the first sentence after the period in the **FINDINGS** paragraph.

2. Press the Footnotes key (`Ctrl`-`F7`).
   RESULT: The following menu appears at the bottom of the screen:

   1 Footnote; 2 Endnote; 3 Endnote Placement: 0

3. Type **1** to select the Footnote option.
   RESULT: The following menu appears at the bottom of the screen:

   Footnote: 1 Create; 2 Edit; 3 New Number; 4 Options: 0

4. Type **1** to create a footnote.
   RESULT: The footnote screen appears as shown in Figure 3.14. Everything that you now type will appear in the footnote.

5. Type **Hughes, M., "Trade Shows: America's Most Misunderstood Marketing Tool," Business Digest, May 1985.**

6. Press Exit (`F7`) when finished.
   RESULT: You are back at the edit screen and the number 1 appears at the end of the sentence. Use the View document option in Print (`Shift`-`F7`) to see how the footnote appears on the page.

Add a Footnote
`Ctrl`-`F7`, *1, 1*

You need one more footnote.

1. Move the cursor after the period at the end of the FINDINGS paragraph.

2. Press the Footnotes key (`Ctrl`-`F7`).

3. Type **1** to select the Footnote option.

4. Type **1** to create a footnote.

5. Type **Hughes. 1985.**

6. Press Exit (`F7`) when finished.

Saving

Press the Save key (`F10`) to save the document as B:FINAL3.

Printing

Print the document using the Print command (`Shift`-`F7`) and selecting the **Full Document** option.

Exiting
`F7`, Y, Y

Exit the document by following these steps:

1. Press the Exit key (`F7`).

2. Type **Y** to save the changes you may have made since last saving the file.

3. Press `Enter`.

4. Type **Y** to save the changes you made to the file.

5. Type **Y** if you want to leave WordPerfect.
    Type **N** if you want to continue working.

Summary

You created styles using the Style key (Alt-F8). To create a new style, you chose the create option, entered the name, type, and description for each style. You then entered the specific codes for each style.

To apply the style to the document, you put the cursor where the style should begin (in the case of paired styles you highlighted the text to be affected). You then pressed the Style key (Alt-F8), highlighted the style that you wanted, and turned it on.

To create hanging indents, you used the Indent key (F4) and the Margin Release key (Shift-Tab) in conjunction.

To create footnotes, you used the Footnote key (Ctrl-F7).

Chapter Review

Key Terms

Footnote key   Paired style
Hanging indents   Style description
Margin release   Style key
Open style   Style name

Review Questions

1. Briefly discuss two major advantages of using styles.
2. Briefly discuss one difference between using macros and using styles to format text.
3. List the two kinds of styles. Provide two examples of when you would use each kind.
4. The open and paired style edit screens are similar to what other screen you have used in WordPerfect?
5. Briefly describe how WordPerfect separates a footnote from the rest of the text.
6. How is the Margin Release key useful for creating hanging indents? Can you think of a way to create hanging indents without using the Margin Release key?

Applications

1. Retrieve the file NEWSREL on the Student Data Disk and follow these instructions to create the document shown in Figure 3.15:

    a. Create styles to
    - Create the news release header and company information.
    - Capitalize the title.
    - Double-space the text.

    b. Apply the styles to the document.

    c. Save the document as B:DRILL3-1.

    d. Print the document.

FIGURE 3.15

```
N E W S   R E L E A S E

Exhibit Place
Computer City, CA 94584

Release:   Immediate
From:      Regina Mitchell, Public Relations Director

KEN TANAKA NAMED DIRECTOR OF NEW WAVE TRADE SHOW

     Computer City, May 1--Ken Tanaka has been appointed director
of the New Wave Trade Show in Computer City. The announcement was
made yesterday by Brigitte Neuendorff, president of the trade show
committee. Tanaka succeeds Dave Bowman, who resigned April 10
after eight years of service.
     The New Wave Trade Show is the largest microcomputer show in
America. Since it will host 2,000 computer vendors from around the
world, it promises to stimulate business in the valley. Mayor Tom
Riggs comments, "I am extremely pleased that Ken (Tanaka) has
taken the position. He understands the city and its people better
than anybody I know."
     A civic leader for 24 years, Tanaka is most known as founder
and chief executive officer of Exhibit Place--a $25 million
company that specializes in developing and promoting expositions,
exhibits, and trade fairs.
```

2.   Retrieve the file RESUME from the Student Data Disk and follow these instructions to create the document shown in Figure 3.16.

   a. Create styles to
   - Bold and center the title.
   - Create the address.
   - Create hanging indents out of bulleted instructions.
   - Bold headings.
   - Set the tabs at 25 (2.5") and 27 (2.7").
   - Right-flush dates.
   - Underline titles.
   - Insert indents.

   b. Apply the styles to the document RESUME.

   c. Save the document as B:DRILL3-2.

   d. Print the document.

FIGURE 3.16

Emily Dickerson
2620 Ardmore Street
Computer City, CA 94583
(619) 792-8100

EDUCATION	M.B.A.	June 1989
	University of California, Los Angeles	
	Major Emphasis: Marketing	
	Minor Emphasis: Information Systems	
	B. A. Graphic Design	June 1982
	University of California, Riverside	
EXPERIENCE	<u>SENIOR EXHIBITION DESIGNER</u>	Nov 1985–
	Exhibit Place	Present

Designed and managed exhibitions for 13 major computer vendors. Received Cy Howard Exhibition Excellence Award 1989.

	<u>INFORMATION SYSTEMS CONSULTANT</u>	May 1986–
	Office Computing Division	Sept 1988
	Metropolitan Electric Company	

Analyzed marketing needs for hydro-electric department. Wrote and coordinated marketing development project. Edited product brochures, business cases, management

MORE

```
briefs and reports.
Specific accomplishments include:
· Designed and co-developed ISPF on-line Bulletin Board
  System used by the Company to communicate changing
  technical information to geographically dispersed work
  groups
· Researched and developed exhibition in local area
  networks and data communication standards
· Co-wrote and edited business cases for electronic mail
  implementation study
· Trouble-shot technical problems on personal computers,
  PC software, and micro-to-mainframe communication
  links.
```

SKILLS
```
IBM Personal Computer: Familiar with PASCAL, Ashton-Tate
and RBASE DataBase Management Systems. Experienced with
WordStar, Microsoft Word, WordPerfect, WordPerfect
Office, DisplayWrite, Ventura Publisher, Harvard
Graphics, GEM Graphics, DOS, OS/2. Mainframe:
Experienced with ISPF Software Development Program,
FOCUS, and SAS.
```

3. Retrieve the file NAUTILUS on the Student Data Disk and follow these instructions to create the document shown in Figure 3.17:

   a. Create styles to
   - Create the memo header.
   - Double-space the text.

   b. Apply the styles to the document.

   c. Save the document as B:DRILL3-3.

   d. Print the document.

FIGURE 3.17

```
DATE:      OCTOBER 15, 19--

FROM:      KEN TANAKA
           PRESIDENT

TO:        ALL EMPLOYEES

SUBJECT:   NAUTILUS DEADLINE


           MORE    ▼
```

You can take advantage of the FREE Nautilus VIP memberships for

one more week. I strongly encourage you and your family to

participate in this fine program. Remember, there is no charge

and membership is valid at any Nautilus location in Computer City.

See Michelle Strongman in the Administrative Office for your

membership!

4. Retrieve the file FORMLET on the Student Data Disk and follow these instructions to create the document shown in Figure 3.18:

    a. Create styles to:
- Enter the date.
- Create hanging indents for the numbered items.
- Enter the closing.

    b. Apply the styles to the document.

    c. Save the document as B:DRILL3-4.

    d. Print the document.

FIGURE 3.18

December 12, 19--

Tom Clancy
President
Red Harbor Graphics
13 Oriel Lane
Houston, Texas 30945

Dear Mr. Clancy:

The information you requested on Thursday has been sent to you.
When you receive the brochure, please review it to get a general
idea of the kind of service the Exhibit Place provides its clients.

In the brochure, you will note the following:

1. Designers who design your exhibit to enhance your company image
    or to create an entirely new one.

MORE

2. Graphics Specialists who create modern, appealing, visual effects through lighting and imagery that attract customer interest.
3. Construction Personnel who specialize in exhibit production to ensure quality workmanship.
4. Marketing Personnel who are experts in helping you sell your products and services through the design strategies of a unique marketing tool--the exhibit itself.

To find out specifically how the Exhibit Place can enhance your company image at a trade show, please call our special hotline number (402) 987-0998. One of our representatives will be available to answer any questions you have.

Sincerely,

Ellen Nasus
Marketing Director

---

5. Retrieve the file MARKLET on the Student Data Disk and follow these instructions to create the document shown in Figure 3.19:

   a. Create styles to
      ▪ Enter the date.
      ▪ Underline text.
      ▪ Bold text.

   b. Apply the styles to the document.

   c. Save the document as B:DRILL3-5.

   d. Print the document.

FIGURE 3.19

November 8, 19--

Bill Durham
Marketing Manager
Shangri-La Computing
431 Howard Avenue
Santa Cruz, CA 93583

Dear Mr. Durham:

 MORE

Are you satisfied with the image your company projects at trade shows? If not, have you ever considered allowing <u>professional image makers</u> create your exhibit?

The **EXHIBIT PLACE** is a company that specializes in creating trade exhibits. Not only does the **EXHIBIT PLACE** work with you to develop an exhibit that will present your company's products and services in the most appealing manner to its customers, but it also will make your job easier by eliminating many of your exhibit worries. The **EXHIBIT PLACE** is a full-service exhibit house. By full service, we mean that you have available to you the following:

1. **Designers** who can enhance your company image.

2. **Graphics Specialists** who can create appealing exhibits.

3. **Construction Personnel** who can ensure quality workmanship.

4. **Marketing Experts** who can help you sell your products.

To find out more about the **EXHIBIT PLACE,** please review the enclosed materials. For your convenience, we have included a list of our clients. We also have a hotline number to give you immediate answers to any questions you might have. Please call (402) 493-0042.

Sincerely,

Ellen Nasus

---

6. Retrieve the file MARKET3 on the Student Data Disk and follow these instructions:

   a. Edit the Indent style so that, in addition to creating hanging indents, it also does these two tasks:

      i. Sets the tabs so that two spaces separate the numbered items from the text in the hanging indents.

      ii. Resets the tabs at the end of the hanging indent so that the paragraphs in the normal text are properly indented.

   b. Apply the styles to the document.

   c. Save the document as B:DRILL3-6.

   d. Print the document.

Advanced Skills

When you save a file that you created using styles, the styles you used are saved along with the file. Sometimes, though, you might want others to be able to use the same styles that you created. You can *save styles* as a separate file and give them to others by following these steps:

1. Press the Style key (⌨Alt⌨-⌨F8⌨).
2. Type **6** to select the Save option.
3. Type a filename with an extension of **STY** and press ⌨Enter⌨. For example, MARKET.STY.
4. Press Exit (⌨F7⌨) to return to the edit screen.

   We recommend you use the STY extension on all your style files so you can identify them at a glance.

Using Style Files

To use a file containing styles in your document, you need to *retrieve the style file* by following these instructions:

1. Press the Style key (⌨Alt⌨-⌨F8⌨).
2. Type 7 to select the Retrieve option.
3. Type the name of the file you want to retrieve and press ⌨Enter⌨. For example, MARKET.STY.

   The styles will then appear on the style screen. If the styles you are retrieving are already on the screen, WordPerfect will ask you if you still want to retrieve them. Typing Y will replace the styles on the screen with the styles in the file. Typing N will end the retrieve option.

Advanced Key Terms

Save a style file   Retrieve a style file

Advanced Review Questions

1. Briefly describe a situation when you would want to save styles as a separate file.
2. Explain in two or three sentences why it is important to give style files an .STY extension.
3. List the step(s) required to retrieve a style file.
4. Briefly describe a situation when you would want to retrieve a style file.

Advanced Applications

1. Retrieve the file ADVAPP1 on the Student Data Disk and follow these instructions:
   a. Create an Indent style that does these tasks:

- Sets the tabs so that two spaces separate the numbered items from the text in the hanging indents.
- Creates hanging indents.
- Resets the tabs at the end of the hanging indent so that the paragraphs in the normal text are properly indented.

    b. Apply the style to the numbered items in the document.
    c. Save the style as INDENT.STY.
    d. Save the document as B:DRILL3-7.
    e. Print the document.
    f. Exit WordPerfect.

2. Start WordPerfect and follow these instructions:
    a. Retrieve the file ADVAPP2 on the Student Data Disk.
    b. Retrieve INDENT.STY.
    c. Apply the style to the numbered items in the document.
    d. Save the document as B:DRILL3-8.
    e. Print the document.

On Your Own

Create your own resume to help you apply for the job of your choice. Use your imagination and format the resume as effectively as possible to emphasize your strengths. Once you have created a resume that satisfies you, prepare a style sheet called RESUME.STY so other people can benefit from your format.

```
                        Exhibit Place
                    1611 N.W. 12th Avenue
                    Computer City, CA 94584



        November 20, 19--


        Mr. Todd Lincoln
        Graphics Extravaganza
        512 Cycle Boulevard
        Rivermore, PA 09745

        Dear Mr. Lincoln:

        This will confirm your registration, aisle, and date
        for the New Wave Trade Show:

                    Aisle B12           August 3

        If I can be of any more service, please feel free to
        give me a call at (408) 555-6434.

        Sincerely,


        Michelle Strongman

        hm
```

In this chapter, you will create a form letter that prompts you to insert information in the correct place.

4

Merging Business Letters and Mailing Lists

Chapter Objectives

After completing this chapter you will be able to

1. Ensure that WordPerfect skips over missing information that you specify.

2. Combine information from a secondary file with information that a WordPerfect user has.

3. Prompt users to enter information.

WordPerfect Commands

Shift - F9 , 1	Enter Field codes
F9	End Field code
Shift - F9 , 2	End Record code
Ctrl - F9 , 1	Merge primary and secondary files
Shift - F9 , 1-?	Skip line if field is blank
Shift - F9 , 3	Input information from the keyboard with a message
Ctrl - F9 , 1, F9	Merge letters that contain an Input code

Overview

The Merge command lets you send the same letter to many people. You can create a letter in one file, called the *primary file,* and a list of names and addresses in another, called the *secondary file,* and merge the two using the Merge key (Ctrl-F9) to create several copies of the same letter.

Figure 4.1 provides an example of a primary file. As you recall, the primary file contains special codes (such as {FIELD}1~, {FIELD}2~, and {FIELD}3~) called *field indicators* that stand in place of data that will be changing from letter to letter, such as the name, address, and salutation.

FIGURE 4.1 *The primary file.*

```
October 5, 19--


{FIELD}1~
{FIELD}2~
{FIELD}3~, {FIELD}4~ {FIELD}5~

Dear {FIELD}6~:

We've seen it happen so many times. A company invests money with a
trade show important to its economic growth only to find that, to
compete, it must spend far more money on exhibits and advertising
than it really can afford. After all, it does not want to look
inferior.

But what can you do? Some of your competitors spend as much as six
figures designing exhibits and displays for the New Wave Trade
Show. Such numbers are far beyond most companies' budgets.

Perhaps we can help. To compete successfully at New Wave, you do
not have to spend several hundred thousand dollars. We have built
our reputation on the fact that good design and interesting,
attention-getting exhibits are more a matter of common sense,
creativity, and ingenuity than of great amounts of money.

Exhibit Place can

1.   Analyze your product.
2.   Create customized marketing strategies for you.
```

MORE ▼

3.   Work with your public relations staff to develop the most
     effective exhibit and trade show campaign possible for your
     budget.

AS A PARTICIPANT OF THE NEW WAVE TRADE SHOW, you are guaranteed
immediate priority for a Stage A marketing analysis performed by
our professional staff. You will not be turned down.
Please read the enclosed material immediately. It provides
complete details on how you can take advantage of this exclusive
offer.

And remember . . . our immediate response is guaranteed.

Sincerely,

Ellen Nasus
Marketing Director

The data for the primary file are supplied by the secondary file, as
shown in Figure 4.2. The secondary file lists the names and addresses that
personalize the letter. Each segment of information before an {END
FIELD} is called a *field*. The first {END FIELD} is field 1, the second
{END FIELD} is field 2, and so on. The {END RECORD} signals the
end of one record and the beginning of another.

FIGURE 4.2   *The secondary file.*

```
Ms. Sarah Stevenson{END FIELD}
143 Beverly Blvd.{END FIELD}
West Los Angeles{END FIELD}
CA{END FIELD}
91232{END FIELD}
Ms. Stevenson{END FIELD}
{END RECORD}
================================================================
Mr. Randy Peynault{END FIELD}
23 Elsinor Drive{END FIELD}
Seattle{END FIELD}
WA{END FIELD}
99492{END FIELD}
Mr. Peynault{END FIELD}
{END RECORD}
================================================================
```

        MORE   ▼

```
Mr. and Mrs. Fred Wyles{END FIELD}
1230 Market Street{END FIELD}
San Francisco{END FIELD}
CA{END FIELD}
91234{END FIELD}
Mr. and Mrs. Wyles{END FIELD}
{END RECORD}
================================================================
Mr. Mike McQuead{END FIELD}
P. O. Box 203{END FIELD}
Santa Fe{END FIELD}
NM{END FIELD}
80945{END FIELD}
Mr. McQuead{END RECORD}
================================================================
Ms. Rosie Requena{END FIELD}
912 Pine Avenue{END FIELD}
Boise{END FIELD}
ID{END FIELD}
73452{END FIELD}
Ms. Requena{END RECORD}
```

It is important when merging files that the field indicators in the primary file correctly match the fields in the secondary file. For example, the heading below contains six field indicators:

```
{FIELD}1~
{FIELD}2~
{FIELD}3~
{FIELD}4~  {FIELD}5~

Dear {FIELD}6~:
```

Each field indicator matches one of the six fields in the first record of the secondary file:

```
Mr. Gil Hadley{END FIELD} (Field 1)
President{END FIELD} (Field 2)
254 Via Los Miradores{END FIELD} (Field 3)
Santa Fe, NM{END FIELD} (Field 4)
65342{END FIELD} (Field 5)
Gil{END FIELD} (Field 6)
{END RECORD} (End of Record)
```

If fields do not correctly match the field indicators, the merge is thrown off. For example, if you do not have a zip code in field 5, the salutation (field 6) will move to field 5 and the secondary record will look like this:

```
Mr. Gil Hadley{END FIELD} (Field 1)
President{END FIELD} (Field 2)
245 Via Los Miradores{END FIELD} (Field 3)
```

```
Santa Fe, NM{END FIELD} (Field 4)
Gil{END FIELD} (Field 5)
{END RECORD} (End of Record)
```

When merged, the salutation will appear where the zip code should have gone:

```
Mr. Gil Hadley
President
245 Via Los Miradores
Santa Fe, NM Gil

Dear :
```

Because it is not always possible to have all the information needed for a merge, WordPerfect provides a method for ensuring that fields and field indicators stay correctly matched. If data for any of the fields in a secondary file is unavailable, you simply press the *End Field* key (F9) where the missing data belongs. For example, to correct the problem shown above, you press F9 where the zip code belongs.

The secondary record will look like this:

```
Mr. Gil Hadley{END FIELD} (Field 1)
President{END FIELD} (Field 2)
245 Via Los Miradores{END FIELD} (Field 3)
Santa Fe, NM{END FIELD} (Field 4)
{END FIELD} (Field 5)
Gil{END FIELD} (Field 6)
{END RECORD} (End of Record)
```

And the first letter will look like this when merged:

```
Mr. Gil Hadley
President
245 Via Los Miradores
Santa Fe, NM

Dear Gil:
```

If you leave an empty field in the secondary file with just an End Field code, WordPerfect leaves a blank space where the field should have been. Often this is fine (such as in the zip code example above), but in other cases it would leave a blank line that you do not want. For example, if Gil Hadley's title were not available, the secondary file would look like this:

```
Mr. Gil Hadley{END FIELD} (Field 1)
{END FIELD} (Field 2)
245 Via Los Miradores{END FIELD} (Field 3)
Santa Fe, NM{END FIELD} (Field 4)
65342{END FIELD} (Field 5)
Gil{END FIELD} (Field 6)
{END RECORD} (End of Record)
```

And the letter would look like the following:

```
Mr. Gil Hadley

245 Via Los Miradores
Santa Fe, NM 65342

Dear Gil:
```

To prevent WordPerfect from leaving a blank line, you must add a question mark on the inside of any field indicator in the primary file that may be missing data:

```
{FIELD}2?~
```

To do this, you place your cursor on the tilde (~) and type the question mark. The primary file would look like this:

```
{FIELD}1~
{FIELD}2?~
{FIELD}3~
{FIELD}4~  {FIELD}5~

Dear {FIELD}6~:
```

And after a merge operation, the letter would appear:

```
Mr. Gil Hadley
245 Via Los Miradores
Santa Fe, NM 65342

Dear Gil:
```

Because the question mark tells WordPerfect to skip the line if data are missing, you must be careful not to use the question mark on lines that contain more than one field. Otherwise, WordPerfect will skip it. For example, if you place a question mark in the zip code field and WordPerfect finds a record that does not have a zip code, it will skip the entire line, including the city and state field.

Merging from Keyboard: The Input Code

What if you send out only one or two copies of a particular form letter a week? Do you still have to create a secondary file just to merge one or two letters? The answer is no. You can enter data directly into a primary file from the keyboard and skip the secondary file entirely.

To enter information manually from the keyboard, you replace the field indicators ({FIELD}1~, {FIELD}2~, {FIELD}3~, and so on) in the primary file with an *Input code*. The Input code tells WordPerfect to stop at a certain point while merging a document so that you can type information from the keyboard. It also displays a message on the status line that prompts the user what information should be entered. This is particularly useful if someone else is using the Merge function and doesn't know what information needs to be keyed in.

To see how this works, suppose you are sending out bank statements to customers and you want to enter their balances from the keyboard. You might then create a primary file that contains a message similar to the following:

```
Your November bank balance is: {INPUT}Type the
customer's balance and press Enter~.
```

During the merge operation, when the cursor moves to the Input code, the message *Type the customer's balance and press Enter* appears in the status line and WordPerfect waits for you to fill in the bank balance. After you have keyed the information, you then press [F9] to continue the merge.

Combining Field and Input Codes

You can also combine field indicators with the Input code in situations where you want to merge data that may be in the secondary file with information that the word processing operator may have. For example, in the bank statement example above, WordPerfect can fill out the name and address from a secondary file and then stop at an Input code and wait for you to enter the customer's balance. The primary file might look like the following:

```
{FIELD}1~
{FIELD}2~
{FIELD}3~  {FIELD}4~

Dear {FIELD}5~:

Your November bank balance is: {INPUT}Type the
customer's balance and press Enter~.
```

While merging, WordPerfect will place names and addresses in the first five fields and stop at the Input code, display a message in the status line, and wait for you to fill in the balance manually.

As you can see, WordPerfect's merge commands are powerful enough for you to create useful merge operations for an entire office.

Tutorial

Michelle Strongman has asked you to send out five letters to customers confirming their registration at the New Wave Trade show. Because not all customers have titles, you must be careful that WordPerfect does not leave blank lines where their titles should appear in the letters.

Michelle does not have exhibits dates confirmed with the New Wave committee yet. Rather than leave a blank field, you decide to create the primary and secondary letters. When Michelle finds out the exhibit date schedule, she will let you know and you will generate the letters.

Looking at the draft of the letter Michelle has given you, you decide to leave a 12-line (2.83") top margin, and 15-space (1.5") left and right margins. Because you will be sending out the letter again, you decide to use a Date code for the date.

To produce the five personalized letters, you will create two files:

1. A primary file containing the letter, field indicators, a Prompt code, and Input code. You will call this file REGIS.PF.

2. A secondary file containing the five names and addresses of customers. You will call this file REGIS.SF.

When you merge the files, WordPerfect will stop at each Input code and wait for you to enter the customer's registration date.

Setting Up

To begin, place the Student Data Disk in drive B and start WordPerfect. You will start by creating the primary letter.

Formatting

Since the personalized letters will eventually be printed on letterhead, you need to increase the top margin to 12 lines (2.83"). You also need to increase the left and right margins to 15 spaces (1.5") each.

Change Top Margin
Shift - F8 , *2, 5, 12*

To change the top margin:

1. Press the Format key (Shift - F8).

2. Type **2** to select the Page option.

3. Type **5** to select the Margin option.

4. Type **12** to change the top margin and press Enter three times to return to the Format menu.

Change Left and Right Margins
Shift - F8 , *1, 7, 15, 15*

To change the left and right margins:

1. Type **1** to select the Line option.

2. Type **7** to select the Margin option.

3. Type **15** to change the left margin and press Enter .

4. Type **15** to change the right margin and press Enter three times to return to the edit screen.

Keyboarding

When you complete the primary file, it will look like Figure 4.3.

Enter Heading and Date Code
Shift - F6 , Shift - F5 , *2*

To begin, first enter the Exhibit Place address and the Date code.

1. Press the Center key (Shift - F6) each time you type the following three lines:

```
Exhibit Place
1611 N.W. 12th Avenue
Computer City, CA 94584
```

2. Press ⸢Enter⸥ four times.

3. Press the Date key (⸢Shift⸥-⸢F5⸥).

4. Type **2** to select the Date code.

5. Press ⸢Enter⸥ five times to put the cursor in position for the first field indicator.

FIGURE 4.3

```
                  Exhibit Place
              1611 N.W. 12th Avenue
              Computer City, CA 94584


July 16, 1990

{FIELD}1~
{FIELD}2?~
{FIELD}3~
{FIELD}4~
{FIELD}5~, {FIELD}6~ {FIELD}7~

Dear {FIELD}8~:

This will confirm your registration, aisle, and date
for the New Wave Trade Show:

          Aisle: {FIELD}9~  {INPUT}Type the
customer's show date.~

If I can be of any more service, please feel free to
give me a call at (408)555-6434.

Sincerely,



Michelle Strongman

hm
```

Enter Field Codes

⸢Shift⸥-⸢F9⸥, *1*

To create the primary letter, you must enter six codes for the data fields. To enter the field codes, follow these steps:

1. Press the Merge Codes key (⸢Shift⸥-⸢F9⸥).

   RESULT: You should see this prompt in the lower left corner of your screen:

```
1 Field; 2 End Record; 3 Input; 4 Page Off; 5 Next
Record; 6 More: 0
```

2. Type **1** to insert the first field code.
    RESULT: You will see this prompt in the lower left corner of your screen:

    `Enter Field:`

3. Type **1** to insert the first field code (recipient's full name) and press `Enter` twice to move to the next line.

Skip Line if Field Is Blank

`Shift`-`F9`, *1, ?*

Because not all addresses have titles, you decide to put a question mark on field 2.

1. Press the Merge Codes key (`Shift`-`F9`).
2. Type **1** and **2** to insert the second field code (title). Press `Enter`.
3. Move the cursor to the tilde (~) in "{FIELD}2~" and Type **?** (a question mark).
    NOTE: WordPerfect should be in Insert mode. Field 2 should now look like {FIELD}2?~.
4. Press the right arrow (`→`) once and press `Enter`.

Enter Field Indicators

`Shift`-`F9`, *1*

You can now finish entering the field indicators.

1. Press the Merge Codes key (`Shift`-`F9`).
2. Type **1** and **3** to insert the third field code (company) and press `Enter` twice.
3. Press the Merge Codes key (`Shift`-`F9`), Type **1** and **4** to insert the fourth field code (street address), and press `Enter` twice.
4. Press the Merge Codes key (`Shift`-`F9`), Type **1** and **5** to insert the fifth field code (city). Press `Enter`.
5. Type **,** (a comma) and press the space bar.
6. Press the Merge Codes key (`Shift`-`F9`).
7. Type **1** and **6** to insert the sixth field code (state) and press `Enter`.
8. Press the space bar once and press the Merge Codes key (`Shift`-`F9`).
9. Type **1** and **7** to insert the seventh field code (zip code). Then press `Enter` three times.
10. Type **Dear** and press the space bar once.
11. Press the Merge Codes key (`Shift`-`F9`).
12. Type **1** and **8** to insert the eighth field code (salutation). Then press `Enter` once.
13. Type **:** (a colon) and press `Enter` twice.

```
                        Exhibit Place
                     1611 N.W. 12th Avenue
                    Computer City, CA 94584


     May 14, 1990



     {FIELD}1~
     {FIELD}2?~
     {FIELD}3~
     {FIELD}4~
     {FIELD}5~, {FIELD}6~ {FIELD}7~

     Dear {FIELD}8~:

     This will confirm your registration, aisle, and date for
     the New Wave Trade Show:

                       aisle: {FIELD}9~              {INPUT}Type t
     show date and press Enter.~
                              Doc 1 Pg 1 Ln 24 Pos 42
```

FIGURE 4.4

The Input Code ({INPUT} message~) appears on the screen.

Enter Text

You are now ready to type the body of the letter.

1. Type:

   This will confirm your registration, aisle, and
   date for the New Wave Trade Show:.

2. Press [Enter] twice to move the cursor down two lines.

3. Move the cursor to position 30 (3")by pressing the [Tab] key three times.

4. Type **Aisle** and press the space bar.

5. Press the Merge Codes key ([Shift]-[F9]).

6. Type **1** and **9** to insert the ninth field code (aisle number). Press [Enter].

   You are now ready to enter an Input code and message.

Enter an Input Code
[Shift]-[F9], *3*

To enter an Input code, follow these steps:

1. Tab to position 50 (5") on the same line as "Aisle."

2. Press the Merge Codes key ([Shift]-[F9]).

3. Type **3** for Input.

   RESULT: The following prompt appears on the status line:

   Enter message:

4. Type the customer's show date.

5. Press [Enter].

   RESULT: The Input code appears on the screen as in Figure 4.4.

6. Press [Enter] twice to move the cursor down two lines.

7. Finish entering the letter by typing:

```
If I can be of any more service, please feel free
to give me a call at (408)555-6434.

Sincerely,



Michelle Strongman
hm
```

Saving

When you finish typing the entire letter, press F10 and save the file under this name: B:REGIS.PF (PF stands for primary file). (Type over Primlett.)

NOTE: We recommend that you put the extension .PF on every primary file you create and .SF on every secondary file.

When the Document Summary screen appears, enter this information:

```
Document Name    Primary letter for confirming
                 dates
Author           Michelle Strongman
Typist           (Your Name)
Subject          New Wave registration
Abstract         Merge this file with REGIS.SF.
                 Contains a console code to enter
                 registration dates manually.
```

8. Clear the screen by pressing F7 and typing N (for No Save) and N (for No Exit).

You are now ready to create the secondary file.

The Secondary File
F9 *and* Shift-F9, *2*

The secondary file contains the information to be merged into the primary file.

1. Type **Todd Lincoln.**
2. Press F9.

RESULT: The {END FIELD} code appears at the end of the line and a hard return [HRt] moves the cursor to the next line.

3. Press F9 again to leave a blank line because we don't know his title.

4. Type the secondary file, as shown in Figure 4.5. At the end of each line, press the End Field key (F9), *not* the Enter key.

5. On the last line of each record (every ninth line), press the Merge codes key (Shift-F9), and Type **2** for End Record. (Type over Secolett.)

RESULT: The End Record code appears. The {End Record} code puts a hard page break between letters so that they print on different sheets of paper. The hard page break appears on screen as a row of double dashes (==========).

FIGURE 4.5

```
Todd Lincoln{END FIELD}
{END FIELD}
Graphics Extravaganza{END FIELD}
512 Cycle Boulevard{END FIELD}
Rivermore{END FIELD}
PA{END FIELD}
09745{END FIELD}
Mr. Lincoln{END FIELD}
B2{END FIELD}
{END RECORD}
================================================================
Noel Larson{END FIELD}
President{END FIELD}
Advanced Publishing Company{END FIELD}
1412 Fredricks Street{END FIELD}
Columbus{END FIELD}
OH{END FIELD}
44367{END FIELD}
Mr. Larson{END FIELD}
B2{END FIELD}
{END RECORD}
================================================================
Lisa Rayes{END FIELD}
Marketing Director{END FIELD}
Northwest Mail Order{END FIELD}
120 Seymour Street, Suite 512{END FIELD}
Seattle{END FIELD}
WA{END FIELD}
99745{END FIELD}
Ms. Rayes{END FIELD}
B2{END FIELD}
{END RECORD}
================================================================
Mary Oshiro{END FIELD}
{END FIELD}
Computer Interface Specialists{END FIELD}
349 Figueroa Street, Suite 1204{END FIELD}
Los Angeles{END FIELD}
CA{END FIELD}
90521{END FIELD}
Ms. Oshiro{END FIELD}
B2{END FIELD}
{END RECORD}
================================================================
Bill Hughes{END FIELD}
{END FIELD}
Hughes Software Games and Innovations{END FIELD}
Route 1A{END FIELD}
```

MORE ▼

```
Porterville{END FIELD}
IN{END FIELD}
43256{END FIELD}
Mr. Hughes{END FIELD}
B2{END FIELD}
{END RECORD}
================================================================
```

Saving

When you finish typing the secondary file, save the file under the name B:REGIS.SF using F10. When the Document Summary screen appears, enter this information:

Document Name	**Secondary letter for confirming dates**
Author	**Michelle Strongman**
Typist	**(Your name)**
Subject	**New Wave registration**
Abstract	**Merges with REGIS.PF. Registration dates will be entered manually.**

Michelle Strongman now gives you the registration dates for each customer as shown in Figure 4.6. You are now ready to create the five personalized letters by merging the secondary file (REGIS.SF) to the primary file (REGIS.PF). You will enter the registration dates when WordPerfect stops at the Input code for each letter.

FIGURE 4.6

NAME	DATE OF REGISTRATION
Todd Lincoln	August 3
Noel Larson	August 5
Lisa Rayes	August 2
Mary Oshiro	August 3
Bill Hughes	August 1

Merging Letters with an Input Code
Ctrl - F9 , *1*, F9

To merge the primary and secondary files with a code, first clear the screen.

1. Press the Exit key (F7) and Type **N N** to clear the screen.
   NOTE: You already saved the secondary file as B:REGIS.SF so it is not lost.

2. Press the Merge/Sort key (Ctrl-F9).
   RESULT: You will see the following prompt at the bottom of the screen:

   1 Merge; 2 Sort; 3 Convert Old Merge Codes: 0

```
                          Exhibit Place
                      1611 N.W. 12th Avenue
                      Computer City, CA 94584


      May 14, 1990



      Todd Lincoln
      Graphics Extravaganza
      512 Cycle Blvd
      Rivermore, PA 09745

      Dear Mr. Lincoln:

      This will confirm your registration, aisle, and date for
      the New Wave Trade Show:

                           aisle: B2


  Type the customer's show date and press Enter.      Doc 1 Pg 1 Ln 22 Pos 50
```

FIGURE 4.7

WordPerfect stops at the Input Code ({INPUT}message~) and provides the prompt to the user in the status line. The user should now enter the customer's date and press the End Field key ([F9]) to go to the next letter.

3. Type **1** to select Merge.
   RESULT: The following prompt appears at the bottom of the screen:

   Primary file:

4. Type **B:REGIS.PF** and press [Enter].
   RESULT: The following prompt appears at the bottom of the screen:

   Secondary file:

5. Type **B:REGIS.SF** and press [Enter].
   RESULT: The letter appears on the screen with your message in the status line as shown in Figure 4.7.

6. Type **August 3**.

7. Press the End Field key ([F9]) to go to the next letter.

8. Repeat steps 6 and 7 for all five letters, using Figure 4.6 to get the date for each customer.

Printing

Print the five letters using the Print command ([Shift]-[F7]) and selecting 1 for Full Document.

Saving

Save the five merged letters in a file called B:REGIS.MRG using [F10]. Because merge files (such as REGIS.MRG) use the same Document Summary as the primary file, you need to create a new Document Summary for REGIS.MRG for following these steps:

1. Press the Format command ([Shift]-[F8]).

2. Type **3** to select the Document option.

3. Type **5** to select the Summary option.

4. Enter the following information:

```
Document Name    5 letters confirming registration
Author           Michelle Strongman
Typist           (Your Name)
Subject          New Wave Trade Show
Abstract         Merged from REGIS.PF and
                 REGIS.SF.
```

Exiting

If you are ready to leave WordPerfect, exit using the Exit key (F7). If you are going to continue working, clear the screen using the Exit key (F7).

Summary

To produce the five personalized letters, you created two files: a primary file and a secondary file. You entered the field indicators in the primary file by using the Merge Codes key (Shift-F9) and typing 1. You entered a question mark (?) on the field indicators of fields for which you did not have all the information.

You entered the End Field codes in the secondary file by pressing F9. For fields that you did not have information, you simply entered {END FIELD} without entering any text. You created {END RECORD} by pressing the Merge Codes key (Shift-F9) and typing 2.

To insert information from the keyboard into a merged document and display a message, you used the {INPUT} message~ command. You created the {INPUT}message~ command by selecting option 3 on the Merge Codes menu.

You then merged the primary and secondary document by pressing the Merge key (Ctrl-F9). Each time WordPerfect stopped at a keyboard command, you typed text and then pressed the End Field key (F9) to move to the next document.

Chapter Review

Key Terms

End Field key
Field indicator
Fields
Input code
Merge command

Merge key
Merge Codes key
Primary file
Prompt code
Secondary file

Review Questions

1. Briefly discuss the roles of the primary and secondary files in the merge function—what does each file provide?

2. What code do you enter at the end of each field in the secondary file?

3. What is a field?

4. What code do you enter at the end of each record in the secondary file?

5. True or False: The final result of the merge function is a third file—the results of the merging of the primary and secondary files.

6. Under what circumstance would you want to include a question mark (?) with the field indicator?

7. Briefly describe how you show that a field is blank in the secondary file.

8. Is the following a proper use of field indicators for the city, state, and zip code of an address?
{FIELD}1~, {FIELD}2~ {FIELD}3?~
Briefly explain why or why not.

9. Describe two situations when you would want to use an Input code.

Applications

Please complete the following merge exercises.

1. Create several copies of a thank you letter by following these instructions.

   a. Retrieve the file called THANKU on the Student Data Disk.

   b. Create the primary file shown in Figure 4.8.

   c. Use the date text option for the date.

   d. Create messages to accompany each Input code, telling the user what information to enter.

   e. Save the document as B:DRILL4-1.PF.

   f. Generate three letters by using the Merge key and inserting the information in Figure 4.9 to fill in each letter.

   g. Save the final letters as B:DRILL4-1.MRG on the Student Data Disk.

2. Generate form letters by following these steps:

   a. Create a secondary file out of the information in Figure 4.9. Save the file as B:DRILL4-2.SF.

FIGURE 4.8

```
December 15, 19--


{INPUT}message~

Dear {INPUT}message~:

Thank you for your generous Christmas contribution of
{INPUT}message~ for the homeless in Computer City. By working
together, we can make this city a home for everyone!

Sincerely,


Mr. and Mrs. Kenny Tanaka
```

b. Retrieve the file called THANKU on the Student Data Disk and create a primary file that can receive the information in the secondary file that you just created. Save the file as B:DRILL4-2.PF.

c. Merge the two files and print the resulting letters.

FIGURE 4.9

```
Mr. Bill Doolay
President
Doolay Pharmaceutical Company
143 Beverly Blvd.
Computer City, CA 94584
Mr. Doolay
$5,000

Mrs. Mandy Reynault
23 Elsinor Drive
Computer City, CA 94584
Mrs. Reynault
$1,000

Mr. and Mrs. Red Hebbard
1230 Market Street
Computer City, CA 94584
Mr. and Mrs. Hebbard
$2,500
```

3. Create several copies of an introduction letter by following these instructions.

    a. Retrieve the file called INTRO on the Student Data Disk.

    b. Create the primary file shown in Figure 4.10.

    c. Use the date text option for the date.

    d. Create messages to accompany each Input code, telling the user what information to enter.

    e. Save the document as B:DRILL4-3.PF.

    f. Generate the letters by using the Merge key and inserting the information in Figure 4.11 to fill in each letter.

    g. Save the final letters as B:DRILL4-3.MRG on the Student Data Disk.

FIGURE 4.10

```
                                    June 20, 19--


     {INPUT}message~

     Dear {INPUT}message~:

          We are sending you a {INPUT}message~ describing what Exhibit
     Place can do for you and its background. As explained in the
     {INPUT}message~, we have built our twenty-five-year-old reputation
     on the simple idea that good design and interesting attention-
     getting exhibits are more a matter of common sense, creativity,
     and ingenuity than of great amounts of money.

     We appreciate your interest in Exhibit Place and its activities.
     We look forward to answering any of your future inquiries.

                                    Sincerely,



                                    Ellen Nasus
                                    Marketing Director
```

4. Generate form letters by following these steps:

    a. Create a secondary file out of the information in Figure 4.11. Save the file as B:DRILL4-4.SF.

b. Retrieve the file called INTRO on the Student Data Disk and create a primary file that can receive the information in the secondary file that you just created. Save the primary file as B:DRILL4-4.PF.

c. Merge the two files and print the resulting letters.

FIGURE 4.11

```
Mr. Bill Birch
Executive President
Baker Circuits, Inc.
511 Forest Lodge Rd.
Glenn Grove, CA 93959
Mr. Birch
catalog

Mr. John Brahms
Vice President
Computer International, Inc.
17110 Lamb Lane
Edina, MN 55435
Mr. Brahms
marketing proposal

Mr. Ralph Night
Cambridge Analysis Co.
32 E. 57 St.
New York, NY 10022
Mr. Night
brochure

Ms. Michele Farley
Career Database, Inc.
Box 15486
Orange, CA 92613
Ms. Farley
prospectus
```

5. Create several copies of the confirmation letter by following these instructions.

   a. Retrieve the file called CONFIRM on the Student Data Disk and create the primary file shown in Figure 4.12.

   b. Use the date text option for the date.

   c. Create messages to accompany each Input code, telling the user what information to enter.

FIGURE 4.12

```
December 12, 19--


{INPUT}message~

Dear {INPUT}message~:

Just a reminder that we have an appointment to meet on
{INPUT}message~, {INPUT}message~ at {INPUT}message~. At that time,
we will be able to more thoroughly explore how we can work
together to provide you with the exhibit you want.

Please start thinking about any questions you have regarding any
of the services the Exhibit House provides.

I am enclosing some information that will help you formulate any
questions you may have and will show you how our services compare
with those of our competitors.

See you soon.

Sincerely,



Carl Mathews

ls
```

    d. Save the document as B:DRILL4-5.PF.

    e. Generate the letters by using the Merge key and inserting the information in Figure 4.13 to fill in each letter.

    f. Save the final letters as B:DRILL4-5.MRG on the Student Data Disk.

6. Generate form letters by following these steps:

    a. Create a secondary file out of the information in Figure 4.13. Save the file as B:DRILL4-5.SF.

    b. Retrieve the file called CONFIRM on the Student Data Disk and create a primary file that can receive the information in the secondary file that you just created. Save the primary file as B:DRILL4-6.PF.

    c. Merge the two files and print the resulting letters.

FIGURE 4.13

```
Mr. Bill Hickey
President
New Enterprise
Box 1353
Portsmouth, NH 03801
Mr. Hickey
Thursday
December 18, 19--
1:00 p.m.

Mr. Larry Baum
Baum Associates, Inc.
1365 Broadway
Hillsdale, NJ 07642
Mr. Baum
Monday
December 14, 19--   .
8:00 a.m.

Mr. James Leaky
President
Leaky, Chimp & Associates
452 Campus Dr., Suite 27
Irvine, CA 92715
Mr. Leaky
Monday
December 14, 19--
1:00 p.m.

Mr. Bill Lowe
National Computing Systems
Box 608
Houston, TX 77252
Mr. Lowe
Tuesday
December 21, 19--
11:30 a.m.
```

Advanced Skills

So far, you have printed merged letters by generating them first on the screen, and then using the Print command (Shift-F7) to print them. If you want to print merged letters during the merge process itself, use the Print code ({PRINT}). The Print code saves you the step of giving WordPerfect the Print command. You enter the Print code by using the

```
{ASSIGN}var~expr~
{BELL}
{BREAK}
{CALL}label~
{CANCEL OFF}
{CANCEL ON}
{CASE}expr~cs1~lb1~...csN~lbN~~
{CASE CALL}expr~cs1~lb1~...csN~lbN~~
{CHAIN MACRO}macroname~                    (^G)
{CHAIN PRIMARY}filename~
```

<Name Search; Arrows; Enter to Select>

FIGURE 4.14

The Merge More menu contains many codes for creating merge operations. Note that the menu contains more codes than can fit on the menu. As a result, to find a code, type the letters of the code you are looking for.

More option of the Merge Codes menu. When you select this option, the menu shown in Figure 4.14 appears on the top right of the screen. This menu contains several commands to help you create sophisticated merge operations; it contains more options, in fact, than can fit on the menu. As a result, to find the Print code, type its beginning letters, just as you do when using the Name Search option of List Files to find a file.

Let's look at how you use the Print command more closely.

Using the Print Code in a Primary Document

Printing documents during the merge process requires these steps:

1. Move the cursor to the bottom of the primary file.

2. Press the Merge Codes key (Shift-F9).

3. Type **6** to select the More option.

4. Type **PR** to find the Print code and press Enter.
   RESULT: The Print code then appears at the bottom of your primary file.

5. Save the file and clear the screen.

6. Press the Merge command (Ctrl-F9) and merge the primary and secondary files as you normally would.

   When you merge the file, WordPerfect will print each merged document without creating a merge file on the screen.

   You should be aware that the Print code belongs at the end of the primary file because WordPerfect prints everything up to that code. When WordPerfect reaches the Print code, it erases the letter from memory (RAM), so that it does not appear on the screen.

By using the Print code creatively, you can often do your job more quickly and easily.

Advanced Key Terms   More option   Print code ({PRINT})

Advanced Review Questions

1. Would you want to print merge files directly to the printer if you have information to enter at an Input code? Briefly explain your answer.

2. What step(s) does/do printing merge files directly to the printer save you?

3. True or False: When you use the Print code ({PRINT}) in a document, the document does not appear on the screen because the code erases it from memory (RAM).

Advanced Applications

1. If a printer is available, print the following document directly to the printer by following these instructions:

   a. Create the primary letter shown in Figure 4.15.

FIGURE 4.15

```
                        Exhibit Place
                  1412 North Pierce Street
                  Computer City, CA 94584


      October 5, 19--

      {FIELD}1~
      {FIELD}2~
      {FIELD}3~
      {FIELD}4~
      {FIELD}5~

      Dear {FIELD}6~:

      I am enclosing change order No. {FIELD}7~ for you to review and
      sign. By signing and returning the pink copy, you will enable our
      builders to make the changes we agreed on.

      Please call me immediately at (302) 432-0493 if this work order
      does not reflect our agreed-on changes.

      Sincerely,


      Carl Mathews
```

b. Create the secondary file shown in Figure 4.16.

c. Merge the two files so that they print directly to your printer and do *not* appear on your screen.

FIGURE 4.16

```
Mr. Harry Cohn{END FIELD}
President{END FIELD}
Atom Software Corp{END FIELD}
355 Chestnut St.{END FIELD}
Westwood, NY 07648{END FIELD}
Mr. Cohn{END FIELD}
09845{END FIELD}
{END RECORD}
==============================================================
Mr. Steven Wharton{END FIELD}
Senior Vice-President{END FIELD}
Advocate Security Systems{END FIELD}
7512 Slate Ridge Blvd.{END FIELD}
Columbus, OH 43068{END FIELD}
Mr. Wharton{END FIELD}
09832{END FIELD}
{END RECORD}
==============================================================
Mr. P. Scott{END FIELD}
President{END FIELD}
Sciences Assembly, Inc.{END FIELD}
20 Cross Rd.{END FIELD}
Albany, NY 13224{END FIELD}
Mr. Scott{END FIELD}
08749{END FIELD}
{END RECORD}
==============================================================
Mr. Ken Hampton{END FIELD}
Vice President{END FIELD}
Certified Accountants Software{END FIELD}
1211 Avenue of the Americas{END FIELD}
New York, NY 10036{END FIELD}
Mr. Hampton{END FIELD}
08976{END FIELD}
{END RECORD}
==============================================================
```

2. If a printer is available, print the following document directly to the printer by following these instructions:

a. Create the primary letter shown in Figure 4.17.

FIGURE 4.17

```
                            Exhibit Place
                       1412 North Pierce Street
                       Computer City, CA 94584


October 5, 19--

{FIELD}1~
{FIELD}2~
{FIELD}3~
{FIELD}4~
{FIELD}5~

Dear {FIELD}6~:

On behalf of the staff at the Exhibit Place, I'd like to thank you
for your confidence and support on this project.  Since we are
completing the final stages of your exhibit, I wanted you to know
how much we appreciated your help.  Through your involvement, our
staff was able to create an exhibit that you will be proud to have
represent your company.

Good luck at the New Wave Trade show.  I'm looking forward to
talking with you.

Sincerely,



Carl Mathews

ls
```

b. Create the secondary file shown in Figure 4.18.

FIGURE 4.18

```
Ms. Pat Walker{END FIELD}
Regional Director{END FIELD}
Mercury Software{END FIELD}
1702 S. Michigan{END FIELD}
South Bend, IN 46618{END FIELD}
Ms. Walker{END FIELD}
{END RECORD}
==============================================================
```

MORE ▼

```
Ms. Judith G. Howard{END FIELD}
President{END FIELD}
ARCsoft Business Systems{END FIELD}
Box 1332{END FIELD}
Woodsboro, MD 21798{END FIELD}
Ms. Howard{END FIELD}
{END RECORD}
===========================================================
Mr. Arthur King{END FIELD}
President{END FIELD}
Atlantis Communications{END FIELD}
542 Hallandale Beach Blvd.{END FIELD}
Hollywood, FL 33023{END FIELD}
Mr. King{END FIELD}
{END RECORD}
===========================================================
Mr. Keith Georgian{END FIELD}
Senior Vice President{END FIELD}
Digital Network, Inc.{END FIELD}
One Penn Plaza{END FIELD}
New York, NY 10119{END FIELD}
Mr. Georgian{END FIELD}
{END RECORD}
===========================================================
```

c. Merge the two files so that they print directly to your printer and do *not* appear on your screen.

On Your Own

You are supervisor for the customer service department of a company that publishes magazines for teenagers. Every week you receive two or three letters from people wanting to cancel their subscriptions. Your staff looks at the number of magazines these customers have left on their subscription and generates a check to refund them the difference.

Write a form letter to accompany each refund check. Design the letter so that your staff need only fill in the name, address, and refund amount for each customer. Be sure that you provide messages in the document so that your staff knows what to enter whenever WordPerfect stops.

Save the primary file as B:3APP4 and print it.

```
Exhibit Place
1611 N.W. 12th Avenue
Computer City, CA 94584




                              Todd Lincoln
                              Graphics Extravaganza
                              512 Cycle Boulevard
                              Rivermore, PA 09745
```

```
Exhibit Place
1611 N.W. 12th Avenue
Computer City, CA 94584




                              Noel Larson
                              President
                              Advanced Publishing Company
                              1412 Fredericks Street
                              Columbus, Ohio 54367
```

In this chapter, you create a file to help you print addresses on envelopes. You will also create a WordPerfect macro that can print envelopes for you.

5

Automatic Mailing Labels

Chapter Objectives   After completing this chapter, you will be able to

1. Create a file that you can use to print envelopes.

2. Create a macro that merges the envelope file for you.

3. Edit your macros.

WordPerfect Commands

Shift-F8, 2, 7, 1	Change form to envelope
Shift-F7, 2	Print envelopes one at a time
Shift-F7, 1	Print envelopes all at once
Ctrl-F10, *macro name description*	Create a macro
Alt-F10, ENVELOPE	Start the envelope macro
Ctrl-F10, ENVELOPE, 2	Edit the envelope macro

Overview

As you know, creating letters is only the first part of the correspondence task. After creating a letter, you also need to create an envelope. Word-Perfect can print envelopes for you. If you used a secondary file to merge letters, you can use the same file to print your envelopes. There are four steps in creating envelopes:

1. Create a primary file that will print the envelopes.

2. Create a secondary file containing the names and addresses for the envelopes (if you have not already created it to generate the letters).

3. Merge the primary file for envelopes with the secondary file that contains the list of names.

4. Print the envelopes.
   Let's look at each of these steps in detail.

Creating a Primary File for Envelopes

To create a primary file for envelopes, you must tell WordPerfect that rather than working with a standard 8 1/2-inch x 11-inch sheet of paper, you are working with an envelope. The simplest way to do this is to use the Page Size/Type option under the Format: Page menu. WordPerfect provides a menu option specifically for standard-sized business envelopes.

You then must add two margin codes. The first goes at the beginning of the file and sets the left and right margins to 10 spaces (1") each. You need this code, even though it is the default, because of the second code. The second code goes at line 8 (2.17") and changes the left margin to 35 spaces (3.5"). These two codes ensure that the addresses line up correctly on the envelope when they are merged.

You also need to change the top margin to 4 (1.5"). Then type the envelope form as shown in Figure 5.1.

Creating a Secondary File for Envelopes

After making the primary file, you need to create a secondary file that lists the names and addresses that go on envelopes. If you have already created a secondary file for personalized letters, you do not need to make another secondary file to print envelopes—WordPerfect can print envelopes from the original secondary file.

If you created a secondary file that has more fields in it than you need in an envelope, don't worry. WordPerfect will only select out of the secondary file the number of fields it needs in the primary file. For example, in the previous chapter you created a secondary file called REGIS.SF that contained nine fields. Note that the ENVELOPE.PF in

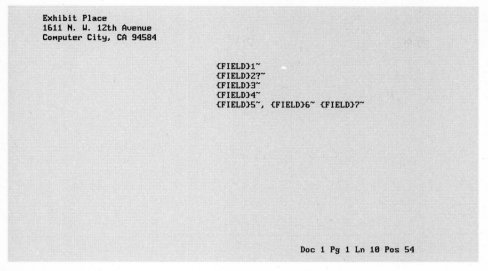

FIGURE 5.1

Figure 5.1 has only seven fields. If you merge the REGIS.SF file with ENVELOPE.PF, WordPerfect will select only the first seven fields of each record from REGIS.SF.

Merge the Primary and Secondary Files

You are now ready to merge the two files using the Merge key ([Ctrl]-[F9]). After merging is completed, each separate envelope will appear on the screen on a page of its own (see Figure 5.2). You are now ready to print the envelopes.

Printing Envelopes

Different printers print envelopes in different ways. Some printers need you to feed in one envelope at a time. Others can print several envelopes at once. WordPerfect can accommodate most kinds of printers for you. If your printer requires you to feed in one envelope at a time, you would feed the envelope into the printer up to the exact spot where you want the first line printed. You would then choose the Page option under the Print menu to print the envelope. When WordPerfect has completed printing, you press the Page Down key to move to the next envelope on the screen and repeat the process. If your printer can print a stack of envelopes at a time, simply put them in the printer's envelope bin and print using the Full Document option under the Print menu.

Creating Macros with Merges

You can simplify the process to create envelopes by making a macro that generates the merged envelope for you. Instead of merging a primary file and secondary file each time you want envelopes, you create a macro that automatically merges a standard secondary file called ADDRESS.SF to a standard primary file called ENVELOPE.PF.

FIGURE 5.2

```
Exhibit Place
1611 N.W. 12th Avenue
Computer City, CA 94584




                        Mary Oshiro
                        Computer Interface Specialists
                        349 Figueroa Street, Suite 1204
                        Los Angeles, CA 94521
```

```
Exhibit Place
1611 N.W. 12th Avenue
Computer City, CA 94584




                        Bill Hughes
                        Hughes Software Games and Innovations
                        Route 1A
                        Porterville, Indiana 43256
```

You do this by making a macro called ENVELOPE with the Macro key (Ctrl-F10) and then starting the merge function. When WordPerfect asks what the primary and secondary files are, you tell it ENVELOPE.PF and ADDRESS.SF. Then, any time you want to merge envelopes, you start the macro.

You should be aware that you do not have to turn the Macro key (Ctrl-F10) off when you combine it with a merge. When the merge starts, macro definition automatically stops. We will show you how to make such a macro in this chapter.

Editing Macros

If you want to check that you performed all the steps correctly or if you want to change the name of the .PF or .SF files in your macro, you can use the macro editor. To use the macro editor, you press the Macro key (Ctrl-F10) and enter the name of the macro. WordPerfect will then tell you that the macro already exists and ask if you want to replace or edit it. You would select the edit option and the macro editor would appear on the screen as shown in Figure 5.3.

Each of your keystrokes in the editor appears in the box. To change the keystrokes, you choose the Action option (2). The cursor jumps inside

```
Macro: Action

     File             A:ENVELOPE.WPM

     Description      creates envelope file

    ┌─────────────────────────────────────────────────────────┐
    │ {Merge/Sort}1a:envelope.pf{Enter}                         │
    │ a:address.f{Backspace}sf{Enter}                           │
    │                                                           │
    │                                                           │
    │                                                           │
    │                                                           │
    │                                                           │
    │                                                           │
    │                                                           │
    └─────────────────────────────────────────────────────────┘

Ctrl-PgUp for macro commands;   Press Exit when done
```

FIGURE 5.3

The macro edit screen allows you to change all your keystrokes in a macro.

the box and you can change any keystrokes that you need to. Like Reveal Codes, any WordPerfect command you give appears on the screen as a code.

Tutorial

Michelle Strongman has asked you to make envelopes for the letters that you created for her in the previous chapter. You will make them by making a primary file called ENVELOPE.PF and merging it with REGIS.SF, the secondary file you made in the previous chapter.

To make your job easier, you will then create a macro called EN-VELOPE that will merge ENVELOPE.PF and REGIS.SF for you. Because the ENVELOPE macro would be most useful if you could use it to generate all your envelopes (not just the envelopes for REGIS.SF), you will then edit the macro so it will merge a generic address file you call ADDRESS.SF. Each time you need to print envelopes, you will create a file called ADDRESS.SF containing the envelope information and use the envelope macro to generate them.

Setting Up

To begin, place the Student Data Disk in drive B and start WordPerfect. You will start by creating the primary file for envelopes.

Formatting

Because you will be printing on envelopes, you need to tell WordPerfect you are working with envelopes. You also need to insert the two margin change codes and change the top margin to 2 lines (1.17").

Change Form to
Envelope
Shift - F8 , *2, 7, 1*

To change the form to envelopes, follow these steps:

1. Press the Format key (Shift - F8).
2. Type **2** to select the Page option.
3. Type **7** to select paper size.
4. Highlight the Envelope-Wide option.
   NOTE: If you do not have an HP LaserJet printer, your Paper Size menu may not have an Envelope-Wide option. If it does not, select the All Others option, then select the Envelope option. Under the Paper Type menu, select Envelope again and go directly to step 6.
   Some printers are unable to handle envelopes. If you have a problem printing envelopes, select the standard paper size and continue with this tutorial. Your results will be different from ours, but you will be able to complete the tutorial by printing on standard paper.
5. Type **1** to select Envelope-wide option.
6. Press Exit (F7) to return to the edit screen.
   WordPerfect has now put a Paper Size/Type code at the beginning of your document for envelopes. You now need to change the top margin so you can print your name close to the top edge.

Change Top Margin
Shift - F8 , *2, 5, 2*

To change the top margin

1. Press the Format key (Shift - F8).
2. Type **2** to select the Page option.
3. Type **5** to select the Margin option.
4. Type **2** to change the top margin to 2 (1.17") and press Enter three times to return to the Format menu.
   Finally, you must insert margin change codes so that the addresses print in the correct places.

Insert First
Left Margin Code
Shift - F8 , *1, 7*

1. Type **1** to select the Line option.
2. Type **7** to select the Margin option.
   NOTE: The left and right margin should both be 10 (1"). If not, change them now.
3. Press Enter four times to return to the edit screen. You have just inserted a hidden code with the margin default values of 10 (1") and 10 (1") into your document.

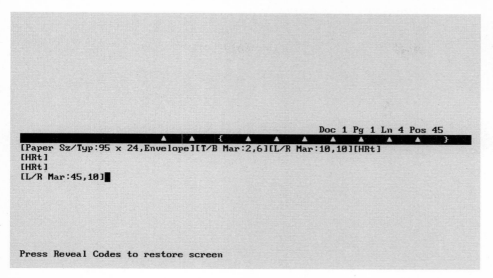

FIGURE 5.4

After entering both margin codes, your reveal codes screen looks like this.

Insert Second Left Margin Code
Shift - F8 , *1, 7*

To insert the second left margin code, follow these steps:

1. Press Enter three times to move the cursor down three lines to ensure that the second margin code is after the return address.
2. Press the Format key (Shift - F8).
3. Type 1 to select the Line option.
4. Type 7 to select the Margin option.
5. Type 45 and press Enter four times to return to the edit screen.
6. Press the Reveal Codes key (Alt - F3) to check that you have the correct codes in the document. Your screen should look like Figure 5.4.
7. Move the cursor to line 1 (1.17"), position 10 (1"). Make sure the cursor appears after all codes.
8. Press the Reveal Codes key (Alt - F3) again to turn it off.

Keyboarding

To create a primary file for envelopes, first create the return address at the top of the envelope by following these steps:

Enter Return Address

1. Type the following:

```
Exhibit Place
1611 N.W. 12th Avenue
Computer City, CA 94584
```

2. Press Home , Home , ↓ to go to the end of the document.
   NOTE: The cursor should now be on line 6 (2"), position 45 (4.5"). If it is not, move the cursor until it is on line 6, position 45. The first line of the mailing address will begin on line 6.
3. Press Enter six times to move to line 12 (3").

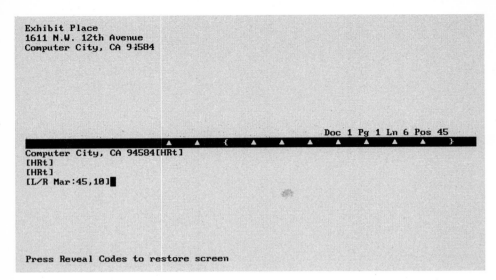

FIGURE 5.5

Move your cursor so that it is after the second margin change code [L/R Mar:45,10] and at position 45 (4.5").

4. Press the Reveal Codes key ([Alt]-[F3]) to turn Reveal Codes on.

5. Move your cursor so that it is after the second margin change code [L/R Mar:45,10] as shown in Figure 5.5, if not there already.

6. Press the Reveal Codes key again to turn it off. You are now ready to enter the field codes for the mailing address.

Enter Mailing Address
[Shift]-[F9], *1, 1*

To enter the field codes for the mailing address, follow these steps:

1. Press the Merge Codes key ([Shift]-[F9]).
   RESULT: The following prompts appear on the screen:

   1 Field; 2 End Record; 3 Input; 4 Page Off; 5 Next Record; 6 More; 0

2. Type 1 to select Field.
   RESULT: The following prompt appears on the screen:

   Enter Field:

3. Type 1 and press [Enter].

4. Enter the field codes for fields 2–7 as shown in Figure 5.6. Be sure that you have a question mark on field 2. When you are done, scroll to the top of the screen and press the Reveal Codes key ([Alt]-[F3]). Your document should look like Figure 5.7.

5. Press Reveal Codes again to turn it off.

Save Primary File
[F7], *Y, Y, N*

Save the primary file for envelopes as B:ENVELOPE.PF using the Exit key ([F7]) and clear the screen by answering N to the prompt that asks if you want to leave the program. Fill out the Document Summary screen as you wish.

```
      Exhibit Place
      1611 N.W. 12th Avenue
      Computer City, CA 94584




                              {FIELD}1~
                              {FIELD}2?~
                              {FIELD}3~
                              {FIELD}4~
                              {FIELD}5~, {FIELD}6~ {FIELD}7~








      A:\FIG5-6.WP5                              Doc 1 Pg 1 Ln 15 Pos 54
```

FIGURE 5.6

Enter the field codes for fields 2–7 as shown in this figure. Be sure that you have a question mark on field 2.

Merge Files

Shift - F9 , *1*

You are now ready to merge ENVELOPE.PF with REGIS.SF.

1. Press the Merge/Sort key (Ctrl - F9).

2. Type **1** to select Merge.

3. Type **B:ENVELOPE.PF** and press Enter .

4. Type **B:REGIS.SF** and press Enter .
   RESULT: The envelopes appear on the screen as shown in Figure 5.8.
   NOTE: If the addresses appear incorrect, check whether your document B:ENVELOPE.PF is the same as shown in Figure 5.7.

Saving

Press F10 and save the envelopes as B:ENVELOPE.MRG. Create a new Document Summary for B:ENVELOPE.MRG using Shift - F8 , 3, 5. Fill in the Document Summary as you see fit, then press Enter . You are now ready to print envelopes.

```
      Exhibit Place
      1611 N.W. 12th Avenue
      Computer City, CA 94584



                              {FIELD}1~
                              {FIELD}2?~
                              {FIELD}3~
                              {FIELD}4~
                              {FIELD}5~, {FIELD}6~ {FIELD}7~

                                      Doc 1 Pg 1 Ln 1 Pos 24
{    ▲   ▲   ▲   ▲   ▲   ▲   ▲   ▲   ▲   ▲   ▲   ▲   ▲   }
[Paper Sz/Typ:95 x 24,Envelope][T/B Mar:2,6][L/R Mar:10,10]Exhibit Place [HRt]
1611 N.W. 12th Avenue[HRt]
Computer City, CA 94584[HRt]
[HRt]
[HRt]
[L/R Mar:45,10][Mrg:FIELD]1~[HRt]
[Mrg:FIELD]2?~[HRt]
[Mrg:FIELD]3~[HRt]
[Mrg:FIELD]4~[HRt]
[Mrg:FIELD]5~, [Mrg:FIELD]6~ [Mrg:FIELD]7~

Press Reveal Codes to restore screen
```

FIGURE 5.7

When you turn on Reveal Codes (Alt - F3), your document should look exactly like this.

```
    Exhibit Place
    1611 N.W. 12th Avenue
    Computer City, CA 94584


                          Todd Lincoln
                          Graphics Extravaganza
                          512 Cycle Blvd
                          Rivermore, PA 09745
    ===============================================================
    Exhibit Place
    1611 N.W. 12th Avenue
    Computer City, CA 94584


                          Noel Larson
                          President
                          Advanced Publishing Company
                          1412 Fredricks Street
                          Columbus, Ohio 44367



    A:\FIG5-8.WP5                        Doc 1 Pg 2 Ln 10 Pos 65
```

FIGURE 5.8
The envelopes appear on the screen.

Printing

Different printers print envelopes in different ways. Some printers need you to feed in one envelope at a time. Others can print several envelopes at once. Below are instructions for both methods.

NOTE: If your printer does not print envelopes, print with standard paper following the steps to print a stack of envelopes.

Print Envelopes One at a Time
Shift - F7 , *2*

If you feed envelopes into your printer one at a time, follow these steps:
1. Insert the envelope in the printer.
2. Press the Print key (Shift - F7).
3. Type **2** to select the Page option.
    RESULT: WordPerfect will print the envelope.
4. Press the PgDn key to move to the next envelope on the screen.
5. Repeat steps 1–4 until all envelopes are printed.

Print All Envelopes at Once

If your printer can print a stack of envelopes at a time, put the envelopes in the printer's envelope bin and follow these steps:
1. Press the Print key (Shift - F7).
2. Type **1** to select the Full Document option.

Revision

You note that your office spends a lot of time printing envelopes. You decide that you would like to create a macro that creates the envelope file for you. To create an envelope macro, follow these steps:

Create Envelope Macro
Ctrl - F10 , *Macro Name Description*

1. Press the Exit key (F7) and Type **N N** to each prompt to clear the screen of the ENVELOPE.MRG file.

2. Press the Macro Definition key (`Ctrl`-`F10`).
    RESULT: The following prompt appears on the screen:

    `Define macro:`

3. Type B:ENVELOPE and press `Enter`.
    RESULT: The following prompt appears on the screen:

    `Description:`

    If this prompt appears:

    `ENVELOPE.WPM is already defined: 1 Replace: 2 Edit:`
    `3 Description: 0`

    Type 1 and continue to the next step.

4. Type **Creates envelope file** and press `Enter`.
    RESULT: The following prompt begins flashing in the Status line:

    `Macro Def`

    Every key you press now will be recorded in the macro.

5. Press the Merge key (`Ctrl`-`F9`).

6. Type 1 to select Merge.

7. Type B:ENVELOPE.PF and press `Enter`.

8. Type B:REGIS.SF and press `Enter`.
    RESULT: The envelopes appear on the screen and the macro definition function is automatically turned off.

Use the Macro
`Alt`-`F10`, `F7`

At the moment, the envelopes are on the screen. To demonstrate how the macro works, follow these steps:

1. Press Exit (`F7`) and Type **N N** to clear the screen.

2. Press the Macro key (`Alt`-`F10`).

3. Type B:ENVELOPE and press `Enter`.
    RESULT: The file for envelopes appears on the screen, ready for you to print.

4. Press the Exit key (`F7`) and Type **N N** to clear the screen.

    You now decide that it would be useful if everyone in the office could use the Envelope macro to print their envelopes. As a result, you decide to edit the Envelope macro to change REGIS.SF to ADDRESS.SF. This way, if anyone wants to use the macro, you can tell them to create a generic secondary file called ADDRESS.SF.

Edit a Macro
`Ctrl`-`F10`, *2*, `F7`

To edit the Envelope macro, follow these steps:

1. Press the Macro Definition key (`Ctrl`-`F10`).

```
Macro: Action

    File              A:ENVELOPE.WPM

    Description       creates envelope file

  ┌─────────────────────────────────────────────────────┐
  │ {Merge/Sort}1a:envelope.pf{Enter}                    │
  │ a:regis.sf{Enter}                                    │
  │                                                      │
  │                                                      │
  │                                                      │
  │                                                      │
  │                                                      │
  │                                                      │
  │                                                      │
  │                                                      │
  │                                                      │
  │                                                      │
  │                                                      │
  └─────────────────────────────────────────────────────┘

Ctrl-PgUp for macro commands;  Press Exit when done
```

FIGURE 5.9
In the box are the keystrokes that you used to create the ENVELOPE macro.

2. Type **B:**ENVELOPE and press [Enter].

    RESULT: The following message appears on the screen:

    ENVELOPE.WPM already exists. 1 Replace; 2 Edit; 3 Description: 0

3. Type **2** to select the Edit option.

    RESULT: The screen as shown in Figure 5.9 appears.

4. Move the cursor to the word "REGIS.SF." Replace it with ADDRESS.SF.

5. Press the Exit key ([F7]) once to leave the macro.

    The macro has now been changed. It will now generate an envelope file by merging the ENVELOPE.PF file and a generic ADDRESS.SF file that the user creates.

Exiting

If you are ready to leave WordPerfect, leave using the Exit key ([F7]). If you are going to continue working, clear the screen using the Exit key ([F7]), if not cleared already.

Summary

You created a file for printing envelopes by using the Merge key ([Ctrl]-[F9]) and merging ENVELOPE.PF and REGIS.SF. ENVELOPE.PF is a primary file you created specially for printing envelopes. To create it, you changed the Page Size/Type under the Format: Page menu. You also changed the top margin to 2 (1.17").

You then created a macro called ENVELOPE that merged EN-VELOPE.PF and REGIS.SF for you. To create it, you used the Macro

Definition key ([Ctrl]-[F10]). To use the macro, you pressed the Macro key ([Alt]-[F10]). To edit the macro, you used the Macro Definition key again, and chose option 2 to edit it.

Chapter Review

Review Questions

1. As you know, you must be careful that the fields in the secondary file match the fields in the primary file. Briefly discuss why when printing envelopes it does not matter if the secondary file has more fields in it than the primary file.

2. List and briefly describe the four steps needed for printing envelopes.

3. What menu do you use to tell WordPerfect that your document is a special size?.

4. True or False: You do not need to turn off the macro definition when you use the Merge key in a macro.

5. True or False: Like Reveal codes, any WordPerfect command that you make while editing a macro will appear on the screen as a code.

Applications

Please complete the following WordPerfect exercises.

1. Print envelopes for the thank you letters created in the previous chapter by following these instructions.

    a. Create a primary file for envelopes with this information in the top left corner:

    ```
    Mr. and Mrs. Ken Tanaka
    1412 Wilmington Ave.
    Computer City, CA 94583
    ```

    b. Save the document as B:DRILL5-1.PF.

    c. Create a secondary file using the data in Figure 5.10. Save it as B:DRILL5-1.SF.

    d. Generate an envelope file using B:DRILL5-1.PF and B:DRILL5-1.SF.

    e. Print the envelopes.

2. Create a macro that automatically generates a merged file from B:DRILL5-1.PF and B:DRILL5-1.SF.

FIGURE 5.IO

```
Mr. Bill Doolay
President
Doolay Pharmaceutical Company
143 Beverly Blvd.
Computer City, CA 94584
Mr. Doolay
$5,000

Mrs. Mandy Reynault
23 Elsinor Drive
Computer City, CA 94584
Mrs. Reynault
$1,000

Mr. and Mrs. Red Hebbard
1230 Market Street
Computer City, CA 94584
Mr. and Mrs. Hebbard
$2,500
```

3. Print envelopes for the introduction letters created in the previous chapter by following these instructions.

   a. Create a primary file for envelopes with this return address:

   ```
   Ellen Nasus
   Marketing Director
   1611 N.W. 12th Avenue
   Computer City, CA 94584
   ```

   b. Save the document as DRILL5-3.PF.

   c. Create a secondary file using the data in Figure 5.11. Save it as B:DRILL5-3.SF.

FIGURE 5.II

```
Mr. Bill Birch
Executive President
Baker Circuits, Inc.
511 Forest Lodge Rd.
Glenn Grove, CA 93959
Mr. Birch
catalog
```

MORE ▼

```
Mr. John Brahms
Vice President
Computer International, Inc.
17110 Lamb Lane
Edina, MN 55435
Mr. Brahms
marketing proposal

Mr. Ralph Night
Cambridge Analysis Co.
32 E. 57 St.
New York, NY 10022
Mr. Night
brochure

Ms. Michele Farley
Career Database, Inc.
Box 15486
Orange, CA 92613
Ms. Farley
prospectus
```

---

    d. Generate an envelope file using B:DRILL5-3.PF and B:DRILL5-3.SF.

    e. Print the envelopes.

4.   Create a macro that automatically generates a merged file from B:DRILL5-3.PF and B:DRILL5-3.SF. Name it B:MERGE5-3.

5.   Print envelopes for the confirmation letters created in the previous chapter by following these instructions.

    a. Create a primary file for envelopes with this return address:

```
Carl Mathews
Marketing Representative
1611 N.W. 12th Avenue
Computer City, CA 94584
```

    b. Save the document as B:DRILL5-5.PF.

    c. Create a secondary file using the data in Figure 5.12. Save it as B:DRILL5-5.SF.

    d. Generate an envelope file using B:DRILL5-5.PF and B:DRILL5-5.SF.

    e. Print the envelopes.

FIGURE 5.12

```
Mr. Bill Hickey
President
New Enterprise
Box 1353
Portsmouth, NH 03801
Mr. Hickey
Thursday
December 18, 19--
1:00 p.m.

Mr. Larry Baum
Baum Associates, Inc.
1365 Broadway
Hillsdale, NJ 07642
Mr. Baum
Monday
December 14, 19--
8:00 a.m.

Mr. James Leaky
Leaky, Chimp & Associates
452 Campus Dr., Suite 27
Irvine, CA 92715
Mr. Leaky
Monday
December 14, 19--
1:00 p.m.

Mr. Bill Lowe
National Computing Systems
Box 608
Houston, TX 77252
Mr. Lowe
Tuesday
December 21, 19--
11:30 a.m.
```

6. Create a macro that automatically generates a merged file from B:DRILL5-5.PF and B:DRILL5-5.SF. Name it B:MERGE5-5.

Advanced Skills

The easiest kind of macro to use is the [Alt] macro. You start [Alt] macros by pressing the [Alt] key and a single character of the alphabet (A through Z). Using them is faster than starting macros as you have done so far because you only press two keys to do it: [Alt] and a single letter key.

For example, to start the macro that merges an envelope file, you needed to press the Macro key ([Alt]-[F10]), type the word ENVELOPE, and press [Enter]. With an [Alt] macro, all you would need to do is press [Alt] and any key you are using to identify the macro, such as E.

To create an [Alt] macro, you simply press [Alt] and a single character when WordPerfect asks you what the name of the macro will be. For example, to make an [Alt] macro that creates envelopes from the EN-VELOPE.PF and REGIS.SF files, follow these steps:

1. Press the Macro Definition key ([Ctrl]-[F10]).
2. Type [Alt]-E and press [Enter].
3. Type **Creates envelope file** and press [Enter].
4. Press the Merge key ([Ctrl]-[F9]).
    Type **1**.
5. Type **B:ENVELOPE.PF** and press [Enter].
6. Type **B:REGIS.SF** and press [Enter]. To start this macro, you simply press [Alt]-E. For all the convenience, there are two disadvantages to this method: (1) You can only create 26 macros (the number of characters in the alphabet). (2) You might start a macro that you do not want by accidentally pressing the wrong key.

We recommend that you *not* use [Alt] macros for tasks that will delete text or clear the screen without saving so that you do not accidentally lose any work.

Advanced Key Term

[Alt] Macro

Advanced Review Questions

1. How many keystrokes are required to start an [Alt] macro?
2. How many [Alt] macros can you create?
3. Briefly describe two major disadvantages to using [Alt] macros.
4. How many keystrokes does an [Alt] macro save you when you compare it to using a macro called ENVELOPE?

Advanced Applications

1. Create an [Alt] macro that automatically generates envelopes by following the instructions on the following page.

a.   Create a primary file for envelopes with this return address:

```
Carl Mathews
Marketing Representative
1611 N.W. 12th Avenue
Computer City, CA 94584
```

b.   Save the document as B:DRILL5-7.PF.

c.   Create a secondary file using the data in Figure 5.13. Save it as B:DRILL5-7.SF.

d.   Create an [Alt] macro called [Alt]-E that generates envelopes using B:DRILL5-7.PF and B:DRILL5-7.SF.

FIGURE 5.13

```
Mr. Harry Cohn
President
Atom Software Corp.
355 Chestnut St.
Westwood, NY 07648
Mr. Cohn
09845

Mr. Steven Wharton
Advocate Security Systems
7512 Slate Ridge Blvd.
Columbus, OH 43068
Mr. Wharton
09832

Mr. P. Scott
President
Sciences Assembly, Inc.
20 Cross Rd.
Albany, NY 13224
Mr. Scott
08749

Mr. Ken Hampton
Vice President
Certified Accountants Software
1211 Avenue of the Americas
New York, NY 10036
Mr. Hampton
08976
```

2.   Create an [Alt] macro that automatically generates and prints envelopes by following the instructions on the next page.

a. Create a primary file for envelopes with this return address:

```
Carl Mathews
Marketing Representative
1611 N.W. 12th Avenue
Computer City, CA 94584
```

b. Save the document as B:DRILL5-8.PF.

c. Create a secondary file using the data in Figure 5.14. Save it as B:DRILL5-8.SF.

d. Create an [Alt] macro called [Alt]-P that generates and prints envelopes using B:DRILL5-8.PF and B:DRILL5-8.SF.

FIGURE 5.14

```
Ms. Pat Walker
Regional Director
Mercury Software
1702 S. Michigan
South Bend, IN 46618
Ms. Walker

Ms. Judith G. Howard
ARCsoft Business Systems
Box 1332
Woodsboro, MD 21798
Ms. Howard

Mr. Arthur King
Atlantis Communications
542 Hallandale Beach Blvd.
Hollywood, FL 33023
Mr. King

Mr. Keith Georgian
Senior Vice President
Digital Network, Inc.
One Penn Plaza
New York, NY 10119
Mr. Georgian
```

On Your Own   Sometimes you want to print just one envelope and do not want to go to the trouble of creating a secondary file and merging it to your primary file. Create a macro that calls up a primary file for envelopes that lets you type a name and address from the keyboard. Use the Console and Message codes where appropriate. See if you can make the macro print the envelope on the printer immediately after you have entered the address.

```
                        Exhibit Place
                   1611 N. W. 12th Avenue
                   Computer City, CA 94584



Invoice Number: 45983                          July 15, 19--

Jan Heverly
Security Systems of America
1920 Wiley Blvd.
San Jose, CA 90356


Statement of your account for your exhibit is as follows:
```

STAGE A--MARKET RESEARCH

Market research	$2,432.20
Research your strategies	448.30
Price studies	328.00
TOTAL A	$3,208.50

STAGE B--DESIGN PRODUCTION

Budget and production	$583.57
Component design	1,200.83
Writers and technicians	8,298.62
TOTAL B	$10,083.02

STAGE C--FOLLOW-UP

Training	$1,024.12
Mailing list	512.65
TOTAL C	$1,536.77
TOTAL DUE	$14,828.29

In this chapter, you will create a form that automatically adds columns of numbers and practically fills itself out.

6

Preparing an Invoice

WordPerfect Commands

Shift - F9 , 3	Enter Input code
Alt - F7 , 2, 1	Create a table
Alt - F7 , 2, 2, 3	Justify a column
Alt - F7 Ctrl - ← or →	Change column width
Alt - F7 , 5, 4	Enter a subtotal code
Alt - F7 , 5, 5	Enter a total code
Alt - F7 , 3, 7, 1	Eliminate all lines in a table
Alt - F7 , 3, 4, 2	Enter a subtotal line
Alt - F7 , 3, 4, 3	Enter a double underline
Alt - F7 , 5, 1	Perform calculations

Overview

Up to now, you have used the Table command to help you lay out text in your documents. But there will also be times when you want to do *math functions* within your documents, such as total budgets or calculate statements. Like a basic calculator, the table feature can quickly add *totals* and *subtotals* for you. For example, say that you want to add the following numbers:

```
   12
  132
5,342
```

You can enter these numbers in a table and have it calculate a subtotal for you.

	12
	132
	5,342
	5,486 <====Subtotal

To provide for flexibility, you can also tell it to add subtotals together into a single total:

	12
	132
	5,342
	5,486 <===Subtotal
	567
	98
	3
	668 <===Subtotal
	6,154 <===TOTAL

Three steps are required to add a column of numbers: (1) creating a table, (2) entering the numbers in the table, and (3) entering a Subtotal or Total code. Let's look at these steps in detail.

1. *Creating a Table.* As you recall, to create a table, you start by using the Columns/Table command (Alt-F7). After you tell WordPerfect how many rows and columns should be in the table, WordPerfect displays the blank table on the screen in *Table Edit mode.* You can then modify the table, as well as enter text and numbers.

2. *Entering Numbers in a Table.* There is no secret to entering numbers in a table. Simply move the cursor to the cell that you want to contain

a number, and then type it. For example, here we have entered the numbers 12, 132, and 5,342 in a table containing two columns and four rows:

	12
	132
	5,342

When making calculations, people usually right-justify numbers to make them easier to read and calculate. Although it makes no difference to WordPerfect whether numbers or not are right-justified when making calculations, you can use the Format option on the Table Edit menu to adjust the numbers.

The Format option asks you if you want to change a single cell or an entire column. By telling WordPerfect that you want everything in a column to be right-justified, the numbers 12, 132, and 5,342 automatically appear like this when you enter them in a table:

	12
	132
	5,342

3. *Entering a Subtotal or Total Code.* After you have entered all the numbers, you then need to tell WordPerfect to add them in a subtotal or total. Totalling a column of numbers takes three steps:

    a. Move the cursor to the first cell beneath the numbers you want to add.
    b. Press the Table command (Alt - F7) to activate the Table edit menu.
    c. Select the Math option and enter the subtotal or total codes.

To add a subtotal, select the plus code (+). To add subtotals into a single total, select the equals code (=). WordPerfect then automatically adds the columns of numbers and puts the results in a cell, shown as follows:

	12
	132
	5,342
Total ===>	5,486

Later, if you change a number in the column, you need to tell WordPerfect to calculate the totals in the table again.

Recalculating the Table

When you change numbers in a column that has already been totaled, WordPerfect does not automatically recalculate and change the totals and subtotals. Instead, you need to tell WordPerfect to recalculate the table by selecting the *Calculate* option in the Math menu of the table edit screen. WordPerfect will then recalculate all the subtotals and totals for you.

Creating Forms

When you start combining features to get a job done, WordPerfect becomes exciting to use. For example, you can combine the merge and table features to create forms that practically fill out and calculate themselves.

Creating such a form requires three steps: (1) creating a table that contains Merge Input codes, (2) formatting the table, and (3) merging the table. Let's look at these steps more closely.

1. *Creating the Form.* By placing Merge Input codes in a table, Word-Perfect will stop in a cell during a merge operation and tell you what kind of information should be entered. To enter an Input code in a cell, use the Merge Codes command ([Shift]-[F9]) and select the Input option.

2. *Formatting the Form.* WordPerfect gives you complete control about how the form will look when it is printed. You can print the form with or without lines in a table or select only certain lines to appear, such as subtotal or total lines.

   To control the lines in a table, use the *Line* option in the Format menu. This option allows you to change the appearance of lines around a single cell or a group of cells. To change lines around a cell, simply move the cursor to the cell, press the Table command ([Alt]-[F7]), and select the Line option under the Format menu.

   To change lines around a group of cells, move the cursor to the first cell in the group, press the Table command ([Alt]-[F7]), and press the Block command ([Alt]-[F4]). You can then highlight all the cells you want to change before invoking the Line option under the Format menu.

   These features are particularly useful if you want to eliminate all the lines in a table and then put single lines under subtotals and double lines under totals.

3. *Merging the Table.* Once you have finished creating and formatting a form, you can fill it out using the Merge command ([Ctrl]-[F9]). When you start the merge process, the cursor jumps to the first Input code in your form and waits for you to enter data.

To go to the next Input code, press the End Field key ($\boxed{\text{F9}}$). By pressing the $\boxed{\text{F9}}$ key, you can move through the form until it is completely filled out.

As you can see, by combining features you enable yourself to create extremely powerful, yet easy to use, applications to help you do your work more effectively.

Tutorial

Michelle Strongman has asked you to create the month end statements to customers shown in Figure 6.1. Rather than type each statement individually, and calculate what each customer owes by hand, you want

FIGURE 6.1

```
                          Exhibit Place
                     1611 N. W. 12th Avenue
                     Computer City, CA 94584


Invoice Number: 45983                      July 15, 19--

Jan Heverly
Security Systems of America
1920 Wiley Blvd.
San Jose, CA 90356


Statement of your account for your exhibit is as follows:



STAGE A--MARKET RESEARCH
Market research                              $2,432.20
Research on your strategies                     448.30
Price studies                                   328.00
        TOTAL A                              $3,208.50

STAGE B--DESIGN PRODUCTION
Budget and production                          $583.57
Component design                             1,200.83
Writers and technicians                      8,298.62
        TOTAL B                             $10,083.02

STAGE C--FOLLOW-UP
Training                                     $1,024.12
Mailing list                                    512.65
        TOTAL C                              $1,536.77

TOTAL DUE                                    $14,828.29
```

to create an invoice that you can quickly fill out and then have Word-Perfect add up what the customer owes.

To make the invoice as easy to fill out as possible, you want to use a Date code for the date and use a table to enter the data.

Setting Up

To begin, put the Student Data Disk in drive B and start WordPerfect. You will start by creating the primary file for envelopes.

Keyboarding

To create the invoice shown in Figure 6.1, follow these steps:

Enter the Heading

1. Starting at line 1 (1"), position 10 (1"), type

    ```
    Exhibit Place
    1611 N.W. 12th Avenue
    Computer City, CA 94584
    ```

2. Center each line using the Center command ([Shift]-[F6]) at the beginning of each line.

    NOTE: Do *not* use the Block Center command to center this text. Early versions of WordPerfect 5.1 fail when combining the Block Center with the Tables and Merge commands.

3. Press [Home] [Home] [↓] to move the cursor to the end of the document. Your cursor should now be on line 3 (1.33").

4. Press [Enter] six times to move the cursor to line 9 (2.33").

Enter Input Code
[Shift]-[F9], *3*

You are now ready to enter the first console code for the invoice number.

1. Type **Invoice Number:** and press the space bar once to leave a space.

2. Press the Merge Codes key ([Shift]-[F9]).

3. Type **3** to enter an Input code.

    RESULT: The following prompt appears on the status line:

    Enter Message:

4. Type **Type the invoice number.**

5. Press [Enter].

    RESULT: Your screen should now look like Figure 6.2.

6. Press the Flush-right command ([Alt]-[F6]) to move the cursor to the right margin.

7. Enter a Date code by pressing the Date key ([Shift]-[F5]) and choosing option 2.

8. Press [Enter] twice to move the cursor to line 11 (2.67"), position 10 (1").

FIGURE 6.2

```
            Exhibit Place
         1611 N.W. 12th Avenue
         Computer City, CA 94584




Invoice Number: {INPUT}Type the invoice number.~








                                    Doc 1 Pg 1 Ln 9 Pos 51
```

FIGURE 6.2

9. Enter another Input code by pressing the Merge Codes key ([Shift]-[F9]) and typing 3.

   RESULT: The following prompt appears:

   Enter Message:

10. Type **Type name and address.**

11. Press [Enter].

12. Press [Enter] three times to move the cursor to line 14 (3.17"), position 10 (1").

13. Type **Statement of your account for your exhibit is as follows:.**

14. Press [Enter] four times to move the cursor to line 18 (3.83"), position 10 (1").

    RESULT: Your screen should now look like Figure 6.3. You are now ready to create the table.

FIGURE 6.3

```
            Exhibit Place
         1611 N.W. 12th Avenue
         Computer City, CA 94584



Invoice Number: {INPUT}Type the invoice number.~   April 27, 1990

{INPUT}Type name and address.~

Statement of your account for your exhibit is as follows:






                                    Doc 1 Pg 1 Ln 18 Pos 10
```

Create a Table
[Alt]-[F7], *2, 1*

To create the table, follow these steps:

1. Press the Table command ([Alt]-[F7]).
2. Type **2** to select the Table option.
3. Type **1** to select the Create option.
4. Type **2** and press [Enter] to create two columns.
5. Type **17** and press [Enter] to create seventeen rows.
   RESULT: The table then appears on the screen.
   You can now change the column widths.

Change Column Widths
[Ctrl]-[←] *or* [→]

To change the column widths, follow these steps:

1. Press [→] once to move to the second column.
2. Press [Ctrl]-[←] 19 times to reduce the size of the second column.
3. Press [←] once to move the cursor bar to the left column.
4. Press [Ctrl]-[→] 20 times to increase the size of the first column.
   You can now start filling in the table.

Enter Data

To fill out the table, follow these steps:

1. Press the Exit key ([F7]) to leave Edit mode.
2. Type **STAGE A--MARKET RESEARCH.**
   NOTE: Be sure that it is bolded, using [F6], and capitalized.
3. Press [↓] once to move the cursor to the next cell below.
4. Type **Market research.**
5. Press [→] once to move the cursor to the second column in the row.
6. Press the Merge Codes key ([Shift]-[F9]).
7. Type **3** to enter an Input code.
   RESULT: The following prompt appears:

   Enter Message:

8. Type **Enter cost for market research** and press [Enter].
9. Press [→] to move to the beginning of the next row.
10. Type **Research your strategies.**
11. Press [→] once to move the cursor to the second column in the row.
12. Press the Merge Codes key ([Shift]-[F9]).
13. Type **3** to enter an Input code.
    RESULT: The following prompt appears:

    Enter Message:

14. Type **Enter cost for research strategies** and press [Enter].

15. Press ⬅️ to move to the beginning of the next row.

16. Type **Price studies**.

17. Press ➡️ once to move the cursor to the second column in the row.

18. Press the Merge Codes key (⬚Shift⬚-⬚F9⬚).

19. Type **3** to enter an Input code.
    RESULT: The following prompt appears:

    Enter Message:

20. Type **Enter cost for price studies** and press ⬚Enter⬚.

21. Press ➡️ to move to the beginning of the next row.

22. Press the space bar twice and type **TOTAL A**.
    RESULT: Your screen should now look like Figure 6.4.

23. Press ➡️ once to move the cursor to the second column in the row. You are now ready to enter the subtotal code.

Enter the Subtotal Code
⬚Alt⬚-⬚F7⬚, *5, 4*

24. Press the Table command (⬚Alt⬚-⬚F7⬚).

25. Type **5** to select the Math option.

26. Type **4** to select the + option.
    RESULT: Now, as shown in Figure 6.5, 0.00 appears in the cell to show that no numbers are available to calculate.

27. Press the Exit key (⬚F7⬚) once to leave the Table Edit mode.

28. Press ➡️ once to move to the beginning of the next row.

29. Press ⬇️ to move down a row in order to leave a space between Stage A and Stage B.

FIGURE 6.4

```
tatement of your account for your exhibit is as follows:


STAGE A--MARKET RESEARCH

Market research


Research your strategies



Price studies


   TOTAL A
                      Cell A5 Doc 1 Pg 1 Ln 33.56 Pos 20.23
```

FIGURE 6.5

30. Repeat steps 2 through 29 for Stage B and Stage C items shown in Figure 6.1. Be sure to enter the proper item names for each line. At the bottom you need to enter the Total Due cell and Total code.

Enter the Total Code
[Alt]-[F7], *5, 5*

To enter the Total Due cell, follow these steps:

1. Move the cursor to the beginning of the last row in the table (after the Total C row).

2. Type **TOTAL DUE:**.

3. Press [→] once to move to the second column in the row.

4. Press the Table command ([Alt]-[F7]).

5. Type **5** to select the Math option.

6. Type **5** to select the = option.

To finish the table, you need to eliminate the lines around the cells and enter lines for the subtotal and total lines.

Eliminate Lines
[Alt]-[F7], [Alt]-[F4], *3, 7, 1*

To eliminate table lines, make sure that the cursor bar is in the second column of the last row of the table and follow these steps:

1. Press the Block command ([Alt]-[F4]).

2. Move the cursor to the top row of the table by pressing [↑].

3. Press [←] once to highlight the entire table.

4. Type **3** to select the Line option.

5. Type **7** to select the All option.

6. Type **1** to select the None option.

RESULT: All lines on the screen disappear.
You can now enter lines for the subtotals.

Making Subtotal Lines
[Alt]-[F7], *3, 4, 2*

To enter subtotal lines, follow these steps:

1. Move the cursor to the last input cell for the Total A row that reads **Enter cost for price studies**.

2. Type **3** to select the Line option.

3. Type **4** to select the Bottom option.

4. Type **2** to select the Single option.
   RESULT: A line appears on the bottom of the cell.

5. Repeat steps 2 through 4 for the input cells for total B and total C. You can now enter double lines for the Total Due.

Making Total Lines
[Alt]-[F7], *3, 4, 3*

To enter double lines, follow these steps:

1. Move the cursor to the input cell for the Total Due row.

2. Type **3** to select the Line option.

3. Type **4** to select the Bottom option.

4. Type **3** to select the Double option.
   RESULT: Because the cell is in the last row, you do not see the double line.

5. Press the Exit key ([F7]) to leave the Table Edit menu. Your screen should look like the one in Figure 6.6.

Saving

Save the file as B:INVOICE using the Exit key ([F7]), create a Document Summary that is meaningful to you, and clear the screen.

You are now ready to use the INVOICE file.

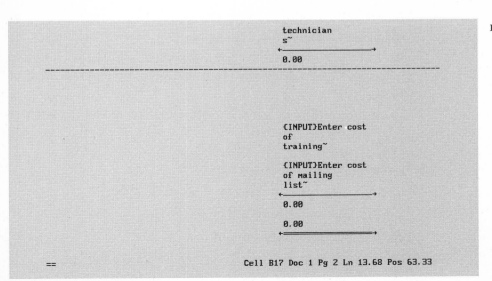

FIGURE 6.6

*Using the Merge Key to
Enter Values*
[Ctrl]-[F9], *1*

To fill out the invoice form, follow these steps:

1. Press the Merge key ([Ctrl]-[F9]).
    RESULT: The following prompt appears on the screen:

    1 Merge: 2 Sort: 3 Convert Old Codes: 0

2. Type 1 to select the Merge option.
    RESULT: The following prompt appears on the screen:

    Primary file:

3. Type **B:**INVOICE and press [Enter].
    RESULT: The following prompt appears on the screen:

    Secondary file:

4. Press [Enter] at the prompt for a secondary file. You are entering data from the keyboard, not from a secondary file.
    RESULT: The top of the B:INVOICE file appears on the screen. The cursor is next to Invoice Number: as shown in Figure 6.7.

5. Type 45983 and press the End Field key ([F9]).
    RESULT: The cursor moves to line 11 (2.67"), where the address goes.

6. Type the following:

    ```
    Jan Heverly
    Security Systems of America
    1920 Wiley Blvd.
    San Jose, CA 90356
    ```

7. When you finish typing the address, press the End Field key ([F9]).
    RESULT: The cursor moves to first item for market research.

8. Type $2,432.20 and press the End Field key ([F9]).

9. Complete the invoice, entering the appropriate value for each line item shown in Figure 6.1. Remember to press End Field ([F9]) after each entry. If you press [Enter] by accident, don't worry. Press the [Backspace] key to delete the Hard Return and then press the End Field key.

    You are now ready to have WordPerfect add up the items on the invoice.

Perform Calculations
[Alt]-[F7], *5, 1*

To calculate columns, follow these steps:

1. Move the cursor so that it is anywhere in the table.

2. Press the Table command ([Alt]-[F7]).

3. Type 5 to select the Math option.

4. Type 1 to calculate the table.

```
                            Exhibit Place
                         1611 N.W. 12th Avenue
                         Computer City, Ca 94584



Invoice Number:






Type the invoice number.                        Doc 1 Pg 1 Ln 9 Pos 26
```

FIGURE 6.7

RESULT: WordPerfect pauses for a moment and calculates the columns.

To complete the document, you now need to right-justify the right column and put dollar signs ($) in front of the totals.

Justify a Column
Alt - F7 , *2, 2, 3*

To format the right column, follow these steps:

1. Type **2** to select the Format option.
2. Type **2** to select the Column option.
3. Type **3** to select the Justify option.
4. Type **3** to select the Right option.
   RESULT: The totals appear right-justified in the second column.
   NOTE: We recommend that you format columns after you calculate totals. Early versions of 5.1 fail when calculating totals in right-justified columns.
5. Press the Exit key (F7) to return to the edit screen.
   You can now enter the dollar signs.

Enter Dollar Sign ($)

To enter a dollar sign ($) on the totals, follow these steps:

1. Move the cursor to the "1" in "14,828.29."
2. Type a dollar sign ($).
3. Repeat step 2 for the subtotals for A, B, and C.
   RESULT: Your screen should now look like Figure 6.8.

Printing

Print the invoice by using the Print key (Shift - F7) and choosing option 2–Page.

Saving/Filing

Save the invoice as B:45983 using the Exit key (F7) and clear the screen.

FIGURE 6.8

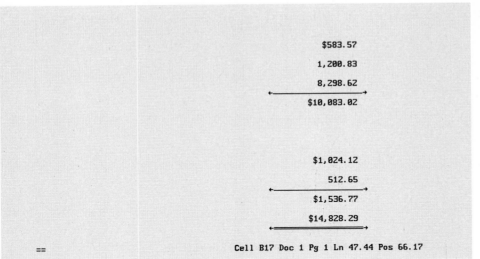

Exiting

If you are ready to leave WordPerfect, leave using the Exit key ([F7]). Otherwise, clear the screen by pressing [F7] and typing N N to continue working.

Summary

You created a form to generate month end statements for customers. To create the form, you created a table using the Table key ([Alt]-[F7]). You then entered text for each invoice line and entered an Input code in the associated cell. You then saved the form as a file called INVOICE and cleared the screen.

To generate invoices, you used the Merge key ([Ctrl]-[F9]) to invoke INVOICE. WordPerfect stopped at each Input code ({INPUT}~) for you to fill in with data. You moved to each Input code by pressing the End Field key ([F9]).

You then asked WordPerfect to calculate the invoice by choosing the Calculate option under Math at the Table menu.

Chapter Review

Key Terms

Format Table option
Math functions
Subtotal code
Table Line option

Table Calculate option
Table Edit mode
Total code

Review Questions

1. List and briefly describe the steps required for adding a column of numbers in a table.

2. What are the keystrokes required to calculate a total in a table column?

3. What keystrokes are required to right-justify numbers in a table column?

4. The _____ sign calculates subtotals. The _____ calculates totals.

5. What key do you press to move to a Input code ({INPUT}~) in a form?

6. What are the keystrokes required to eliminate all the lines from a table?

7. What are the keystrokes required to double-underline a number in a cell?

Applications

Please do the following WordPerfect exercises.

1. Retrieve the invoice form that you created in this chapter and follow these instructions:

   a. Fill out the form with this information:

   ```
   Invoice 45976
   Nancy Howard Gonzales
   First Computer Center
   320 First Avenue
   San Diego, California 94909

   STAGE A        432.69
                  553.00
                  234.44
   STAGE B        321.94
                5,022.54
                   21.32
   STAGE C        654.84
                3,234.64
   ```

   Calculate the form. Save it as B:45976 and print the file.

   b. Fill out the form with this information:

   ```
   Invoice 45921
   Karl Torgeson
   Database Incorporated
   21 Bayside Avenue
   Alameda, California 98756
   ```

```
STAGE A          762.99
                 355.08
                 364.25
STAGE B          634.34
                 322.73
                  43.32
STAGE C          368.88
               2,317.89
```

Calculate the form. Save it as B:45921 and print the file.

c. Fill out the form with this information:

```
Invoice 46001
Brian Starkey
Logos Inc.
2375 Waylon Avenue
Oakhurst, Tennessee 45374

STAGE A           22.69
                 143.00
                 734.44
STAGE B          221.94
                 302.54
                 105.50
STAGE C          364.90
               6,784.70
```

Calculate the form. Save it as B:46001 and print the file.

2. Assume you are creating a sample travel budget to help clients plan their trip to the New Wave Trade Show.

   a. Create the table in Figure 6.9. Instead of the data, insert Input codes in the figure. Save the form as B:FORM6-2.

   b. Use the Merge key to fill out the form with the data shown in Figure 6.9.

   c. Use the Calculate option to calculate the subtotals and totals.

FIGURE 6.9

```
              ANALYSIS OF TRAVEL COSTS


   Transportation          $340.00
   Lodging                  550.00
        Subtotal


   Car Rental              $150.00
   Insurance                 30.00
        Subtotal


   Food                    $200.00
   Gratuities                40.00
        Subtotal
```

MORE

```
Entertainment                    $50.00
Miscellaneous Expense             75.00
     Subtotal

GRAND TOTAL
```

3. Create the document shown in Figure 6.10 by following these instructions:

   a. Use the Table Math function to total the donations for both months.

   b. Save the document as B:DRILL6-3.

   c. Print the document.

FIGURE 6.10

```
              EXHIBIT PLACE STAFF
              UNITED WAY DONATIONS

        Winter and Summer Quarter 19--
```

NAME	WINTER	SUMMER
A. Ackroyd	32.43	45.62
R. Adams	23.65	19.43
L. Adent	19.22	25.00
R. Ardrey	11.23	14.56
R. Basel	12.32	35.69
J. Birchman	56.83	12.43
R. Blane	9.47	3.21
K. Brown	56.89	62.43
N. Burns	23.78	98.22
A. Camus	25.85	56.93
L. Hutton	34.25	67.37
B. Joad	32.45	35.00
M. Laursen	88.76	76.32
M. Lincoln	56.43	45.83
I. Malone	19.21	18.77
R. Merle	19.12	34.56
E. Murphey	18.98	19.04
F. Neckerbow	14.12	9.27
R. Olson	56.75	65.32
M. Perkins	54.23	45.32
R. Ricardo	42.14	32.55
N. Silver	21.45	65.32
P. Smith	53.21	51.22
M. Strongman	75.87	87.00
K. Tanaka	81.25	93.14
TOTAL	**$939.89**	**$1,119.55**

4.   Create the memo shown in Figure 6.11 by following these instructions:

a. Use the Table Math function to total the donations for both years.

b. Save the document as B:DRILL6-4.

c. Print the document.

FIGURE 6.11

TO: Michelle Strongman

FROM: Holly Myers

DATE: August 23, 19--

SUBJECT: United Way Donations Compared to Previous Year

Below I have listed what employees in your department donated this year compared with what they donated last year.

If you have any questions, be sure to let me know.

NAME	LAST	CURRENT
A. Ackroyd	32.43	45.62
R. Adams	23.65	19.43
L. Adent	19.22	25.00
R. Ardrey	11.22	14.56
J. Baldwin	0.00	0.00
A. Basel	12.32	35.69
R. Basel	0.00	0.00
J. Birchman	56.83	12.43
R. Blane	9.47	3.21
D. Bonet	0.00	0.00
K. Brown	56.89	62.43
N. Burns	23.78	98.32
A. Camus	112.32	45.67
A. Caron	12.56	12.43
H. Caulfield	19.22	54.32
K. Clark	0.00	0.00
D. Curtis	43.12	76.34
E. Dickerson	19.21	26.88
F. Ditterow	123.56	183.12
P. Dow	43.56	45.12
R. Emilio	21.90	52.43
A. Florio	25.00	25.00
L. Goldberg	31.14	42.87
A. Hamil	15.00	20.00
TOTAL	**712.41**	**900.87**

5.   Create the memo shown in Figure 6.12 by following these instructions:

   a.   Create the memo as a form so that you can enter different entries for each aisle location.

   b.   Use the Table Math function to calculate the subtotal bookings for each aisle and the total of all aisles.

   c.   Fill out the form with this information:

```
Aisle A          Bookings
A1                36
A2                32
A3                51
A4                59
A5                67
A6                01


Aisle B          Bookings
B1                64
B2                63
B3                42
B4                31
B5                33


Aisle C          Bookings
C1                67
C2                01
C3                21
C4                43
C5                12
C6                64


Aisle D          Bookings
D1                63
D2                42
D3                31
D4                33
D5                36
D6                32
```

   Calculate the form. Save it as B:FORM651 and print the file.

FIGURE 6.12

```
     TO:  Ken Tanaka

   FROM:  Michelle Strongman

   DATE:  August 23, 19--

SUBJECT:  New Wave Bookings to Date

Please examine the September booking statistics for exhibits at
the New Wave Trade Show. Note that the occupancy rate has
```

MORE

increased 12 percent since last month, but we are still below our projections for September by 8 percent.

Aisle A	Bookings
A1	36
A2	32
A3	51
A4	59
A5	67
A6	01
	246.00

Aisle B	Bookings
B1	64
B2	63
B3	42
B4	31
B5	33
	233.00

Aisle C	Bookings
C1	67
C2	01
C3	21
C4	43
C5	12
C6	64
	208.00

Aisle D	**Bookings**
D1	63
D2	42
D3	31
D4	33
D5	36
D6	32
	237.00
TOTAL	**924.00**

d. Fill out the form with this information:

Aisle A	Bookings
A1	12
A2	34
A3	43
A4	75
A5	45
A6	61

Aisle B	Bookings
B1	32
B2	64

MORE ▼

```
B3              78
B4              32
B5              64


Aisle C         Bookings
C1              43
C2              56
C3              24
C4              64
C5              67
C6              32


Aisle D         Bookings
D1              21
D2              36
D3               5
D4              24
D5              56
D6              67
```

Calculate the form. Save it as B:FORM652 and print the file.

e. Fill out the form with this information:

```
Aisle A         Bookings
A1              43
A2              56
A3              34
A4              61
A5              96
A6              21


Aisle B         Bookings
B1              44
B2              53
B3              67
B4              35
B5              33

Aisle C         Bookings
C1              37
C2              51
C3              22
C4              43
C5              81
C6              74


Aisle D         Bookings
D1              68
D2              49
D3              21
D4              43
D5              56
D6              62
```

Calculate the form. Save it as B:FORM653 and print the file.

6. Create the memo shown in Figure 6.13 by following these instructions:

a. Use the Table Math function to calculate the subtotal donations for each department and the total of all departments.

b. Save the document as B:DRILL6-6.

c. Print the document.

FIGURE 6.13

EXHIBIT PLACE STAFF
UNITED WAY DONATIONS
BY DEPARTMENT

Winter Quarter 19--

MARKETING	WINTER	SUMMER
M. Perkins	$54.23	45.32
R. Ricardo	42.14	32.55
R. Ardrey	11.23	14.56
R. Basel	12.32	35.69
E. Murphey	18.98	19.04
F. Neckerbow	14.12	9.27
	$766.02	$769.43

OPERATIONS		
J. Birchman	$56.83	$12.43
N. Burns	23.78	98.22
N. Silver	21.45	65.32
L. Adent	19.22	25.00
A. Camus	25.85	56.93
	$147.13	$257.90

ADMINISTRATION		
L. Hutton	$34.25	$67.37
B. Joad	32.45	35.00
R. Adams	23.65	19.43
M. Lincoln	56.43	45.83
I. Malone	19.21	18.77
R. Blane	9.47	3.21
M. Laursen	88.76	76.32
A. Ackroyd	32.43	45.62
	$296.65	$311.55

DESIGN		
K. Brown	$56.89	$62.43

MORE ▼

```
R. Merle              19.12       34.56
R. Olson              56.75       65.32
P. Smith              53.21       51.22
M. Strongman          75.87       87.00
K. Tanaka             81.25       93.14
                    $343.09     $393.67

TOTAL             $1,552.89    1,732.55
```

Advanced Skills

In this chapter you added subtotals and totals using the + and = codes under the math function of the Table Edit menu. This is only the beginning of WordPerfect's mathematical capabilities. You can also add totals into grand totals and subtract totals from each other. Let's look more closely at how this is done.

Calculating a Grand Total

The asterisk (*) in option 6 of the Table Math menu is the command for producing the *grand total*. You use it in the same way that you use the + and = codes. When you want to add up a series of totals made with the = code, you enter an asterisk (*) code. For example:

```
ITEMS A
      2.83
      5.32
      8.15+

ITEMS B
     92.45
     12.84
    105.29+
    _____

    113.44=    <==== Total of A and B

ITEMS C
      1.53
      4.90
      6.43+




ITEMS D
      2.87
      5.23
      8.10+
     _____

     14.53=    <==== Total of C and D

    127.97*    <==== Grand Total of B and D
```

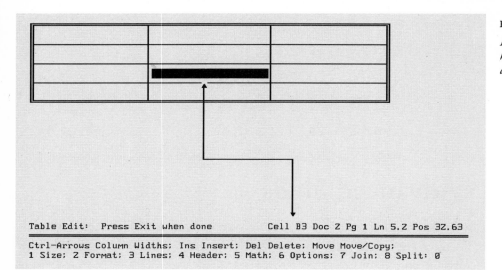

```
Table Edit:   Press Exit when done          Cell B3 Doc 2 Pg 1 Ln 5.2 Pos 32.63

Ctrl-Arrows Column Widths: Ins Insert: Del Delete: Move Move/Copy:
1 Size: 2 Format: 3 Lines: 4 Header: 5 Math: 6 Options: 7 Join: 8 Split: 0
```

FIGURE 6.14

Note that the highlighted cell's address is B3.

The Grand Total sign (*) adds all the totals. But WordPerfect can do more than add columns of numbers. You can also subtract columns from each other.

Subtracting with WordPerfect

If Ken Tanaka, president of Exhibit Place, asks you to calculate the net profit made on an exhibit for a major client at the New Wave Trade Show, you need to add up revenues and subtract expenses. To do so, you create a *Table formula* that subtracts a number in one cell from a number in another cell.

Each cell in a table has a *cell address,* which helps you to refer to specific cells when creating a formula. Each row in your table has a number and each column has a letter:

	A	B	C
Row 1			
Row 2			
Row 3			
Row 4			

The address for each cell is the row number and cell letter where it appears. WordPerfect displays this address in the middle of the Table Edit menu. For example, in Figure 6.14 the cursor bar is in Cell B3.

To create a formula that subtracts the number in one cell from a number in another cell, use the *Formula option* in the Table Math menu. With this option you can use the arithmetic operands (+ and −) to add and subtract numbers in cells. For example, to calculate the net profit, you might create a table like the following:

REVENUE	
Stage A	1,500.00
Stage B	3,500.00
Stage C	13,000.00
	18,000.00
EXPENSES	
Salaries	8,532.87
Overhead	4,436.21
Supplies	1,312.43
	14,281.51
NET PROFIT	**3,718.49**

<=== *Subtotal (+) in cell B5*

<=== *Subtotal (+) in cell B10*

<=== *Formula (B5 – B10)*

When you tell WordPerfect to calculate the document table, it will subtract the expense subtotal in cell B10 from the revenue subtotal in cell B5.

Creating a Formula

To create the formula shown in the preceding example, follow these steps:

1. Move the table to the second column of the last row.
2. Press the Table command (Alt-F7).
3. Type **5** to select the Math option.
4. Type **2** to select the Formula option.
5. Type **B5 – B10** and press Enter.

The result automatically appears in the cell. The formula itself, however, appears to the left of the cell address.

Advanced Key Terms

Cell Address   Grand total

Formula option

Advanced Review Questions

1. The code to create a grand total is _____.
2. The grand total symbol adds up totals made with the _____ code.
3. List the cell addresses for each of the cells in the following table. Use the letter in each cell to identify each address you list.

A	B	C
D	E	F
G	H	I

4. Create a table that calculates this equation:
   (12 + 42) – (543.23 + 97)

Advanced Applications

1. Create the memo shown in Figure 6.15 by following these instructions:

   a. Use the Table Math function to subtotal the donations for men and women for each department, total the donations for each department, and calculate a grand total for both departments.

   b. Save the document as B:DRILL6-7.

   c. Print the document.

FIGURE 6.15

```
         TO:  Michelle Strongman

       FROM:  Holly Myers

       DATE:  July 13, 19--

    SUBJECT:  Returns of Ugly Tie Contest by Gender and Department

    Below I have listed what employees in your department donated in
    the Ugly Tie contest compared by gender and department.


                         MARKETING WOMEN
                             $23.83
                              31.32
                             $55.15

                          MARKETING MEN
                             $92.45
                              42.84
                            $135.29
           Marketing Total   $190.44

                        ADMINISTRATION MEN
                             $51.53
                              34.90
                             $86.43

                       ADMINISTRATION WOMEN
                             $22.87
                              35.23
                             $58.10
        Administration Total   $144.53
               Grand Total   $334.97
```

2.   Create the memo shown in Figure 6.16 by following these instructions:

   a.   Use the Table Math function to subtract expenses from revenues and calculate the net profit for Exhibit Place.

   b.   Save the document as DRILL6-8.

   c.   Print the document.

FIGURE 6.16

```
        TO:   Ken Tanaka

      FROM:   Michelle Strongman

      DATE:   December 31, 19--

   SUBJECT:   Exhibit Place Quarterly Standing

   Please examine the Winter Quarter financial standings for each
   city. If you have any questions, please give me a call.

   REVENUE

       New York                  $211,554.94
       Atlantic City              433,556.78
       Los Angeles              2,383,670.40
       Computer City              512,432.65
                               $3,544,948.77

   EXPENSES

       Salaries                $2,432,532.87
       Overhead                   234,436.21
       Supplies                    91,321.43
       Travel                      32,905.00
                               $2,791,195.51

   NET PROFIT                     $753,753.26
```

On Your Own   Prepare a monthly budget for your personal finances. Estimate your expenses for food, lodging, transportation, clothing, and other expenses that come to mind for the next month. Use the Math key to calculate these costs.

SPEECH OUTLINE

I. Introduction
    A. Story of the farmer
    B. Why we are here
II. Description of Product
    A. Education of your staff
    B. What we create for you
    C. Economical choices
    D. Possible formats
        1. Panel wall with cases brought in from behind
        2. Built-in case with curving panel wall
        3. Display stages
        4. Glass-top shallow case supported on a sloping-top floor base
        5. Small cases supported on shelves
III. Description of Market
    A. Five elements of effective selling
        1. Involve sales and marketing management in setting specific objectives for the show
        2. Construct a sales scenario
        3. Prepare an exhibit that augments the sales plan
        4. Train staff to work in the specific medium
        5. Follow-up leads obtained at the show
    B. Perils of inexperience at trade shows
    C. Benefits of Stage A research proposal
IV. Design Development
    A. Role of designer
    B. Role of writers
    C. Role of technicians
V. Stages of Development
    A. Market research and company report
    B. Design development and production
    C. Trade show consulting and follow-up services
VI. Projected Costs
    A. Stage A
        1. Rationale
        2. Cost
    B. Stage B
        1. Rationale
        2. Cost
    C. Stage C
        1. Rationale
        2. Scope
    D. Exclusivity of letter

In this chapter, you will create outlines using WordPerfect's outline feature.

7

Speech Outline

Chapter Objectives	After completing this chapter, you will be able to

1. Create an outline seven levels deep.

2. Insert and delete outline headings.

3. Move and change outline headings.

WordPerfect Commands	[Shift]-[F5], 4, 1	Turn outline on
	[Enter] [F4]	Enter first-level section
	[Tab]	Go one level deeper
	[Enter] [Tab] [F4]	Enter second-level section
	[Enter] [Tab] [Tab] [F4]	Enter third-level section
	[Shift]-[Tab]	Back up a level
	[Backspace], [Del]	Delete a section
	[Shift]-[F5], 4, 2	Turn outline off

Overview

Most successful professionals organize their work with *outlines,* especially if they are planning a major project, giving a presentation, or writing an important document. A strong outline ensures a clear flow of ideas and a unity of presentation.

WordPerfect's outline feature can help you develop and polish your important projects by providing a blueprint of your ideas that you can quickly change. It gives you the freedom to move ideas around and see what happens if you veer off in a new direction to see where a new thought takes you. Each time you make a change, WordPerfect adjusts the outline automatically.

Polishing Ideas with Outlines

Depending on your project, WordPerfect can break ideas and topics down into parts, sections, headings, and subheadings—all the way down to eight *levels* deep, if necessary. For example, WordPerfect can automatically structure the following outline for you:

```
              PLAN FOR SUCCESS
    I.    ORGANIZE THOUGHTS
          A. Develop an outline
             1. Use WordPerfect outline feature
                a. Learn its keystrokes
                   (1)  Be proficient with  Tab  and  Enter  keys
                       (a)  Practice until it is a habit
                           i) Show other people how it works
                              a) Become a teacher
                              b)
    II.   DEVELOP A PLAN
          A. Write a Plan
             1. Schedule each step
             2. Allocate resources
                a. People
                b. Materials
             3. Assign responsibilities
          B.
    III. WORK THE PLAN
          A. Ensure accountability
             1. Audit progress
             2.
          B. Provide incentives
             1. Increase pay
             2.
```

If you move section Part II, "DEVELOP A PLAN," to be first, in the outline, WordPerfect renumbers the headings as follows:

```
    I.    DEVELOP A PLAN
          A. Write a plan
             1. Schedule each step
             2. Allocate resources
```

```
            a. People
            b. Materials
         3. Assign responsibilities
      B.
  II.  ORGANIZE THOUGHTS
      A. Develop an outline
         1. Use WordPerfect Outline feature
            a. Learn its keystrokes
               (1)  Be proficient with  Tab  and  Enter  keys
                  (a)  Practice until it is a habit
                     i) Show other people how it works
                        a) Become a teacher
                        b)
 III. WORK THE PLAN
      A. Ensure accountability
         1. Audit progress
         2.
      B. Provide incentives
         1. Increase pay
         2.
```

Few word processors can help you create outlines as easily as Word-Perfect. Let's take a look at how you use WordPerfect to create an outline.

Using the Outline Key

To create an outline, you use the *Date/Outline* key (Shift - F5 , 4, 1) to turn the Outline feature on. You need to do only three steps to create an outline: (1) Turn outline mode on, (2) enter topics and ideas, and (3) turn outline off.

1. *Turning Outline Mode on.* You start the outline mode by pressing the Date/Outline key (Shift - F5). You have already used this key to access the automatic date feature. First, you choose option 4 (Outline), at this prompt:

    1 Date Text; 2 Date Code; 3 Date Format; 4 Outline; 5 Para Num; 6 Define: 0

    Second, you choose option 1 (On), at this prompt:

    Outline: 1 On; 2 Off; 3 Move Family; 4 Copy Family; 5 Delete Family: 0

    The word "Outline" appears in the status line and WordPerfect goes into outline mode.

    When the outline function is turned on, the Enter , Tab , and Margin Release (Shift - Tab) keys work differently and become quite powerful for creating outlines.

2. *Creating an Outline with the* Enter , Tab , *and* (Shift - Tab) *keys.* It will take you a few moments to get used to the new functions that the Enter , Tab , and (Shift - Tab) keys take on when you are in outline mode. Each time you press Enter , a new level number automatically appears

on the screen. For example, if you press Enter, the following number appears:

```
I.
```

To change the Roman numeral heading "I." to the next level, press the Tab key. For example, if you press Tab, the "I." indents five spaces and automatically becomes an "A." as follows:

```
     A.
```

Each time you press Tab, the number indents another five spaces and changes to the next level. WordPerfect has eight outline levels:

```
I.
     A.
          1.
               a.
                    (1)
                         (a)
                              i)
                                   a)
```

To move an entry left 5 spaces and change it to a higher level, press (Shift-Tab). Each time you press (Shift-Tab) an entry changes to another level.

3. *Turning the outline option off.* When you are finished working on your outline, you return WordPerfect back to normal edit mode by pressing the Date/Outline key (Shift-F5) and selecting option 4 (Outline) and option 2 (Off). When you turn the outline option off, the "Outline" prompt in the status line will disappear.

Typing Text with the Indent Key

Because the Tab key moves an outline heading, you must use the Indent key (F4) to move the cursor and type text. The Indent key works the same in Outline mode as it does in normal Edit mode. For example, to create the following heading:

```
I. DEVELOP A PLAN
```

You would press Enter once so that "I." appears on the screen, press the Indent key (F4), and type your heading: "DEVELOP A PLAN."

Insert a New Entry

As you work in outline mode, you will want to add new entries and delete old entries. To add a new entry, you move the cursor to where you want the new entry to start and press Enter. For example, say that you want to insert a new entry between headings "a." and "b." in the outline below:

```
I.    DEVELOP A PLAN
      A. Write a plan
         1. Schedule each step
```

```
      2. Allocate resources
         a. People
         b. Materials
      3. Assign responsibilities
```

You would move the cursor to the end of the word: "People" after heading "a." and press ⎡Enter⎤. The outline would then look like this:

```
I.     DEVELOP A PLAN
       A. Write a plan
          1. Schedule each step
          2. Allocate resources
             a. People
             b.
             c. Materials
          3. Assign responsibilities
```

To enter text at the new heading, you would press the Indent key (⎡F4⎤) and type your heading.

Deleting an Entry

Each time you create a new entry, you are inserting an Outline code in a document. For example, when you added the new heading "b." in the preceding outline, you actually inserted the following code: Par Num: Auto into the document. To delete the entry, you need to move the cursor to the right of the new entry code and use the Backspace key (⎡Backspace⎤) to delete it and the ⎡Tab⎤ codes that precede it. WordPerfect will then renumber your remaining entries. You may want to turn Reveal Codes on (⎡Alt⎤-⎡F3⎤) the first few times you delete outline entries in order to see the codes that you are deleting.

Decreasing Outline Levels with Margin Release

When people first start working with the outline option, they commonly press ⎡Tab⎤ when they do not mean to. For example, if you want to type text at the "b." level, you might accidentally press the ⎡Tab⎤ key instead of the Indent key. As a result, the outline level "b." will indent five spaces and become level "(1)." To move "(1)" back five spaces and return "i" to "b.," you press the *Margin Release* key (⎡Shift⎤-⎡Tab⎤). For example, say that the cursor is at the "a." heading in the following outline:

```
II.    DEVELOP A PLAN
       A. Write a plan
          1. Schedule each step
          2. Allocate resources
             a.
             b. Materials
          3. Assign responsibilities
```

If you want to type a heading to "a." and instead of pressing Indent, you accidentally press ⎡Tab⎤, the outline will look like this:

```
II.   DEVELOP A PLAN
      A. Write a plan
         1. Schedule each step
         2. Allocate resources
               (1)
            b. Materials
         3. Assign responsibilities
```

The "a." has indented five spaces and changed to "(1)." You can move the "(1)" back five spaces and change it to the previous level by pressing the Margin Release key ([Shift]-[Tab]). You can then enter text by pressing the Indent key and typing your text.

Moving Parts of an Outline

You move a part of an outline to another place in the same way that you move normal text. As you recall, there are five steps for moving text:

1. Highlight the text that you want to move with the Block key ([Alt]-[F4]).

2. Press the Move key ([Ctrl]-[F4]).

3. Select the Block and Move options.

4. Move the cursor to where you want the new part to go.

5. Press [Enter] to insert the text in the new place.

Moving text in Outline mode can be exciting because it quickly shows you the power of WordPerfect to renumber and keep your outline organized. With a little practice, creating and changing ideas in outlines can become second nature and a lot of fun as you see your project ideas develop before your eyes.

Tutorial

Ken Tanaka, president of Exhibit Place, is going to give a talk to the senior executives at a major corporation about how best to use trade show exhibits as a marketing tool.

Your task is to create a typed, polished outline that he can use while giving his speech. To start the outline, you work from scribbled notes that he gave you, as shown in Figure 7.1. Each time you give him a draft of his notes, you should expect that he will change the outline in order to polish and develop his ideas. As a result, you must be prepared to make several drafts of the outline before it is completed.

Setting Up

To begin, put the Student Data Disk in drive B and start WordPerfect.

Formatting

To put WordPerfect into Outline mode, follow these two steps:

FIGURE 7.1 *Notes that Ken Tanaka created for his speech.*

```
                         Speech Outline

   I.   Description of Product
        A. Education of your staff
        B. What we create for you
        C. Economical choices
        D. Possible formats
           1. Panel wall with cases brought in from behind
           2. Built-in case with curving panel wall
           3. Display stages
           4. Glass-top shallow case supported on a sloping-top
              floor base
           5. Small cases supported on shelves

  II.   Description of Market
        A. Perils of inexperience at trade shows
        B. Five elements of effective selling
           1. Involve sales and marketing management in setting
              specific objectives for the show
           2. Construct a sales scenario
           3. Prepare an exhibit that augments the sales plan
           4. Train staff to work in the specific medium
           5. Follow up leads obtained at the show
        C. Benefits of Stage A research proposal

 III.   Design Development
        A. Role of designer
        B. Role of writers
        C. Role of technicians

  IV.   Stages of Development
        A. Market research and company report
        B. Design development and production
        C. Trade show consulting and follow-up services

   V.   Projected Costs
        A. Stage A
        B. Stage B
        C. Stage C
        D. Exclusivity of letter
```

Turn Outline On
Shift - F5 , *4, 1*

1. Press the Date/Outline key (Shift - F5).

    RESULT: The following menu appears on the status line:

    **1 Date Text; 2 Date Code; 3 Date Format; 4 Outline;
    5 Para Num; 6 Define; 0**

2. Type 4 to select the Outline option.

    RESULT: The following menu appears on the status line:

    ```
    Outline: 1 On; 2 Off; 3 Move Family; 4 Copy Family;
    5 Delete Family: 0
    ```

3. Type 1 to select Outline On.

    RESULT: The word "Outline" appears on the status line. You are now ready to create your outline.

Keyboarding

Ken Tanaka hands you the piece of paper shown in Figure 7.1. To create the first-level section, follow these steps:

Enter First-Level Section

Enter , F4

1. Press Enter .

    RESULT: The Roman numeral heading "I." appears on the screen.

2. Press the Indent key (F4).

    RESULT: The cursor jumps to the right five spaces.

3. Type **Description of Product**.

Enter Second-Level Section

Enter Tab F4

To create the second-level section, follow these steps:

1. Press Enter .

    RESULT: The Roman numeral "II." appears on the next line.

2. Press the Tab key Tab .

    RESULT: The Roman numeral "II." moves to the right five spaces and turns into "A." The screen should now look like this:

    ```
    I.   Description of Product
         A.
    ```

3. Press the Indent key (F4) and type **Education of your staff**. Press Enter .

4. Press the Indent key (F4) and type **What we create for you**. Press Enter .

5. Press the Indent key (F4) and type **Economical choices**. Press Enter .

6. Press the Indent key (F4) and type **Possible formats**.

Enter Third-Level Section

Enter Tab F4

To enter a third-level section, follow these steps:

1. Press Enter .

2. Press the Tab key Tab once.

3. Press the Indent key (F4) and type **Panel wall with cases brought in from behind**. Press Enter .

4. Repeat step 3 to enter headings 2 through 5 of Part I. Press Enter after typing heading 5.

RESULT: 6 appears below heading 5.

Before you enter the rest of the speech, practice what you do in case you make a mistake.

Going a Level Too Deep
[Tab]

If you press the [Tab] key too many times, you will go too deep into the outline hierarchy. To fix this problem, you use the Margin Release key ([Shift]-[Tab]).

1. Press ([Shift]-[Tab]) twice.
   RESULT: The Roman numeral heading "II." appears on the screen.
2. Press the Tab key.
   RESULT: The letter heading "E." appears on the screen.

Back Up with Margin Release
[Shift]-[Tab]

You had meant to press the Indent key and type the new heading. Instead you created a new level. To back up to the previous level, you use the Margin Release key ([Shift]-[Tab]).

1. Press Margin Release ([Shift]-[Tab]).
   RESULT: The "E." moves to the left five spaces and turns into "II."
2. Press [Enter] once to move the Roman numeral heading "II." down one line (to separate it from the section above).
3. Press the Indent key ([F4]) and type **Description of Market**.

Add an Extra Section
[Enter], [Tab], [F4]

We'll now show you how to delete a section that you don't want. First, let's add a few sections:

1. Press [Enter] and [Tab].
2. Press the Indent key ([F4]) and type **Perils of inexperience at trade shows**. Press [Enter].
3. Press the Indent key ([F4]) and press [Enter].
4. Press the Indent key ([F4]) and type **Five elements of effective selling**.
   RESULT: Your screen should now look like this:

```
II.  Description of Market
     A. Perils of inexperience at trade shows
     B.
     C. Five elements of effective selling
```

Let us say you want to delete the "B." section.

Delete a Section
[Alt]-[F3], [Del]

To delete a section, follow these steps:

1. Move the cursor until it is to the right of the "B."
2. Turn on Reveal Codes ([Alt]-[F3]).
   RESULT: Your screen should now look like Figure 7.2.

```
I.  Decription of Product
    A.    We educate your staff
    B.    What we create for you
    C.    Economical choices
    D.    Possible formats
          1.Panel wall with casaes brought in from behind

II. Description of Market
    A.    Perils of inexperience at trade shows
    B.
Outline                                           Doc 1 Pg 1 Ln 11 Pos 17
{   ▲   ▲   ▲   ▲   ▲   ▲   ▲   ▲   ▲   ▲   ▲   }   ▲   ▲
[HRt]
[Par Num:Auto][→Indent]Description of Market[HRt]
[TAB][Par Num:Auto][→Indent]Perils of inexperience at trade shows[HRt]
[TAB][Par Num:Auto][→Indent][HRt]
[TAB][Par Num:Auto][→Indent]Five elements of effective selling



Press Reveal Codes to restore screen
```

FIGURE 7.2

To delete a section you must delete the [Par Num:Auto] code, the tab(s) code, and the [HRt] code that precede it.

3. Move the cursor to the right of the Par Num:Auto code (if it is not already to the right of it).

4. Press the Backspace key (⌫ Backspace) three times to delete the Par Num:Auto code, the Tab code, and the Indent code.

    RESULT: Your screen should now look like Figure 7.3.

5. Press the Del key once to delete the [HRt] code.

6. Turn Reveal Codes off (Alt-F3).

    RESULT: Your screen should now look like this:

```
II.  Description of Market
     A. Perils of inexperience at trade shows
     B. Five elements of effective selling
```

FIGURE 7.3

```
I.  Decription of Product
    A.    We educate your staff
    B.    What we create for you
    C.    Economical choices
    D.    Possible formats
          1.Panel wall with casaes brought in from behind

II. Description of Market
    A.    Perils of inexperience at trade shows
    B.    Five elements of effective selling
Outline                                           Doc 1 Pg 1 Ln 10 Pos 57
{   ▲   ▲   ▲   ▲   ▲   ▲   ▲   ▲   ▲   ▲   ▲   }   ▲   ▲
[TAB][TAB][Par Num:Auto]Panel wall with casaes brought in from behind[HRt]
[HRt]
[Par Num:Auto][→Indent]Description of Market[HRt]
[TAB][Par Num:Auto][→Indent]Perils of inexperience at trade shows[→Indent][HRt]
[TAB][Par Num:Auto][→Indent]Five elements of effective selling



Press Reveal Codes to restore screen
```

7. Enter the remaining text for Part II. If you press [Tab] when you don't want to, correct the mistake with the Margin Release key ([Shift]-[Tab]).

Enter Text

Complete creating the outline by entering Parts III, IV, and V.

Turn Outline Off
[Shift]-[F5], *4*

You are now ready to turn Outline Off.

1. Press the Date/Outline key ([Shift]-[F5]).
2. Type 4 to select Outline.
3. Type 2 to turn Outline off.
   RESULT: The word "Outline" disappears on the status line.

Saving

Save the outline as B:OUTLINE using the Save key ([F10]).

Printing

Print the outline using the Print command ([Shift]-[F7]) and selecting Full Document.

Revisions

Ken Tanaka reviews the outline and would like to make a series of changes. First he decides he would like to add an introduction as shown in Figure 7.4.

FIGURE 7.4 *Ken Tanaka would like to add an introduction to his outline.*

```
  I.   Introduction
       A. Story of the farmer
       B. Why we are here
 II.   Description of Product
       A. Education of your staff
       B. What we create for you
       C. Economical choices
       D. Possible formats
          1. Panel wall with cases brought in from behind.
          2. Built-in case with curving panel wall
          3. Display stages
          4. Glass-top shallow case supported on a sloping-top floor
             base.
          5. Small cases supported on shelves
```

Add a New Section

To add a new section, follow these steps:

1. Move the cursor *on top of* the Roman numeral heading "I." at the beginning of the outline.
2. Press [Enter].
   RESULT: The screen should now look like this:
   I.II. Description of Product

3. Press the Indent key ($\boxed{\text{F4}}$).

4. Press $\boxed{\text{Enter}}$ twice to move "II. Description of Product" two lines.
   RESULT: The line now should look like this:
   II.III. Description of Product

5. Press the $\boxed{\text{Del}}$ key once to delete "III."

6. Press the left arrow ($\boxed{\leftarrow}$) three times to move the cursor to the right of the "I." on the first line.

7. Type

   ```
   Introduction
   A. Story of the farmer
   B. Why we are here
   ```

8. Press $\boxed{\text{Home}}$ $\boxed{\text{Home}}$ $\boxed{\downarrow}$ to move to the bottom of the document.
   RESULT: The Roman numeral part headings renumber to show six sections.

Move Sections
$\boxed{\text{Alt}}$-$\boxed{\text{F4}}$, $\boxed{\text{Ctrl}}$-$\boxed{\text{F4}}$,
1, 1, $\boxed{\text{Enter}}$

Tanaka also wants to reverse the order of sections A and B in what is now Part III as shown in Figure 7.5.

FIGURE 7.5 *Ken Tanaka would like to add more detail to the Projected Costs section.*

```
III. Description of Market
    A. Perils of inexperience at trade shows
    B. Five elements of effective selling
        1. Involve sales and marketing management in setting
           specific objectives for the show
        2. Construct a sales scenario
        3. Prepare an exhibit that augments the sales plan
        4. Train staff to work in the specific medium
        5. Follow up leads obtained at the show
    C. Benefits of Stage A research proposal
```

1. Move the cursor to the "A." in "A. Perils of inexperience at trade shows."

2. Press the left arrow ($\boxed{\leftarrow}$) once to move the cursor to position 10.

3. Highlight the line by turning on the Block key ($\boxed{\text{Alt}}$-$\boxed{\text{F4}}$) and pressing $\boxed{\text{Enter}}$.

4. Press the Move key ($\boxed{\text{Ctrl}}$-$\boxed{\text{F4}}$).

5. Type **1** to select Block.

6. Type **1** to select Move.

7. Move the cursor to the left margin (position 10 or 1") of the line **Benefits of Stage A research proposal.**"

8. Press Enter.

RESULT: The two lines at your cursor should now look like this:

B. Perils of inexperience at trade shows

C. Benefits of Stage A research proposal

Your screen should now look like Figure 7.6.

FIGURE 7.6

```
III. Description of Market
    A. Five elements of effective selling
        1. Involve sales and marketing management in setting
           specific objectives for the show
        2. Construct a sales scenario
        3. Prepare an exhibit that augments the sales plan
        4. Train staff to work in the specific medium
        5. Follow up leads obtained at the show
    B. Perils of inexperience at trade shows
    C. Benefits of Stage A research proposal
```

Add Subsections

Home, →, Tab, F4

Ken would also like to add more detail in the last section, Projected Costs as shown in Figure 7.7.

FIGURE 7.7 *Ken Tanaka would like to add more detail to the Projected Costs section.*

```
VI.  Projected Costs
     A. Stage A_____→   1. Rationale
     B. Stage B                        2. Cost
     C. Stage C
     D. Exclusivity of letter
```

1. Move the cursor *anywhere* in level A of Part VI ("Stage A").

2. Press Home-→ to move the cursor to the end of the line.

3. Press Enter.

4. Press the Tab key Tab once.

5. Press the Indent key (F4).

6. Type **Rationale** and press Enter to move to the next line.

7. Press the Indent key (F4).

8. Type **Cost.**

RESULT: Part VI should now look like Figure 7.8.

FIGURE 7.8

```
VI.  Projected Costs
     A. Stage A
        1. Rationale
        2. Cost
     B. Stage B
     C. Stage C
     D. Exclusivity of letter
```

9. Move the cursor after the "B" in "Stage B" in Part VI.

10. Repeat steps 3 through 9 to insert the same headings "1." and "2." to stage B.

11. Move the cursor after the "C" in "Stage C" in Part VI.

12. Repeat steps 3 through 9 to insert the same headings "1." and "2." to stage C.

RESULT: Your document should look like the outline at the beginning of the chapter.

Saving

Save the file again, with the Save key ([F10]).

Printing

Proofread the document for errors, and print it using the Print key ([Shift]-[F7]) and 1 for Full Document.

Exiting
[F7], **Y, Y**

Leave the document by following these steps:

1. Press the Exit key ([F7]).

2. Type **Y** to save the changes you may have made since last saving the file.

3. Press [Enter].

4. Type **Y** to replace the file.

5. Type **Y** if you want to leave WordPerfect. Type **N** if you want to continue working.

Summary

You began creating an outline by turning Outline Mode on with option 4 (Outline) of the Date/Outline key ([Shift]-[F5]) and option 1 of the outline option. When Outline mode was turned on, every time you pressed [Enter] you created a new outline section. Each time you pressed the Tab key [Tab], you went a level deeper in the outline format. To back out of an outline level, you pressed the Margin Release key ([Shift]-[Tab]).

You selected option 2 of the Date/Outline key Outline option again to turn the outline mode off.

Chapter Review

Key Terms

Date/Outline key
Margin Release key
Outline levels

Outline Mode Off
Outline Mode On
Outlines

Review Questions

1. Briefly describe two situations when you would want to create an outline to accomplish your work more effectively.
2. How many levels deep can WordPerfect outline information?
3. Discuss two reasons why it is more convenient to use the outline feature than to create an outline manually.
4. When WordPerfect is in outline mode, what does [Enter] do when you press it? What does [Tab] do?
5. If you press [Tab] too many times and get "1." instead of "A.," what key do you press to go back a level?
6. What key should you press before you type text in a section?
7. True or False: To let WordPerfect renumber an outline, you need to move the cursor through the area that you changed.

Applications

Please do the following WordPerfect exercises.

1. Create the memo shown in Figure 7.9 using the Date/Outline key and follow these instructions:

    a. Turn the outline mode on when you start the outline and off when you finish the outline.

    b. Save the file as B:DRILL7-1.

    c. Print the file.

FIGURE 7.9

November 9, 1989

TO: Middle Managers

FROM: Ken Tanaka

SUBJECT: Speech Class

I have recently returned from a class on effective speaking at the Speaking Institute of America in Minneapolis. For those interested in attending, here's an outline of the course:

SIX STAGES OF SPEAKING EXCELLENCE

I.   Develop an Idea and Test It
    A. Discuss the idea with friends
    B. Research what other people have written about the idea
      1. Local library
        a. Encyclopedias
        b. Card catalogs
      2. On-Line databases
        a. CompuServe
        b. Others
II.   Develop a Conflict
    A. Find three aspects that interest people about the idea
    B. Find three items about the idea that cause problems
    C. Rank the items in Sections IIA and B in order of importance
III. Develop a Theme
    A. What is your interpretation of the problem or idea?
    B. What is your point of view?
IV.   Write a First Draft
    A. Introduction
    B. Body
    C. Conclusion
V.   Develop Speaking Skills
    A. Provide perspectives for the listener
    B. Provide many points of view and explain why people have them
    C. Revise the draft several times over several days
    D. Practice giving the speech
      1. Alone
      2. With an audience
VI.   Body Language
    A. Make every gesture and word count
    B. Project enthusiasm!

If any of you are interested in improving your public speaking skills, I strongly recommend that you enroll in this program. It was excellent and I enjoyed it very much. See me if you have any questions.

2. Retrieve the file called EXCEL on the Student Data Disk, and make the editing changes shown in Figure 7.10. Save the file as B:DRILL7-2 and print the outline.

FIGURE 7.10

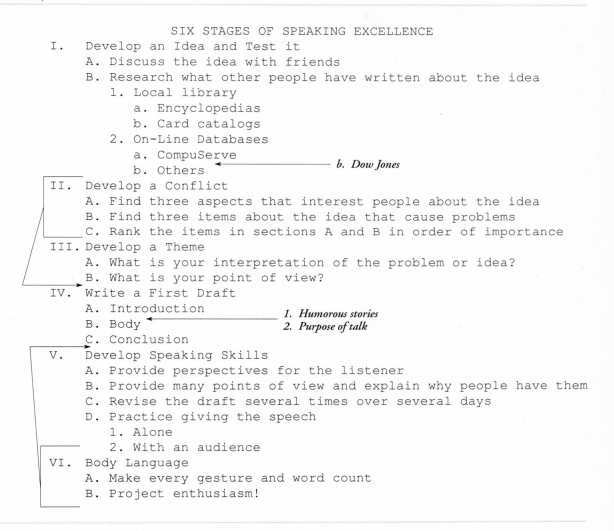

```
                     SIX STAGES OF SPEAKING EXCELLENCE
      I.   Develop an Idea and Test it
           A. Discuss the idea with friends
           B. Research what other people have written about the idea
              1. Local library
                 a. Encyclopedias
                 b. Card catalogs
              2. On-Line Databases
                 a. CompuServe
                 b. Others                     b. Dow Jones
      II.  Develop a Conflict
           A. Find three aspects that interest people about the idea
           B. Find three items about the idea that cause problems
           C. Rank the items in sections A and B in order of importance
      III. Develop a Theme
           A. What is your interpretation of the problem or idea?
           B. What is your point of view?
      IV.  Write a First Draft
           A. Introduction              1. Humorous stories
           B. Body                      2. Purpose of talk
           C. Conclusion
      V.   Develop Speaking Skills
           A. Provide perspectives for the listener
           B. Provide many points of view and explain why people have them
           C. Revise the draft several times over several days
           D. Practice giving the speech
              1. Alone
              2. With an audience
      VI.  Body Language
           A. Make every gesture and word count
           B. Project enthusiasm!
```

3. Create the outline shown in Figure 7.11 using the Date/Outline key and follow these instructions:

   a. Turn the outline mode on when you start the outline and off when you finish the outline.

   b. Save the file as DRILL7-3.

   c. Print the file.

FIGURE 7.11

```
              HOW TO WRITE THE STORY OF YOUR LIFE

    I.   Why Write Your Story?
         A. Problems and goals
            1. Courage
            2. Motives
            3. Truths and secrets
   II.   When You Were Young
         A. Experiences
         B. Education
         A. Body contact
         B. Friends
         C. Transitions
  III.   Adulthood
         A. Priorities
         B. Goals
         C. Missing parts of life
         D. Great successes
         E. Great failures
   IV.   Research
         A. Diaries
            1. Reasons for writing diaries
            2. Diaries over years
            3. Rereading old diaries
         B. Unsent letters
         C. Privacy
    V.   Writing It Down
         A. Myths about writing
         B. Audience
         C. Discipline
            1. Schedules
            2. Personal deadlines
         D. Writer's block
   VI.   Publishing
         A. Length
         B. Preparing manuscript
         C. Polishing
         D. Marketing
            1. Road trips
            2. Interviews
         E. Finding your way to the bank
```

4.   Retrieve the file called STORY on the Student Data Disk and make the editing changes shown in Figure 7.12. Save the file as DRILL7-4 and print the outline.

FIGURE 7.12

HOW TO WRITE THE STORY OF YOUR LIFE

Why Write Your Story?
    A. Problems and Goals
        1. Courage
        2. Motives
        3. Truths and secrets

II. When You Were Young
    A. Experiences
    B. Education   *1. Courage*
       Body contact   *2. Motives*
       Friends   *3. Truths and secrets*
       Transitions

III. Adulthood
    A. Priorities
    B. Goals
    C. Missing parts of life
    D. Great successes
    E. Great failures

IV. Research
    A. Diaries
        1. Reasons for writing diaries
        2. Diaries over years
        3. Rereading old diaries
    B. Unsent letters
    C. Privacy

V.   Writing it Down
    A. Myths about Writing ——————— *Switch*
    B. Audience ———————
    C. Discipline
        1. Schedules
        2. Personal Deadlines
    D. Writer's Block ——————→ *Indent one more level*

VI. Publishing
    A. Length
    B. Preparing manuscript
    C. Polishing
    D. Marketing
        1. Road trips
        2. Interviews ——————— *a. Newspapers*
    E. Finding your way to the bank   *b. TV*

5.   Create the outline shown in Figure 7.13, using the Date/Outline key, and follow these instructions:

   a.   Turn the outline mode on when you start the outline and off when you finish the outline.

   b.   Save the file as DRILL7-5.

   c.   Print the file.

FIGURE 7.13

```
            HOW TO WRITE MOVIE AND TELEVISION SCRIPTS THAT SELL

     I.   Starting Out
          A. Putting the script on paper
          B. Tell a story
          C. Rough draft

     II.  The Essentials
          A. Characterization
               1. The protagonist
               2. The antagonist as counterthrust
               3. Conflict
               4. Suspense
          B. Dialogue
               1. Not telling it all
               2. Content and emotion

     III. Writing the Script
          A. Beginning your screen play
               1. Where the problem begins
               2. Exposition
               3. The build-up
          B. Ending a dramatic story
          C. Resolution

     IV.  Writing for Television
          A. Your idea for a television series
          B. The regulars in an episodic series
          C. Situation comedy

     V.   Mastering the Business
          A. Getting an agent
          B. Sales procedures
          C. "Spec" scripts
          D. Copyrights, contracts, options
```

6. Retrieve the file called SCRIPTS on the Student Data Disk, and make the editing changes shown in Figure 7.14. Save the file as B:DRILL7-6 and print the outline.

FIGURE 7.14

HOW TO WRITE MOVIE AND TELEVISION SCRIPTS THAT SELL

```
  I.   Starting Out
       A. Putting the script on paper
       B. Tell a story
       C. Rough draft

 II.   The Essentials
       A. Characterization                    a. Insiders and outsiders
          1. The protagonist                  b. Likeable or unlikeable
          2. The antagonist as counterthrust  a. Antagonist within
          3. Conflict                         b. One or more
          4. Suspense
       B. Dialogue
          1. Not telling it all
          2. Content and emotion
       C. Plot
          1. Advance
          2. Setback

III.   Writing the Script
       A. Beginning your screen play
          1. Where the problem begins
          2. Exposition
          3. The build-up                     a. Thrust and counter
       B. Ending a dramatic story             b. The open show
       C. Resolution                          c. The closed show
       D. Analysis of screenplay

 IV.   Writing for Television
       A. Your idea for a television series
       B. The regulars in an episodic series
       C. Situation comedy

  V.   Mastering the Business
       A. Getting an agent
       B. Sales procedures
       C. "Spec" scripts
       D. Copyrights, contracts, options
```

Advanced Skills

So far in this chapter you have worked with the default numbering style, called *outline style.* The first level is marked by a Roman number *I*, second is a capital letter *A*, third is an Arabic number *1.* and so on as follows:

```
I.
II.
III.
        A.
        B.
        C.
            1.
            2.
            3.
                a.
                b.
                c.
                    (1)
                    (2)
                    (3)
                        (a)
                        (b)
                        (c)
                            i)
                            ii)
                            iii)
                                a)
                                b)
                                c)
```

If you prefer another style, you can use the *Define Outline option* on the Date/Outline key (Shift - F5) to change it. WordPerfect supplies three other styles to choose from: Paragraph, Legal, and Bullets.

Paragraph Style

Paragraph outline style is as follows:

```
1.
2.
3.
        a.
        b.
        c.
            i.
            ii.
            iii.
                (1)
                (2)
                (3)
                    (a)
                    (b)
                    (c)
                        (i)
                        (iii)
                            1)
```

```
                                    2)
                                    3)
                                        a)
                                        b)
                                        c)
```

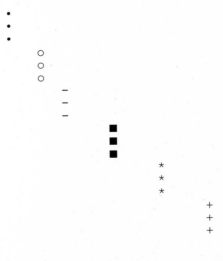

Legal Style

Legal outline style is as follows:

```
1.
2.
3.
        3.1
        3.2
        3.3
                3.3.1
                3.3.2
                3.3.3
                        3.3.3.1
                        3.3.3.2
                        3.3.3.3
                                3.3.3.3.1
                                3.3.3.3.2
                                3.3.3.3.3
                                        3.3.3.3.3.1
                                        3.3.3.3.3.3
                                                3.3.3.3.3.3.1
                                                3.3.3.3.3.3.2
                                                3.3.3.3.3.3.3
                                                        3.3.3.3.3.3.3.1
                                                        3.3.3.3.3.3.3.2
                                                        3.3.3.3.3.3.3.3
```

Bullet Style

Bullet outline style is as follows:

```
Paragraph Number Definition                                    FIGURE 7.15

   1 - Starting Paragraph Number           1
       (in legal style)
                                        Levels
                           1    2    3    4    5    6    7    8
   2 - Paragraph           1.   a.   i.  (1)  (a)  (i)  1)   a)
   3 - Outline             I.   A.   1.   a.  (1)  (a)  i)   a)
   4 - Legal (1.1.1)       1    .1   .1   .1   .1   .1   .1   .1
   5 - Bullets             •    o    -    ■    *    +    ·    x
   6 - User-defined

   Current Definition      I.   A.   1.   a.  (1)  (a)  i)   a)
   Attach Previous Level        No   No   No   No   No   No   No

   7 - Enter Inserts Paragraph Number      Yes

   8 - Automatically Adjust to Current Level  Yes

   9 - Outline Style Name


Selection: 0
```

Selecting Outline Styles

If you want to change the outline style, use the Define option on the Date/Outline key ([Shift]-[F5]). When you select this option, you'll see the *Paragraph Number Definition menu* shown in Figure 7.15.

To choose another style, follow these steps:

1. Press the Date/Outline key ([Shift]-[F5]).

2. Type **6** to select Define.

3. Type **2** to select the Paragraph option (or 4 to select Legal style, or 5 to select Bullets style).

4. Press [Enter] twice to return to the Edit menu.

5. Scroll to the end of the outline to reformat the outline levels.

You can quickly test various outline styles in your document by moving the cursor to the top of the outline and performing the previous five steps. Each time you select a style and scroll through the outline, the format will change. When you change a style, WordPerfect inserts the following code into your document:

[Par Num:Def]

Like all WordPerfect codes, it takes effect from that point in the document forward.

If you change a style, scroll through the outline, and the style does not change, chances are another Par Num:Def code follows the code you entered. You must then delete the code that follows your new one. The outline will then format correctly.

Figure 7.16 shows the outline you created in this chapter as it would look if you used the bullet style.

FIGURE 7.16

Speech Outline

- Introduction
  - o Story of the farmer
  - o Why we are here
- Description of Market
  - o Five elements of effective selling
    - Involve sales and marketing management in setting specific objectives for the show
    - Construct a sales scenario
    - Prepare an exhibit that augments the sales plan
    - Train staff to work in the specific medium
    - Follow up leads obtained at the show.
  - o Dangers of inexperience at trade shows
  - o Benefits of Stage A research proposal
- Description of Product
  - o Education of your staff
  - o What we create for you
  - o Economical choices
  - o Possible formats
    - Panel wall with cases brought in from behind.
    - Built-in case with curving panel wall
    - Display stages
    - Glass-top shallow case supported on a sloping top floor base.
    - Small cases supported on shelves
- Design Development
  - o Role of flagship designer
  - o Role of writers
  - o Role of technicians
  - o Economy of good design
  - o Necessity of timeliness
- Stages of Development
  - A. Market research and company report
  - B. Design development and production
  - C. Trade show consulting and follow-up services
- Projected Costs
  - o Stage A
    - Rationale
    - Scope
  - o Stage B
    - Rationale
    - Scope
  - o Stage C
    - Rationale
    - Scope
  - o Exclusivity of letter

Advanced Key Terms	Define Outline option Paragraph outline style	Legal outline style Paragraph Number Definition menu

Advanced Review Questions

1. Identify the four possible outline styles WordPerfect can use. Briefly list how each level appears in each style.

2. List the keystrokes required to define a paragraph outline style.

3. If you define a new outline style and nothing changes when you scroll through the document, what is probably happening?

Advanced Applications

1. Retrieve the file EXCEL from the Student Data Disk and follow these instructions:
   a. Define the outline style as legal.
   b. Define only Parts III and IV as bullet style.
   c. Save the outline as B:DRILL7-7.
   d. Print the outline.

2. Retrieve the file SCRIPTS from the Student Data Disk and follow these instructions:
   a. Define the outline style as paragraph style.
   b. Define all third-level sections as bullet style.
   c. Save the outline as B:DRILL7-8.
   d. Print the outline.

On Your Own

Michelle Strongman, the administrative manager at Exhibit Place, has asked you to develop a class to teach new employees how to use Word-Perfect to outline and plan major projects.

Use your imagination and develop an outline of the class. Possible class topics include the benefits of using WordPerfect to plan projects, how to use the outline feature, project planning, how to get help, examples of projects and documents outlined with WordPerfect, and so on.

November 10, 19--

TO: Ken Tanaka

FROM: Michelle Strongman

SUBJECT: OVERDUE ACCOUNTS

Here is the data you requested. Table 1 lists delinquent
accounts by client name. Table 2 lists clients by the amount
that they still owe.

TABLE 1
DELINQUENT CLIENTS

Name	SSN	Invoice	Amount Due
Bill Doolay	867-48-6982	34598	942
Red Hebbard	394-69-9384	44384	15,763
Bill Howard	567-58-9685	43875	150
Nancy Howard	495-93-4854	45976	6,892
Noel Larson	349-95-4837	44120	2,983
Todd Lincoln	352-48-4859	44099	12,940
Alfred Mann	345-39-2809	45870	65
Mary Oshiro	345-67-3994	42060	2,300
Lisa Rayes	885-48-9584	44129	143,452
Mandy Reynault	568-35-8743	43098	32,933
Brian Stark	139-59-2107	46001	4,763
Fred Stone	283-93-4822	45097	12,994
Karl Torey	385-86-0932	45921	9,938

TABLE 2
DELINQUENT CLIENTS BY AMOUNT THEY OWE

Name	SSN	Invoice	Amount Due
Lisa Rayes	885-48-9584	44129	143,452
Mandy Reynault	568-35-8743	43098	32,933
Red Hebbard	394-69-9384	44384	15,763
Fred Stone	283-93-4822	45097	12,994
Todd Lincoln	352-48-4859	44099	12,940
Karl Torey	385-86-0932	45921	9,938
Nancy Howard	495-93-4854	45976	6,892
Brian Stark	139-59-2107	46001	4,763
Noel Larson	349-95-4837	44120	2,983
Mary Oshiro	345-67-3994	42060	2,300
Bill Doolay	867-48-6982	34598	942
Bill Howard	567-58-9685	43875	150
Alfred Mann	345-39-2809	45870	65

In this chapter, you will sort information in alphabetic and numeric order.

8

Sorting

WordPerfect Commands

Ctrl - F9 , 3, a Enter Enter - F7 , 1	Sort alphanumerics
Ctrl - F9 , 3, n Enter Enter - F7 , 1	Sort numbers
Ctrl - F9 , 6, 1, 1	Sort in ascending order
Ctrl - F9 , 6, 2, 1	Sort in descending order

Overview

The mark of the professional is a passion for order. The more organized you are, the faster and easier you can generally get a job done. You can often tell exceptional office workers from average workers by how well they organize the material with which they work. Exceptional workers often sort a stack of invoices alphabetically or numerically as soon as they get the stack, even if they are not told to. Such people understand that all information in offices will eventually need to be quickly found later and should be properly sorted.

WordPerfect's powerful sorting capability can help you manage your work and stay organized. Many people do not realize that WordPerfect not only helps you create documents, but also helps you organize and manage business information.

What WordPerfect Can Sort

WordPerfect can sort either alphabetically or numerically any list of items, such as names, addresses, telephone numbers, classes, products, or anything you need to keep track of for later use.

You can sort items by a series of criteria, called *Keys*. Keys allow you to control the result of your sort. For example, say that you want to sort all your company's customers by their names. In this case, the last name is the Key by which you sort the list. But what do you do if two people have the same last name, such as

Silver, Blake
Silver, Nancy

Clearly, you need to sort them by first name as well. Using WordPerfect, you would tell the program to sort the list by two Keys: (1) last name, and (2) first name. To arrange this list:

Smith, Bob R.
Smith, Bob B.
Smith, Bob W.

you need to sort by three Keys: (1) last name, (2) first name, and (3) middle initial. WordPerfect can sort up to nine Keys—more than you probably will ever need.

What makes sorting with WordPerfect exciting is that it is flexible enough to sort both *lines* or *paragraphs* of text. If data is arranged in rows and columns, such as in Figure 8.1, you use line sort. If your data is longer than a line, you use paragraph sort. Let's begin by looking at line sorting in more detail.

FIGURE 8.1

Name	Status	Social Security No.
Mary Basel	Full	372-39-4875
Paul Dow	Consult	674-34-8567
Richard Ardrey	Full	346-09-5843
Jerry Baldwin	Temp	234-34-4856
Andy Basel	Part	475-34-3485
Jay Birchman	Full	382-22-1903
Lynn Goldberg	Part	568-35-5208

Sorting Lines of Data

To sort lines, text must be arranged in rows and columns such as the list of names in Figure 8.1. In the list, each column contains either a name, status code, or social security number. Each row contains data for only one person and is called a *record*. In Figure 8.1, there are seven records, one for each person.

WordPerfect calls every entry in each column of a record a *field*. There are three fields in the record for Mary Basel:

1. Mary Basel
2. Full
3. 372-39-4875

As you can see, each field contains the same kind of data for each record—Names contains names, Status contains status codes, and Social Security Number contains people's social security numbers. Each field is separated by a Tab or Indent code. Each line ends with a Hard Return ([HRt]). The Tab and Hard Return [HRt] codes are what WordPerfect uses to identify keys and sort lines of records.

To sort these records by last name, you use the Sort screen shown in Figure 8.2 to tell WordPerfect what Key you want to use for sorting and where the Key is located. This procedure is called *defining the sort criteria*. To define a sort, you press the Sort key (Ctrl-F9) and select 2 (Sort). Let's look at the sort screen more closely. The more familiar you are with it, the easier sorting becomes.

Using the Sort Screen to Define Your Sort

Like Reveal Codes, the sort screen divides the screen into two parts: in the top half are the lines that you will sort, and in the bottom half is the Sort menu, as shown in Figure 8.2. Note the numbered items 1 through 9. These are the nine Keys that you can use to sort your list. (Rarely, though, will you need to use all nine!)

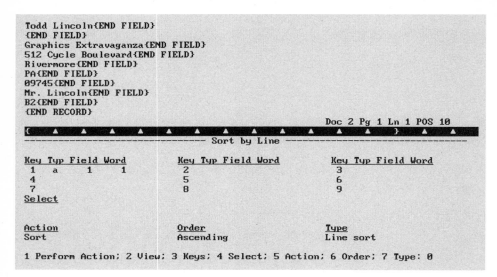

FIGURE 8.2

The sort screen enables you to sort records with up to nine keys. You define the type, field, and word for each key.

WordPerfect needs to know three things about each Key: (1) what kind of data the Key is, (2) where in the record it can find the Key (the field), and (3) if there is more than one word in a field, which word is the Key.

1. *Sort Type.* WordPerfect can sort two kinds of information: alphanumeric or numeric. *Alphanumeric* are alphabet letters, or numbers that you are not going to calculate. For example, social security numbers are alphanumeric because you are not going to add them. *Numerics* are numbers that you are going to perform calculations on, such as prices, wages, or the number of items.

    To sort the records in Figure 8.1 by name, you would make the last name your first Key. Key 1 would be "a" for alphanumeric.

2. *Sort Field.* WordPerfect now needs to know where it can find Key 1 in the record. Figure 8.1 contains three fields: name, status, and social security number. Name is field 1, status is field 2, and social security number is field 3. You need to tell WordPerfect that Key 1 is in field 1.

3. *Sort Word.* As you can see, Field 1 contains two *words:* the first name and last name. You need to tell WordPerfect which word is Key 1. WordPerfect can sort by either name. If you want to sort by first name, you specify word 1. If you want to sort by last name, you choose word 2.

    To sort Figure 8.1 by last name, you would fill out the Sort options like this:

Key	Type	Field	Word
1	a	1	2

    Key 1 (last name) is the second word of field 1 and is alphanumeric.

Because there are two people with the same last name in Figure 8.1 (Basel), you need to tell WordPerfect to sort the list by two Keys: (1) last name, and (2) first name. Key 2 (first name) is the first word of field 1 and is alphanumeric.

```
Key     Type    Field   Word
1       a       1       2       <==== last name
2       a       1       1       <==== first name
```

You are now ready to sort the list.

How to Sort Lines of Records

There are three steps required for sorting any list of lines:

1. Select your input and output options.

2. Define the sort criteria.

3. Perform the sort.

1. *Select Input and Output Options.* When you first press the Merge/Sort key ([Ctrl]-[F9]) and select Sort, the following prompt appears on the screen:

    Input file to sort: (Screen)

    WordPerfect is asking you what file contains the lines that you want to sort. Usually, you will want to sort the lines that are on the screen and you will press ([Enter]), but you can, if you like, also enter a filename and WordPerfect will sort a file on your disk. WordPerfect assumes that you want to sort the document on the screen.

    After telling WordPerfect what Input file you want to sort, you will then see this prompt:

    Output file for sort: (Screen)

    WordPerfect wants to know if you want to see the results of the sort on the screen, or if it should put the sort in a file on disk. If you wanted to send the results of a sort to a file, you could type a filename at this point. As you can see, WordPerfect assumes that you want to see the output file on the screen.

2. *Define the Sort Criteria.* At this stage, you tell WordPerfect what Keys it should sort and where they are located.

3. *Perform the Sort.* Performing the sort is a lot of fun because you can watch WordPerfect do all the work for you. After you select the Perform Action option in the sort screen, WordPerfect pauses and the screen disappears for a moment. When it reappears, your lines are all sorted!

FIGURE 8.3

Star Wars. **** A dazzling science fiction film for all ages. Cheer the good guys (rebels) as they fight the wicked empire.

War Games. *** Matthew Broderick saves the world from global holocaust, after nearly setting it off!

It's a Wonderful Life. **** A man (James Stewart) facing ruin is sent help from a guardian angel. Has great warmth and humor. Get your Kleenexes.

Halloween XVIII. * Watch fifteen teenagers discover the meaning of boredom as Michael, now aged 82, chases them from a wheelchair.

Somewhere in Time. ** Is there a love so strong that you can travel back in time to discover it? With enough emotion, it seems, anything is possible. Charming.

Jules and Jim. **** A tantalizing woman challenges the art and friendship of two men. Lovely and lyrical.

Sorting a Block

Often you will not want to sort an entire file. If you are typing a memo that contains a list of names, you can sort the names without affecting the rest of the memo. *Sorting a block* of lines is faster to do because you do not have to tell WordPerfect what the input and output files are.

To quickly sort a list of items, highlight the items with the Block key ([Alt]-[F4]). When you press the Merge/Sort key ([Ctrl]-[F9]), the sort screen appears.

Sorting Paragraphs

So far we have been talking about sorting lines of text. You can also sort paragraphs either alphabetically or numerically by the first word in each paragraph by choosing the Type option of the sort screen (see Figure 8.2). For example, you can sort the paragraphs in Figure 8.3 so that the movie titles are in alphabetical order. Sorting paragraphs can be useful for creating catalogs, glossaries, or lists of citations.

Because WordPerfect defines as a paragraph any text that ends with two [HRt] commands, the paragraph can be as brief as one line or as long as a page.

Paragraph sort works the same way as Line sort, except that because paragraphs can have multiple lines (text separated by one Hard Return

[HRt]), you can specify a line number when defining your keys. For example, the movie titles in Figure 8.3 are in the first line of each paragraph.

Tutorial

By four o'clock this afternoon, Ken Tanaka needs to know which Exhibit Place clients are delinquent on their accounts. He wants a list that he can glance at to find a client's name and also find out immediately who owes the company the most money. Michelle Strongman has asked you to create a memo to Tanaka with two tables. Table 1 should list clients by their names in alphabetical order. Table 2 should list clients by how much they owe the company. Strongman has told you that she wants the people who owe Exhibit Place the most money at the top of the list.

You call the Exhibit Place computer room and ask them to generate two reports listing delinquent clients by name and listing them in order of what they owe. The technicians in the computer room tell you that it will take five days to get the report—clients are organized in the computer by their social security number and a special program has to be written to get the information in the order that you need. But they can get you a list of delinquent clients sorted by social security number in an hour.

You ask them to get the list to you right away. An hour later a technician hands you the list in Figure 8.4.

You are now ready to create the memo shown in Figure 8.5. You will call it B:8LIST.

Setting Up

To begin, place the Student Data Disk in drive B and start WordPerfect. You will start by creating the memo to Ken Tanaka.

Formatting

To create the columns for the tables, you need to set left tabs at 20 (2"), 30 (3"), and 50 (5"). You also need a right tab at 70 (7").

Set Tabs
[Shift]-[F8], *1, 8, T, 1*

1. Press the Format key ([Shift]-[F8]).
2. Type **1** to select Line.
3. Type **8** to select Tabs.
4. Type **T** to select type.
5. Type **1** to select absolute
6. Press [Ctrl]-End to delete all tab settings.
7. Type **20** and press [Enter].
8. Type **30** and press [Enter].

FIGURE 8.4

Name	Social Security No.	Account No.	Amount Due
Brian Stark	139-59-2107	46001	4,763
Fred Stone	283-93-4822	45097	12,994
Alfred Mann	345-39-2809	45870	65
Mary Oshiro	345-67-3994	42060	2,300
Noel Larson	349-95-4837	44120	2,983
Todd Lincoln	352-48-4859	44099	12,940
Karl Torey	385-86-0932	45921	9,938
Red Hebbard	394-69-9384	44384	15,763
Nancy Howard	495-93-4854	45976	6,892
Bill Howard	567-58-9685	43875	150
Mandy Reynault	568-35-8743	43098	32,933
Bill Doolay	867-48-6982	34598	942
Lisa Rayes	885-48-9584	44129	143,452

9. Type **50** and press [Enter].

10. Move the cursor to position 70 (7") on the tab ruler, using the right arrow key ([→]).

11. Type **R**.

12. Press the Exit key ([F7]) twice to return to the edit screen.

Keyboarding

You are now ready to begin entering the text of the memo.

Center the Date
[Shift]-[F6], [Shift]-[F5], *1*

To center the date, follow these steps:

1. Press the Center key ([Shift]-[F6]).

2. Press the Date key ([Shift]-[F5]).

3. Type **1** to select Date text and press [Enter] twice to move the cursor to line 3 (1.33").

Enter Text

To enter the memo heading, follow these steps:

1. Type the following:

   TO: Ken Tanaka

   FROM: Michelle Strongman

   SUBJECT: OVERDUE ACCOUNTS

   Here is the data you requested. Table 1 lists
   delinquent accounts by client name. Table 2 lists
   clients by the amount that they still owe.

   NOTE: Use the space bar to align the heading information.

FIGURE 8.5 *You are going to create this memo.*

November 10, 19--

TO: Ken Tanaka

FROM: Michelle Strongman

SUBJECT: OVERDUE ACCOUNTS

Here is the data you requested. Table 1 lists delinquent
accounts by client name. Table 2 lists clients by the amount
that they still owe.

TABLE 1
DELINQUENT CLIENTS

Name	SSN	Invoice	Amount Due
Bill Doolay	867-48-6982	34598	942
Red Hebbard	394-69-9384	44384	15,763
Bill Howard	567-58-9685	43875	150
Nancy Howard	495-93-4854	45976	6,892
Noel Larson	349-95-4837	44120	2,983
Todd Lincoln	352-48-4859	44099	12,940
Alfred Mann	345-39-2809	45870	65
Mary Oshiro	345-67-3994	42060	2,300
Lisa Rayes	885-48-9584	44129	143,452
Mandy Reynault	568-35-8743	43098	32,933
Brian Stark	139-59-2107	46001	4,763
Fred Stone	283-93-4822	45097	12,994
Karl Torey	385-86-0932	45921	9,938

TABLE 2
DELINQUENT CLIENTS BY AMOUNT THEY OWE

Name	SSN	Invoice	Amount Due
Lisa Rayes	885-48-9584	44129	143,452
Mandy Reynault	568-35-8743	43098	32,933
Red Hebbard	394-69-9384	44384	15,763
Fred Stone	283-93-4822	45097	12,994
Todd Lincoln	352-48-4859	44099	12,940
Karl Torey	385-86-0932	45921	9,938
Nancy Howard	495-93-4854	45976	6,892
Brian Stark	139-59-2107	46001	4,763
Noel Larson	349-95-4837	44120	2,983
Mary Oshiro	345-67-3994	42060	2,300
Bill Doolay	867-48-6982	34598	942
Bill Howard	567-58-9685	43875	150
Alfred Mann	345-39-2809	45870	65

FIGURE 8.6

Name	SSN	Invoice	Amount Due
Brian Stark	139-59-2107	46001	4,763
Fred Stone	283-93-4822	45097	12,994
Alfred Mann	345-39-2809	45870	65
Mary Oshiro	345-67-3994	42060	2,300
Noel Larson	349-95-4837	44120	2,983
Todd Lincoln	352-48-4859	44099	12,940
Karl Torey	385-86-0932	45921	9,938
Red Hebbard	394-69-9384	44384	15,763
Nancy Howard	495-93-4854	45976	6,892
Bill Howard	567-58-9685	43875	150
Mandy Reynault	568-35-8743	43098	32,933
Bill Doolay	867-48-6982	34598	942
Lisa Rayes	885-48-9584	44129	143,452

2. Press [Enter] twice to move the cursor to line 14 (3.17") and turn on the Bold key ([F6]), the CAPS LOCK key ([CapsLock]), and the Center key ([Shift]-[F6]).

3. Type the following:

   TABLE 1
   DELINQUENT CLIENTS

   NOTE: Make sure that "DELINQUENT CLIENTS" is also centered. Turn off the CAPS LOCK key ([CapsLock]).

4. Press [Enter] twice to move the cursor to line 17 (3.67").

5. Type **Name** and press [Tab] twice to move the cursor to position 20 (2").

6. Type **SSN** and press [Tab].

7. Type **Invoice** and press [Tab].

8. Type **Amount Due** and press [Enter].

9. Press the Bold key ([F6]) to turn it off.

   Next is the table information. Do not worry that it is not in the order that you need.

Enter Table

To create the table, type the records shown in Figure 8.6. Be sure to press [Tab] between each entry in a column. When you have finished, you are ready to sort the table alphabetically by last name.

STOP! HAVE YOU SAVED YOUR FILE USING THE SAVE KEY ([F10])? IF NOT, SAVE IT NOW AS B:8LIST. WE STRONGLY RECOMMEND THAT YOU SAVE YOUR DOCUMENT *BEFORE* YOU BEGIN A SORT OPERATION!

```
Brian Stark        139-59-2107        46001      4,763
Fred Stone         283-93-4822        45097      12,994
Alfred Mann        345-39-2809        45870      65
Mary Oshiro        345-67-3994        42060      2,300
Noel Larson        349-95-4837        44120      2,983
Todd Lincoln       352-48-4859        44099      12,940
Karl Torey         385-86-0932        45921      9,938
Red Hebbard        394-69-9384        44384      15,763
Nancy Howard       495-93-4854        45976      6,892
Bill Howard        567-58-9685        43875      150
                                            Doc 2 Pg 1 Ln 1 Pos 10
[                       ▲                  ▲          ▲            ]
--------------------------------- Sort by Line ---------------------------------

Key Typ Field Word        Key Typ Field Word        Key Typ Field Word
 1   a     1     1          2                         3
 4                          5                         6
 7                          8                         9
Select


Action                    Order                     Type
Sort                      Ascending                 Line sort

1 Perform Action; 2 View; 3 Keys; 4 Select; 5 Action; 6 Order; 7 Type: 0
```

FIGURE 8.7

The sort screen allows you to define the keys with which you will sort the records.

*Sorting Names
Alphabetically*

Ctrl - F9 , *3, a,*
Enter , Enter , F7 , *1*

To sort the records so that the names are in alphabetical order, follow these steps:

1. Move the cursor to the "B" in the name "Brian Stark" at the beginning of the list.

2. Highlight the list by turning on the Block key (Alt - F4) and pressing Home Home - ↓ to move the cursor to the bottom of the list.

3. Press the Merge/Sort key (Ctrl - F9).
   RESULT: The Sort screen appears, as shown in Figure 8.7.
   NOTE: Because there are two people with the same last name, you need to sort the list using two keys: one for the last name and the second for the first name.

4. Type **3** to select the Keys option.
   RESULT: The cursor jumps to the Type column of Key 1.

5. Type **a** for alphanumeric. If an "a" is already in the field, simply press Enter .
   RESULT: The cursor jumps to the Field column.

6. Type **1** and press Enter .
   RESULT: The cursor jumps to the Word column.

7. Type **2** and press Enter .
   RESULT: The cursor jumps to the Type column of Key 2.

8. Press Enter .
   RESULT: WordPerfect fills in the default values for field and word: 1 and 1.

9. Press the Exit key (F7) to accept the default values.

10. Type **1** to select the Perform Action option.

RESULT: WordPerfect pauses for a moment, the screen flickers, and the list appears with each record sorted in alphabetical order by last name, as shown in Figure 8.5.

NOTE: If you did something wrong and the list does not appear as it should, clear the screen using the Exit key and start the sort process again on B:8LIST.

Let's now move to begin entering Table 2.

Enter Heading

To create Table 2, follow these steps:

1. Move the cursor to line 33 and turn on the Bold key (F6), the CAPS LOCK key (CapsLock), and the Center key (Shift-F6).

2. Type the following:

```
TABLE 2
DELINQUENT CLIENTS BY AMOUNT THEY OWE
```

NOTE: Make sure that "DELINQUENT CLIENTS BY AMOUNT THEY OWE" is also centered. Then turn off Bold and CapsLock.

3. Press Enter twice to move the cursor to line 36.

Rather than retype the table in Figure 8.6, you will make a copy of Table 1 with the Move key (Ctrl-F4).

Copy Table 1
Ctrl-F4, *1, 2*

1. Move the cursor to the "N" in "NAME" in the heading of Table 1.

2. Highlight the entire table by turning on the Block key (Alt-F4) and pressing the down arrow (↓) fourteen times.

3. Press the Move key (Ctrl-F4).

4. Type **1** to select the Block option.

5. Type **2** to select the Copy option.

6. Move the cursor to line 36, position 10 and press Enter.

You are now ready to sort this list in order of who owes the company the most money.

STOP! HAVE YOU SAVED YOUR FILE USING THE SAVE KEY (F10)? IF NOT, SAVE IT NOW AS B:LIST8.

Sort Numerics
Ctrl-F9, *3, n,*
Enter, Enter, F7, *1*

1. Move the cursor to the "B" in the name "Bill Dooley" at the beginning of the list in Table 2.

2. Highlight the entire list using Block On (Alt-F4).

3. Press the Merge/Sort key (Ctrl-F9).

4. Type **3** to select the Keys option.

5. Type **n** for numeric in the Type column.
    RESULT: The cursor jumps to the Field column.
6. Type **4** and press [Enter].
    RESULT: The cursor jumps to the Word column.
7. Type **1** and press [Enter].
8. Press the Exit key ([F7]).

Sort Numbers in
Descending Order
[Ctrl]-[F9], *8, 6, 2, 1*

You now need to tell WordPerfect to sort the Amount Due column in descending order.

9. Type **6** to select the Order option.
    RESULT: The following message appears on the status line:

    Order: 1 Ascending; 2 Descending: 0

10. Type **2** to select the Descending option.
11. Type **1** to select Perform Action. The memo is now complete, with the two tables correctly sorted.

Saving

Save the file as B:LIST8.

Printing

Print the file using the Print key ([Shift]-[F7]) and selecting the Page option.

Exiting

If you would like to continue working, clear the screen using the Exit key ([F7]). Otherwise, exit WordPerfect.

Summary

To put the names in Table 1 in alphabetical order, you first highlighted the records you wanted to alphabetize and selected Sort under the Merge/Sort key ([Ctrl]-[F9]). You sorted the names after defining two keys under the Keys option of the sort screen. Key 1 (last name) was the second word of Field 1 and was alphanumeric. Key 2 (first name) was the first word of Field 1 and was alphanumeric.

To sort the list, you selected the Perform Action option in the sort screen.

You then created a second table by making a copy of the first and then sorting the records by the amount of money delinquent clients owed the company. To sort the records, you repeated the same steps as in Table 1, except that you only defined one Key (AMOUNT DUE). Key 1 was the first word of Field 4 and was numeric. You then chose the Order option in the sort screen to select "Descending" so WordPerfect would put the people who owed the company the most money at the top of the list.

Chapter Review

Key Terms

Alphanumerics
Block sort
Defining sort criteria
Keys
Line sort
Numerics

Paragraph sort
Record
Sort screen
Sort word
Sort field
Sort type

Review Questions

1. Briefly discuss the difference between alphanumeric and numeric data.

2. WordPerfect can sort two kinds of information: _____ and _____.

3. How many Keys would you need to sort the following:
   Williams, Robert B.
   Williams, Richard C.
   Williams, Bob, B.
   Williams, Bob R.
   Explain your answer.

4. How does WordPerfect identify a record during a sort? A paragraph?

5. Can a field have more than one word in it? How does WordPerfect define a field?

6. List and briefly discuss two advantages of highlighting your records before you sort them. Discuss one possible disadvantage.

7. How does WordPerfect identify a line during a paragraph sort?

Applications

Please do the following WordPerfect exercises:

1. Retrieve the file on the Student Data Disk called STATES, and follow these instructions:

   a. Sort the file (by line) in ascending order of abbreviations.

   b. Save the file as B:DRILL81A.

   c. Sort the file again in descending order of state names.

   d. Save the file as B:DRILL81B.

   e. Print both files.

2. To sort a paragraph, you must select the Type option in the Sort screen and choose paragraph. Retrieve the file called MOVIES off the Student Data Disk, and follow these instructions:

   a. Select the paragraph option at the sort screen by selecting the Type option (7).

   b. Alphabetize the movie listing by Keying off the title.

   c. Save the file as B:DRILL82.

   d. Print the file.

3. Retrieve the file on the Student Data Disk called DONATE, and follow these instructions:

   a. Sort the list in ascending order of donations from the previous year. Save the file as B:DRILL83A.

   b. Sort the list in descending order of donations from the previous year. Save the file as B:DRILL83B.

   c. Sort the list in ascending order of donations from the current year. Save the file as B:DRILL83C.

   d. Sort the list in descending order of donations from the current year. Save the file as B:DRILL83D.

4. Retrieve the file on the Student Data Disk called INVENTRY, and follow these instructions:

   a. Sort the list in ascending numerical order of price for an item. Save the file as B:DRILL84A.

   b. Sort the list in alphabetic order of the description of an item. Save the file as B:DRILL84B.

   c. Sort the list in numeric order of part number of an item. Save the file as B:DRILL84C.

5. Retrieve the file on the Student Data Disk called AISLE, and follow these instructions:

   a. Sort the list in ascending alphabetic order by aisle name. Save the file as B:DRILL85A.

   b. Sort the list in numeric order of the number of bookings. Save the file as B:DRILL85B.

   c. Sort the list in numeric order of the rate. Save the file as B:DRILL85C.

6. Retrieve the file on the Student Data Disk called UNTWAY, and follow these instructions:

   a. Sort the list in ascending alphabetic order by name. Save the file as B:DRILL86A.

   b. Sort the list in descending numeric order of the winter donations. Save the file as B:DRILL86B.

   c. Sort the list in ascending numeric order of summer donations. Save the file as B:DRILL86C.

Advanced Skills

You can use the sort feature to reorganize your merge files, if you need to. Say, for instance, that you plan to use the REGIS.SF file you created in Chapter 4 to do a bulk mailing (see Figure 8.8). Because the U.S. Post Office prefers that you sort your letters by zip code before you mail them, you decide to sort the records in REGIS.SF by zip code.

Let's look at how this is done in more detail.

FIGURE 8.8 *You created this secondary merge file (REGIS.SF) in Chapter 4.*

```
Todd Lincoln{END FIELD}
{END FIELD}
Graphics Extravaganza{END FIELD}
512 Cycle Boulevard{END FIELD}
Rivermore{END FIELD}
PA{END FIELD}
09745{END FIELD}
Mr. Lincoln{END FIELD}
B2{END FIELD}
{END RECORD}
================================================================
Noel Larson{END FIELD}
President{END FIELD}
Advanced Publishing Company{END FIELD}
1412 Fredricks Street{END FIELD}
Columbus{END FIELD}
Ohio{END FIELD}
44367{END FIELD}
Mr. Larson{END FIELD}
B2{END FIELD}
{END RECORD}
================================================================
```

MORE ▼

```
Lisa Rayes{END FIELD}
Marketing Director{END FIELD}
Northwest Mail Order{END FIELD}
120 Seymour Street, Suite 512{END FIELD}
Seattle{END FIELD}
Washington{END FIELD}
99745{END FIELD}
Ms. Rayes{END FIELD}
B2{END FIELD}
{END RECORD}
==================================================================
Mary Oshiro{END FIELD}
{END FIELD}
Computer Interface Specialists{END FIELD}
349 Figueroa Street, Suite 1204{END FIELD}
Los Angeles{END FIELD}
CA{END FIELD}
90521{END FIELD}
Ms. Oshiro{END FIELD}
B2{END FIELD}
{END RECORD}
==================================================================
Bill Hughes{END FIELD}
{END FIELD}
Hughes Software Games and Innovations{END FIELD}
Route 1A{END FIELD}
Porterville{END FIELD}
Indiana{END FIELD}
43256{END FIELD}
Mr. Hughes{END FIELD}
B2{END FIELD}
{END RECORD}
==================================================================
```

Sorting Secondary Merge Files

The first step in *sorting secondary merge files* is to define the Key that WordPerfect will use to perform the sort. Since the records will be sorted by zip code, your Key will be the zip code. To define it, you must identify the zip code Key type, field, line, and word.

Zip Code Key Type. Because you will not be performing any mathematical operations on the zip code, the Key type is alphanumeric.

Zip Code Key Field. Each record in Figure 8.8 has nine fields. The zip code Key is field 7.

Zip Code Key Line. Since there is only one line in this field, the Key line will be 1.

Zip Code Key Word. Since there is only one word in this field, the Key word will be 1.

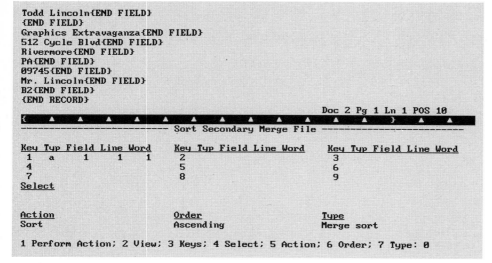

FIGURE 8.9

The sort secondary merge file screen lets you sort a secondary file by any field you choose.

You are now ready to perform the merge sort by following these steps:

1. Press the Sort key ([Ctrl]-[F9]).

2. Type **2** to select Sort.

3. Type B:REGIS.SF to tell WordPerfect what the input file will be.

4. Press [Enter] to accept the screen as the output file.
   RESULT: A sort screen will appear with some of the records from REGIS.SF above it.

5. Type **7** to select the Type option.

6. Type **1** to select the Merge option.
   RESULT: The *Sort Secondary Merge File screen* shown in Figure 8.9 will appear.

7. Enter the Key field options as follows:

   ```
   Key  Type Field  Line Word
   1    a    7      1    1
   ```

8. Type **1** to perform the sort.
   The records in REGIS.SF will then be sorted in zip code order on the screen.

Advanced Key Terms   Sort Secondary Merge File screen   Sorting secondary merge files

Advanced Review Questions

1. True or False: The first step in sorting secondary merge files is to define the Key that WordPerfect will use to perform the sort.

2. List the four items you must identify in order to identify a Key for a secondary merge file. Briefly describe each type in two or three sentences.

Advanced Applications

1. Retrieve the file on the Student Data Disk called NAMES, and follow these instructions:
   a. Sort the list in ascending alphabetic order by last name. Save the file as B:DRILL87A.
   b. Sort the list in descending alphabetic order by company name. Save the file as B:DRILL87B.
   c. Sort the list in ascending numeric order by zip code. Save the file as B:DRILL87C.

2. Retrieve the file on the Student Data Disk called COMPANYS, and follow these instructions:
   a. Sort the list in ascending alphabetic order by last name. Save the file as B:DRILL88A.
   b. Sort the list in descending alphabetic order by company name. Save the file as B:DRILL88B.
   c. Sort the list in ascending alphabetic order by the person's title. Save the file as B:DRILL88C.
   d. Sort the list in descending numeric order by zip code. Save the file as B:DRILL88D.

On Your Own

Make a mailing list using the addresses and phone numbers of all members of your class—if they allow it. Alphabetize the list by last and first name, and print it. Save it as 3APP8.

Sort the list again by zip code in ascending order as though you were to do a bulk mailing and needed all your letters organized by zip code. Save the file as 3ZIP8 and print it.

In this chapter, you will quickly create a table of contents and index for a document.

9

Table of Contents and Index

Chapter Objectives   After completing this chapter, you will be able to

1. Create a table of contents.

2. Create an index.

WordPerfect Commands   [Alt]-[F4] [Alt]-[F5], 1, 1   Mark first-level heading in table of contents
[Alt]-[F4] [Alt]-[F5], 1, 2   Mark second-level heading in table of contents
[Alt]-[F5] 5, 1   Define a table of contents
[Alt]-[F5], 6, 5, Y   Generate a table of contents
[Alt]-[F5], 5, 3   Define an index
[Alt]-[F5], 6, 5, Y   Generate an index

Overview

To help provide the professional touch to your documents, you can tell WordPerfect to generate a *table of contents* and *index* for you automatically. Let's look in more detail how WordPerfect does this.

Creating a Table of Contents

After you complete your document, WordPerfect can make a table of contents with up to five levels of entries:

```
                          CONTENTS
                                                      Page
        Level 1    .  .  .  .  .  .  .  .  .  .  .  .  .  .  .  .  .  .   1
          Level 2 .  .  .  .  .  .  .  .  .  .  .  .  .  .  .  .  .  .   1
            Level 3  .  .  .  .  .  .  .  .  .  .  .  .  .  .  .  .  .   3
              Level 4  .  .  .  .  .  .  .  .  .  .  .  .  .  .  .  .   4
                Level 5  .  .  .  .  .  .  .  .  .  .  .  .  .  .  .   4
```

Each *table of contents level* represents a heading in your document and is indented five spaces to the right of the one above it. WordPerfect attaches a *dot leader* (. . ., etc.) to each level and a page number where the heading can be found. Although WordPerfect provides five levels, in most cases you would probably need only two or three levels.

Creating a table of contents requires four steps:

1. Mark each heading that you want in the table.

2. Move the cursor to where you want the table to go in the document.

3. Define the style for the table.

4. Tell WordPerfect to generate the table.

1. *Marking Table of Contents Entries.* The first step in creating a table of contents is to move the cursor to each entry in the document that will be in the table and mark it. To mark a heading, you highlight it with the Block key and then press the *Mark Text* key ([Alt]-[F5]). The following menu will then appear in the status line:

Mark for: 1 ToC; 2 List; 3 Index; 4 ToA: 0

You type 1 to select ToC (Table of Contents). This prompt will then appear in the status line:

ToC level:

WordPerfect is asking you to enter the level number for the heading. You can choose among the five levels (1–5). After you type a number, you can move the cursor to the next heading that you want to mark.

For example, say that on page 3 of your document you have the following major-level heading that you want in your table of contents:

"FIVE RULES FOR A HAPPY MARRIAGE." To mark it, you would highlight it with the Block key (Alt-F4) and then press the Mark Text key (Alt-F5). You select the first option (ToC) and WordPerfect asks you what level the marked text should be. Since "FIVE RULES FOR A HAPPY MARRIAGE" is a first-level heading, you type "1" and move the cursor to the next heading that you want to mark. Later, when you generate the table, this heading will appear in the table with a leader and the page number in front of it.

You can mark headings as you type your document, or you can wait until you complete the document. Either way, we recommend that you have a good idea of what level each heading will be before you mark it. Otherwise, you may end up deleting and re-entering Mark Text codes several times before the table of contents is to your liking.

2. *Moving the Cursor to Where the Table Will Go.* After you have marked all the headings that you want in the table, move the cursor to the beginning of the document and press the Hard Page key Ctrl-Enter to create a new first page. If you like, center and type the main title, "CONTENTS."

You are now ready to define the style of the table.

3. *Defining the Table's Style.* Move the cursor to where the table will start on the page and press Mark Text (Alt-F5). The following menu will appear:

```
1 Auto Ref; 2 Subdoc; 3 Index; 4 ToA Short Form; 5
Define; 6 Generate
```

To define the *style* of the table, choose the Define option. The Mark Text: Define menu shown in Figure 9.1 will appear. At this menu, you

```
Mark Text: Define

    1 - Define Table of Contents

    2 - Define List

    3 - Define Index

    4 - Define Table of Authorities

    5 - Edit Table of Authorities Full Form




Selection: 0
```

FIGURE 9.1

The mark text definition screen lets you define several different tables. Choose option 1 to make a table of contents.

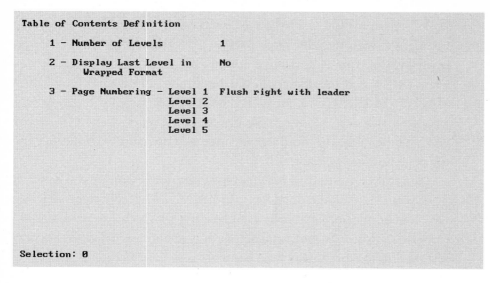

FIGURE 9.2

This menu let you choose the number of levels and page-numbering style for your table of contents.

select the option to define a table of contents. The Table of Contents Definition menu shown in Figure 9.2 appears.

Here you select the number of levels that you want in the table of contents and the page-numbering style for each level. Unless you want a different numbering style, we recommend the style default, which is page numbers flush right with leader for each level.

After you define a style, WordPerfect inserts a table of contents definition code into the document (Def Mark:ToC,n:5,5,5). You are now ready to generate the table.

4. *Generating the Table.* When you have finished defining the table, you *generate* the list by pressing the Mark Text (Alt - F5) key. WordPerfect will automatically create the table with entries, leaders, and page numbers for you, starting at the point where the definition code appears in the document.

You create an index in almost the same way that you create a table of contents.

Creating a Document Index with a Concordance File

An index is similar to tables of contents; it lists the page numbers on which items occur in a document. However, it is easier to create than a table of contents because you do not need to mark each entry that you want to appear in the list as you did with the table of contents. Instead, you can use a *concordance file* that lists each of the entries you want WordPerfect to index.

For example, if you have a ten-page document called REPORT that you want to index, and you also have a second file called CONCORD that contains the following list:

> Green eggs
> Ham
> Black hats
> Stray cats

WordPerfect can search REPORT for every occurrence of the items in CONCORD and then build your index.

Creating an index requires four steps:

1. Make a concordance file.
2. Move the cursor to where you want the index to go in the document.
3. Define the style for the index.
4. Tell WordPerfect to generate the index.

1. *Making a Concordance File.* To create a concordance file, you simply create a file that lists the entries you want in your index. Each entry must be followed by a Hard Return code ([HRt]).

   In this chapter, you will create a concordance file by scrolling through the document that you want to index and each time you locate an index item, use the Switch key ([Shift]-[F3]) to open Document 2 and type the indexed term. When you have finished, you will save the list in Document 2 as CONCORD.

   To speed the indexing process, we recommend that you sort the concordance file before you use it.

2. *Moving the Cursor to Where the Index Will Go.* After you have created the concordance file, move the cursor to the end of the document and press the Hard Page key ([Ctrl]-[Enter]) to create a new last page. If you like, center and type the main title, INDEX.

   You are now ready to define the style of the index.

3. *Defining the Index Style.* You define the *index style* in almost the same way that you defined a table of contents style. First, move the cursor to where the table will start on the page and press Mark Text ([Alt]-[F5]). The Mark Text menu appears on the status line. After you select Define (5) and Define Index (3) (shown in Figure 9.1), the following prompt will appear on the status line:

   Concordance Filename (Enter = none).

   WordPerfect wants you to type the name of the concordance file. After you enter a file, the index definition screen appears, as shown in Figure 9.3. Unless you want a different numbering style, we recommend

```
Index Definition

    1 - No Page Numbers

    2 - Page Numbers Follow Entries

    3 - (Page Numbers) Follow Entries

    4 - Flush Right Page Numbers

    5 - Flush Right Page Numbers with Leaders
```

```
Selection: 5
```

FIGURE 9.3

The index definition screen lets you choose the numbering style for the index.

the style default, which is page numbers flush right with leader for each item.

After you define a style, WordPerfect inserts an index code into the document (Def Mark:Index,5).

4. *Generating the Table.* When you have finished defining the index, you then generate the list by pressing the Mark Text (Alt-F5) key. WordPerfect can automatically locate every page where an item is located and build an index for you, as follows:

```
Green eggs  . . . . . . . . . . .  1, 2, 4, 7, 10

Ham . . . . . . . . . . . . . . . . . . . . . . 1

Black hats  . . . . . . . . . . . .  2, 3, 5, 7

Stray cats  . . . . . . . . . . . . . . . . . . 2
```

Tutorial

Ellen Nasus has completed a proposal document for sending to clients. She has asked you to create a table of contents and index for it.

Setting Up

To begin, put the Student Data Disk in drive B and start WordPerfect. Use the Retrieve key (Shift-F10) to bring the file B:PROPOSAL to the screen. You will start by creating a table of contents for this document.

Keyboarding

To create a table of contents, you must first mark the headings that you want in the table.

*Mark Table of Contents
First Heading*
Alt -F4 , Alt -F5 , *1, 1*

1. Move the cursor to the "1." in the title of the first heading, "1. Description of Market"

2. Highlight it by turning on the Block key (Alt -F4) and pressing the letter t twice.
   NOTE: Do not highlight the Hard Return code (HRt).

3. Press the Mark Text key (Alt -F5).
   RESULT: The following menu will appear in the status line:

   `Mark for: 1 ToC: 2 List: 3 Index: 4 ToA: 0`

4. Type **1** to select the ToC (Table of Contents) option.
   RESULT: The following prompt appears in the status line:

   `ToC level:`

5. Type **1**, since this is a first-level heading, and press Enter .

6. Move the cursor to the "2" in "2. Description of Product—Exhibits"

7. Repeat steps 2 through 5 to mark it as a first-level heading.

8. Move the cursor to the "3" in "3. Design Development"

9. Repeat steps 2 through 5 to mark it as a first-level heading.

10. Move the cursor to the "4" in "4. Stages of Development"

11. Repeat steps 2 through 5 to mark it as a first-level heading.

*Mark Second-level
Heading*
Alt -F4 , Alt -F5 , *1, 2*

To mark a second-level heading, follow these steps:

1. Move the cursor to the "A" in "A. Market Research and Company Report"
   NOTE: "A. Market Research and Company Report" is in "Section 4: Stages of Development"

2. Highlight A. Market Research and Company Report.

3. Press the Mark Text key (Alt -F5).

4. Type **1** to select the Table of Contents option.

5. Type **2** to select second-level heading, and press Enter .

6. Move the cursor to the "B" in "B. Design Development and Production"

7. Highlight **B. Design Development and Production**

8. Repeat steps 3 through 5 to mark it as a second-level heading.

9. Move the cursor to the "C" in "C. Trade Show Consulting and Follow-up Services"

10. Highlight **C. Trade Show Consulting and Follow-up Services.**

11. Repeat steps 3 through 5 to mark it as a second-level heading.

Mark Text

To complete marking the proposal for a table of contents, follow these steps:

1. Mark "5. Cost of Development and Production" as a first-level heading.
2. Mark "Stage A" on the next line as a second-level heading.
3. Mark the section "Stage B" in the line, "Stage B: $2,500 Rationale:" as a second-level heading.
4. Mark the section "Stage C" in the line, "Stage C: $2,500 Rationale:" as a second-level heading.

Now that your headings are marked, you are ready to create the table of contents page.

Create Table of Contents Page

To create the table of contents page, follow these steps:

1. Move the cursor to the top of the document by pressing `Home` `Home`-`↑`.
2. Press the Hard Page key (`Ctrl`-`Enter`) to create a new page.
3. Press the Up Arrow key (`↑`) once to move to the beginning of the new page.
4. Press the Center key (`Shift`-`F6`).
5. Press the Bold key (`F6`).
6. Type **TABLE OF CONTENTS** and press `Enter` 3 times to move the cursor down 3 lines.
    NOTE: Do not turn Bold off.
7. Press the Flush-Right command (`Alt`-`F6`).
    RESULT: The cursor jumps to the far right margin.
8. Type **Page**.
9. Press the Bold key (`F6`) again to turn it off, or the entire table of contents will be boldfaced ("bolded").
10. Press `Enter` twice to move the cursor down 2 lines.
    You are now ready to define the table of contents.

Define Table of Contents
`Alt`-`F5`, *5, 1*

To define the table of contents, follow these steps:

1. Press the Mark Text key (`Alt`-`F5`).
    RESULT: The following menu appears at the bottom of the screen:

    ```
    1 Cross-Ref; 2 Subdoc; 3 Index; 4 ToA Short Form; 5
    Define; 6 Generate: 0
    ```

```
Mark Text: Define

    1 - Define Table of Contents

    2 - Define List

    3 - Define Index

    4 - Define Table of Authorities

    5 - Edit Table of Authorities Full Form
```

```
Selection: 0
```

The mark text definition screen lets you define several different tables. Choose option 1 to make a table of contents.

2. Type **5** to select the Define option.
   RESULT: The Mark Text: Define screen appears as shown in Figure 9.4.

3. Type **1** to select the Define Table of Contents option.
   RESULT: The table of contents definition screen appears as shown in Figure 9.5.

4. Type **1** to select the number-of-levels option.

5. Type **2** to enter two levels.
   RESULT: The cursor jumps to the bottom of the screen and the defaults for levels 1 and 2 of the page-numbering options are entered.

6. Press [Enter] to accept the defaults.
   RESULT: You are returned to the edit screen.

```
Table of Contents Definition

    1 - Number of Levels          1

    2 - Display Last Level in     No
        Wrapped Format

    3 - Page Numbering - Level 1  Flush right with leader
                         Level 2
                         Level 3
                         Level 4
                         Level 5
```

```
Selection: 0
```

FIGURE 9.5

This menu lets you choose the number of levels and page-numbering style for your table of contents.

```
Mark Text: Generate

    1 - Remove Redline Markings and Strikeout Text from Document

    2 - Compare Screen and Disk Documents and Add Redline and Strikeout

    3 - Expand Master Document

    4 - Condense Master Document

    5 - Generate Tables, Indexes, Cross-References, etc.













Selection: 0
```

FIGURE 9.6

After you have defined your table of contents and indexes, you use the fifth option of the Mark Text: Generate screen to tell WordPerfect to create them.

You are now ready to generate the table.

Generate Table of Contents
Alt - F5 , *6, 5, Y*

To generate a table of contents, follow these steps:

1. Press the Mark Text key (Alt - F5).
2. Type **6** to select the Generate option.
    RESULT: The Mark Text: Generate screen appears as shown in Figure 9.6.
3. Type **5** to generate tables.
    RESULT: The following prompt appears on the screen:

    Existing tables, lists, and indexes will be replaced. Continue? Yes (No)

    NOTE: WordPerfect is asking if you are sure you want to generate the table. If you have already used this feature to generate other tables, WordPerfect will renumber those tables as well when it numbers your table of contents.
4. Type **Y** to generate the table of contents.
    RESULT: WordPerfect pauses for a moment. The following prompt appears:

    Generation in progress. Pass: n, Page n

    When it completes the task, a table of contents appears.
    If the leaders (the row of dots) start at the left margin beneath an item as shown in Figure 9.7, you accidentally highlighted the Hard Return code (HRt) when you marked that particular line. Don't attempt to edit the table of contents. To fix the problem, follow these steps:

1. Find that problem line in the document.

FIGURE 9.7

```
                    Contents

                                                     Page
     1. Description of Market
        . . . . . . . . . . . . . . . . . . . . . . . . . 2
     2. Description of Product—Exhibits
        . . . . . . . . . . . . . . . . . . . . . . . . . 3
     3. Design Development
        . . . . . . . . . . . . . . . . . . . . . . . . . 4
```

2. Delete the hidden Mark code.

3. Re-mark the problem line *without* highlighting the Hard Return.

4. Generate the table again.

Saving

Save the file as B:PROP9 using the Save key ([F10]). Do *not* clear the screen. You will now create an index.

Make a Concordance File

[Shift]-[F3]

To create an index, you must first make a concordance file. To create a concordance, follow these steps:

1. Press the Switch key ([Shift]-[F3]).

   RESULT: Document 2 screen appears and the words "Doc 2" appear on the status line.

2. Type the following list:

```
Built-in case
Cost of development and production
DEC
Description of market
Description of product
Display stages
Designers
Follow-up services
Hospitality suite
IBM
Market research and company report
Mishandled exhibits
Panel wall
Portable pop-up frames
Prime computer
Production of exhibit
Qualified sales prospects
Sales goal
Sales scenario
Specific objectives
Stage A
Stage B
Stage C
```

```
Stages of development
Technicians
```

Be sure to press [Enter] after each entry.

Saving

Save the file as B:CONCORD. Make a Document Summary that is meaningful to you. Now that you have created a concordance, you are ready to create the index page.

Create Index Page

To create the index page, follow these steps:

1. Press the Switch key ([Shift]-[F3]) to return to B:PROP9.
2. Move the cursor to the end of the proposal by pressing [Home] [Home]-[↓].
3. Press the Hard Page key ([Ctrl]-[Enter]) to create a new page.
4. Press the Center key ([Shift]-[F6]).
5. Press the Bold key ([F6]).
6. Type **INDEX** and press [Enter] three times to move the cursor down 3 lines.
   NOTE: Do not turn Bold off.
7. Press the Flush-Right command ([Alt]-[F6]).
   RESULT: The cursor jumps to the far right margin.
8. Type **Page**.
9. Press the Bold key ([F6]) again to turn it off, or the entire index will be boldfaced.
10. Press [Enter] twice to move the cursor down 2 lines.
    You are now ready to define the index.

Define the Index
[Alt]-[F5], *5, 3*

To define the index, follow these steps:

1. Press the Mark Text key ([Alt]-[F5]).
2. Type **5** to select the Define option.
3. Type **3** to select the Define Index option.
   RESULT: The following prompt appears on the screen.

   Concordance Filename (Enter = none):

4. Type **B:CONCORD** and press [Enter].
   RESULT: The index definition screen appears as shown in Figure 9.8.
5. Type **5** to select leaders with right flush page numbers.
   RESULT: The edit screen appears. You can now generate the index.

```
Index Definition

    1 - No Page Numbers

    2 - Page Numbers Follow Entries

    3 - (Page Numbers) Follow Entries

    4 - Flush Right Page Numbers

    5 - Flush Right Page Numbers with Leaders




Selection: 5
```

FIGURE 9.8
The index definition screen lets you choose the numbering style for the index.

Generate Index
Alt - F5 , *6, 5, Y*

To generate an index, follow these steps:

1. Press the Mark Text key (Alt - F5).

2. Type **6** to select the Generate option.

3. Type **5** to generate tables.
   RESULT: The following prompt appears on the screen:

   Existing tables, lists, and indexes will be replaced. Continue? (Y/N): Yes

   NOTE: Because you have already used this feature to generate the table of contents, WordPerfect is asking if you want to renumber the table of contents when you generate the index.

4. Type **Y** to generate the index and renumber the table of contents.
   RESULT: WordPerfect pauses for a moment. When it completes the task, an index appears on the screen.

Saving
Save the file as B:PROP9 using the Save key (F10).

Printing
Print the table of contents page by putting the cursor on the page and selecting the page option of the Print key (Shift - F7). Print the index page in the same way.

Exiting
If you would like to continue working, clear the screen using the Exit key (F7) and Type **N N**. Otherwise, exit WordPerfect by using the Exit key (F7) and Type **N Y**.

Summary

You created a table of contents by marking each heading that would appear in the table. To mark headings, you first decided what level they were, highlighted them with the Block key (⟦Alt⟧-⟦F4⟧), and then pressed the Mark Text key (⟦Alt⟧-⟦F5⟧). You selected the first option to mark a table of contents and then typed the level number for the heading. You repeated this process for every heading that would appear in the table.

You then created a table of contents page and defined the table by choosing the Define option under the Mark Text key (⟦Alt⟧-⟦F5⟧). After defining the table, you created it by using the Generate option under Mark Text. To create an index, you first created a concordance file that contained all the files you wanted to index. You then made an index page at the end of the document and defined the index using the Define option of the Mark Text key (⟦Alt⟧-⟦F5⟧). Finally, you generated the index by choosing the Generate option under Mark Text.

Chapter Review

Key Terms

Concordance file	Index style
Dot leader	Mark Text key
Generate index	Table of contents level
Generate a table of contents	Table of contents
Index	Table of contents style

Review Questions

1. How many levels can you have in a table of contents?
2. How does WordPerfect show the difference between levels in a table of contents?
3. True or False: You can mark headings either as you type them or after you complete the document.
4. Briefly discuss one advantage and one disadvantage to marking table of contents headings as you type. Discuss one advantage and one disadvantage to marking headings after you complete a document.
5. True or False: You generate a table of contents with the same keystrokes that you generate an index.
6. Briefly describe what a concordance file is and what it does.
7. Briefly describe what a dot leader is.

Applications

Please complete the following exercises.

1. Retrieve the file named SENSES on the Student Data Disk, and follow these instructions:

   a. Create a table of contents for this file using the Mark Text key. The sections called "Sight," "Sound," "Touch," "Smell," and "Taste" should be first-level headers. The three subsections, "Fluorescent," "Incandescent," and "Natural light" are second-level headers.

   b. Print the table of contents.

   c. Save the file as DRILL9-1.

2. Retrieve the file called SENSES on the Student Data Disk, and follow these instructions:

   a. Create a concordance for this document using the following terms:

   ```
   Metropol
   Sight
   Sound
   Touch
   Smell
   Taste
   Lighting
   Fluorescent light
   Incandescent light
   Natural light
   Organ music
   Carnival music
   Magnifying glass
   Pine
   New car smell
   Orange juice
   ```

   b. Sort the concordance and use it to create an index at the end of the document.

   c. Print the index.

   d. Save the file as B:DRILL9-2.

3. Retrieve the file named RESEARCH on the Student Data Disk, and follow these instructions:

   a. Create a table of contents page for this file and generate a table of contents. The sections called "Introduction," "Findings," "Preliminary Recommendation," "Recommended Strategy," and "Reading List" should be first-level headers. The subsections "Recommendation 1," "Recommendation 2," "Strategy 1," "Strategy 2," and "Strategy 3" are second-level headers.

    b. Print the table of contents.

    c. Save the file as B:DRILL9-3.

4. Retrieve the file called RESEARCH on the Student Data Disk, and follow these instructions:

    a. Create a concordance for this document using the following terms:

```
Introduction Findings
Preliminary Recommendation
Recommended Strategy
Reading List
Recommendation 1
Recommendation 2
Strategy 1
Strategy 2
Strategy 3
National Trade Shows
Regional Trade Shows
Specific Sales Objectives
Main Audience
Product Demonstration
Games and Raffles
Cotterell, P.
Campbell, R.
Francisco, R.
```

    b. Sort the concordance, and use it to create an index at the end of the document.

    c. Print the index.

    d. Save the file as B:DRILL9-4.

5. Retrieve the file named BUSPLAN on the Student Data Disk, and follow these instructions:

    a. Create a table of contents page for this file and generate a table of contents. First-level headers are:

```
Purpose of the BBS
Implementation
Benefits and Considerations
Administering the Bulletin Board
Marketing and Training
Future Services
Conclusion
Appendix A
Appendix B
```

Second-level headers should be every underlined section title in the document.

    b. Print the table of contents.

    c. Save the file as B:DRILL9-5.

6. Retrieve the file called BUSPLAN on the Student Data Disk, and follow these instructions:

a. Create a concordance for this document using the following terms:

```
Purpose of the BBS
Implementation benefits and considerations
Administering the bulletin board
Marketing and training
Future services
Conclusion
Appendix A
Main menu
CLIST
ISPF
Dialogue manager
PROFS version
TSO version
Administrative tiers
Area editors
Supervisors
BBS editor
On-line help
Appendix B
Article themes
Coordinating writers
```

b. Sort the concordance, and use it to create an index at the end of the document.

c. Print the index.

d. Save the file as B:DRILL9-6.

Advanced Skills

WordPerfect provides six *page-numbering styles* for your table of contents and five for your index. You can have the following five styles for both table of contents and index:

1. No page numbers
2. Page numbers following entries
3. Page numbers in parentheses following entries
4. Flush-right page numbers
5. Flush-right page numbers with leaders

Let's look at each of these more closely.

1. *No Page Numbers.* Using the *No Page Numbers* option, the table of contents you created in this chapter would look like this:

CONTENTS

```
1.   Description of Market
2.   Description of Product—Exhibits
3.   Design Development
```

```
4.  Stages of Development
    A.  Market Research and Company Report
    B.  Design Development and Production
    C.  Trade Show Consulting and Follow-up Services
5.  Cost of Development and Production
    Stage A
    Stage B
    Stage C
```

2. *Page Numbers Following Entries.* Using the *Page Numbers Following Entries* option, the table of contents you created in this chapter would look like this:

CONTENTS

```
1.  Description of Market  2
2.  Description of Product—Exhibits  3
3.  Design Development  4
4.  Stages of Development  4
    A.  Market Research and Company Report  4
    B.  Design Development and Production  4
    C.  Trade Show Consulting and Follow-up
        Services  4
5.  Cost of Development and Production  4
    Stage A 4
    Stage B 5
    Stage C 5
```

3. *Page Numbers in Parentheses Following Entries.* Using the *Page Numbers in Parentheses Following Entries* option, the table of contents you created in this chapter would look like this:

CONTENTS

```
1.  Description of Market (2)
2.  Description of Product—Exhibits (3)
3.  Design Development (4)
4.  Stages of Development (4)
    A.  Market Research and Company Report (4)
    B.  Design Development and Production (4)
    C.  Trade Show Consulting and Follow-up
        Services (4)
5.  Cost of Development and Production (4)
    Stage A (4)
    Stage B (5)
    Stage C (5)
```

4. *Flush-Right Page Numbers.* Using the *Flush-Right Page Numbers* option, the table of contents you created in this chapter would look like this:

CONTENTS

```
1.  Description of Market                      2
2.  Description of Product—Exhibits            3
```

```
3.    Design Development                        4
4.    Stages of Development                     4
      A.   Market Research and Company Report   4
      B.   Design Development and Production    4
      C.   Trade Show Consulting and Follow-up
           Services                             4
5.    Cost of Development and Production        4
      Stage A                                   4
      Stage B                                   5
      Stage C                                   5
```

5. *Flush-Right Page Numbers with Leaders.* The *Flush-Right Page Numbers with Leaders* option is the most popular and the one you used to create the table of contents in this chapter. It places the page number at the right margin preceded by a row of dots called *leaders,* which guide the eye across the page.

You can also have a wrapped format for the last entry level of your table of contents. Wrapped format means that entries in the last level of your table will no longer occupy a line of their own, but will line up next to each other, separated only by a semicolon, as shown below:

CONTENTS

```
1.    Description of Market  . . . . . . . . . .  2

2.    Description of Product—Exhibits  . . . . .  3

3.    Design Development . . . . . . . . . . . .  4

4.    Stages of Development  . . . . . . . . . .  4
      A.  Market Research and Company Report (4);
      B. Design Development and Production (4); C.
      Trade Show Consulting and Follow-up Services (4)

5.    Cost of Development and Production   . . .  4
      Stage A (4); Stage B (5); Stage C (5)
```

Selecting a Page-Numbering Style

Choosing a page-numbering style for your table of contents or index is easy. You simply enter the option number for the style you want while at the definition screen for the table of contents or index.

However, if you want to change a page-numbering style for a table or index that already exists, you must first be aware of how WordPerfect inserts hidden codes in your document when it creates an index or table of contents.

Changing a Page-Numbering Style

When WordPerfect generates a table of contents or index, it sets them off from the rest of a document by putting a *Definition Mark* (Def Mark) code at the beginning of the table of index and an *End Mark* (End Mark) code at the end. If you want to change the page numbering style, you need to delete the original Def Mark code and define a new table with the new page numbering style. If you leave the old Def Mark code in the document, WordPerfect will make two lists!

To change a page-numbering style, you need to follow these steps:

1. Find and delete the original Def Mark code.
2. Define the table again, choosing the page-numbering option you prefer.

With a little practice, you can make tables of contents and indexes that turn your files into professional documents.

Advanced Key Terms

Definition mark
End mark
Flush-Right Page Numbers
with Leaders option
Flush-Right Page Numbers
   option
Index-numbering style

No Page Number option
Page Numbers Following
   Entries option
Table of contents numbering
   style
Wrapped format

Advanced Review Questions

1. How many page-numbering styles are available for an index? For a table of contents?
2. Below are six numbering styles for a table of contents. Identify each style.

<u>Style 1</u>

```
4.    Stages of Development 4
      A. Market Research and Company Report 4
      B. Design Development and Production 4
      C. Trade Show Consulting and Follow-up
         Services 4
```

<u>Style 2</u>

```
4.    Stages of Development
      A. Market Research and Company Report
      B. Design Development and Production
      C. Trade Show Consulting and Follow-up Services
```

<u>Style 3</u>

```
    4.  Stages of Development                        4
        A. Market Research and Company Report        4
        B. Design Development and Production         4
        C. Trade Show Consulting and Follow-up
           Services                                  4
```

Style 4

```
4.      Stages of Development . . . . . . . . . . 4
        A. Market Research and Company Report (4); B.
        Design Development and Production (4); C. Trade
        Show Consulting and Follow-up Services (4)
```

Style 5

```
   4.   Stages of Development  . . . . . . . . . 4
        A. Market Research and Company Report   . . 4
        B. Design Development and Production   . . . 4
        C. Trade Show Consulting and Follow-up
           Services . . . . . . . . . . . . . . . 4
```

Style 6

```
4.      Stages of Development (4)
        A. Market Research and Company Report (4)
        B. Design Development and Production (4)
        C. Trade Show Consulting and Follow-up
           Services (4)
```

3. List and briefly describe in two or three sentences how you can redefine an existing page-numbering style.

4. What happens if you generate a document with two Def Mark codes in it?

Advanced Applications

1. Retrieve the file called B:DRILL9-6 that you created in Question 6 of the office applications section of this chapter and follow these instructions:
   a. Change the numbering style to flush-right page numbers. Print the index and save it as B:DRILL97A.
   b. Change the numbering style to page numbers following entries. Print the index and save it as B:DRILL97B.
   c. Change the numbering style to page numbers in parentheses following entries. Print the index and save it as B:DRILL97C.

2. Retrieve the file called B:DRILL9-5 that you created in Question 5 of the office applications section of this chapter and follow these instructions:
   a. Change the numbering style to wrapped format. Print the table of contents and save it as B:DRILL98A.
   b. Change the numbering style to page numbers following entries. Print the index and save it as B:DRILL98B.

c.   Change the numbering style to flush-right page numbers.
Print the index and save it as DRILL98C.

On Your Own   Make a document that contains all your completed exercises that you saved on the Student Data Disk. Create a table of contents for the file and an index.

A P P E N D I X

A

Using Pull-Down Menus and the Mouse

Overview

To help you use WordPerfect's many features, version 5.1 provides a comprehensive series of pull-down menus containing the same 40 commands as those on the template. These pull-down menus appear across the top of the screen as shown in Figure A.1 and are organized in a new way.

Understanding the Pull-Down Menu Structure

The pull-down menu displays nine major categories of tasks for using WordPerfect:

    File Edit Search Layout Mark Tools Font Graphics
    Help

File Edit Search Layout Mark Tools Font Graphics Help

The nine pull-down menus appear at the top of the screen when you press Alt *-=.*

FIGURE A.2   *The pull-down menu structure organizes WordPerfect's command menus under nine categories.*

PULL-DOWN MENU SYSTEM STRUCTURE

FILE	EDIT	SEARCH	LAYOUT	MARK	TOOLS	FONT	GRAPHICS	HELP
Retrieve	Move Cut	Forward	Line	Index	Spell	Base Font	Figure	Index
Save	Copy	Backward	Page	Table of Cont	Thesaurus	Normal	Table Box	Template
Text In	Paste	Next	Document	List	Macro	Appearance	Text Box	
Text Out	Append	Previous	Other	Cross-Refrnce	Date Text	Superscript	User Box	
Password	Delete	Replace	Columns	Table of Auth.	Date Code	Subscript	Equation	
List Files	Undelete	Extended	Tables	Define	Date Format	Fine	Line	
Summary	Block	Goto	Math	Generate	Outline	Small		
Print	Select		Footnote	Master Docs	Para Number	Large		
Setup	Comment		Endnote	Subdocument	Define	Very Large		
Goto DOS	Convert Case		Justify	Doc Compare	Merge Codes	Extra Large		
Exit	Protect Block		Align		Merge	Print Color		
	Switch Doc		Styles		Sort	Characters		
	Window				Line Draw			
	Reveal Codes							

Figure A.2 displays the possible commands under each option. Here we will look at each of these categories a little more closely.

Commands in the File Menu

By combining the Retrieve, Save, Exit, List Files, Print, Shell, and Text In-Out commands, the File menu provides all the options needed to handle entire disk files. You can save your document, retrieve a document, or convert a file to and from DOS Text format. You can also list files in a directory, print the contents of files, or change WordPerfect's Setup defaults.

Commands in the Edit Menu

The Edit menu lets you move, copy, and delete text. You can also use it to block sentences, paragraphs, or pages.

Commands in the Search Menu

Like the Search command, the Search menu allows you to search forward or backward through a document for a specific word or phrase.

Commands in the Layout Menu

The Layout menu provides all the format options for the layout of text in lines, pages, and the entire document, such as for setting margins or tabs, right-justifying the document, and so on.

Commands in the Mark Menu

The Mark menu allows you to create advanced document management tools such as indexes, tables of contents, and lists of items in a document.

Commands in the Tools Menu

The Tools menu presents special word processing features, such as line draw, spell-checking, and thesaurus.

Commands in the Font Menu

The Font menu allows you to control the size, appearance, and typestyle of text in a document.

Commands in the Graphics Menu

The Graphics menu enables you to insert graphic images in a document.

Commands in the Help Menu

The Help menu provides access to screens displaying information about the program.

When you start WordPerfect, the edit screen is blank, except for the information in the status line in the lower-right corner. You can activate the pull-down menu system in two ways: (1) with the keyboard, or (2) with the mouse. We will first look at how to activate and use the pull-down menus with the keyboard.

Using the Pull-Down Menu System with a Keyboard

Activate the pull-down menu system by pressing [Alt]-= (hold the [Alt] key and the equals sign (=) at the same time). After pressing [Alt]-=, the main menu appears on the top line of the edit screen:

```
File Edit Search Layout Mark Tools Font Graphics
Help
```

You can select a pull-down menu command in two ways: by typing the command letter or highlighting it and pressing [Enter].

Typing a Command

To select a command, press any of the boldfaced letters. Pressing a boldfaced letter will "pull down" the corresponding menu. For example, pressing **F** pulls down the File menu as shown in Figure A.3.

Highlighting a Command

You can also press the [→] or [←] keys to move the highlight bar onto a complete menu name, and then press [Enter] to select a menu.

As you can see in Figure A.3, each menu consists of a series of choices. You can select any option by either typing the boldfaced letter, or using the [↑], [↓], [←], and [→] keys to highlight a specific choice and pressing [Enter]. For example, if you type the P option shown in Figure A.3, the WordPerfect Print menu appears.

Do you notice that beside the Setup option in Figure A.3 there is a solid triangle (➤)? The triangle (➤) means that the item beside it contains a submenu. By selecting Setup, a second-level menu appears as shown in Figure A.4.

In essence, by providing a series of main and submenus, the pull-down menu system provides a fast, visual way to remember and use all of WordPerfect's command screens without having to use the Control, Shift, Alt, and Function key combinations.

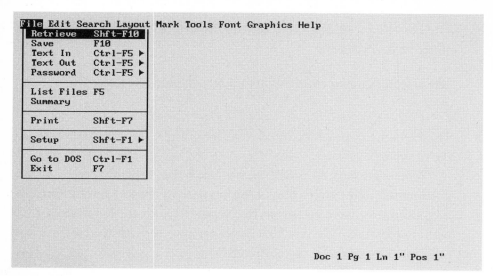

FIGURE A.3

Each pull-down menu consists of a series of choices.

Using the Pull-Down Menu System with a Mouse

When a mouse is installed, a solid rectangular pointer (↗) appears on the edit screen and moves as you move the mouse. Activate the pull-down menu system by pressing the right button. After pressing the right button, the main pull-down menu appears on the top line of the edit screen.

To select a menu option, move the mouse pointer (↗) over a choice and press the left button. That is all there is to it. If your mouse has three buttons, it works the same way: press the right button to activate the pull-down menu and press the left button to make a menu choice. The middle button will cancel any command you have made.

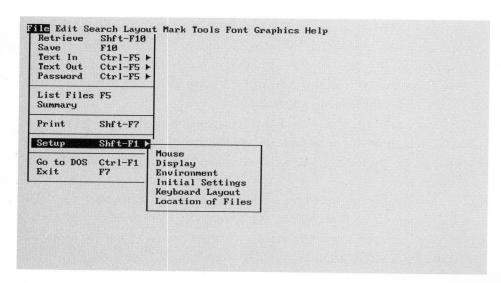

FIGURE A.4

By selecting an option with a triangle (▶) beside it, a second-level menu appears.

By pressing the left button, you can use the mouse to select commands that appear in three areas:

1. The pull-down menu system.

2. The status line.

3. Any menu screen.

   You can also use the mouse to block text.

Highlighting Text with a Mouse

To block text with the mouse, follow these steps:

1. Move the mouse pointer to the beginning of the text to be blocked.

2. Press the left button and hold it down.

3. Move the mouse to the end of the blocked text.

4. Release the left button.

   Your selected text will be highlighted in reverse video on the screen, and you can edit or change the format of the text in any way you like.

B

Starting WordPerfect on a Two-Floppy-Disk System

If your computer system contains two floppy disk drives (A and B) and no hard disk, you will start WordPerfect by turning on your machine and loading DOS manually. Here are the procedures for doing so:

1. Place your copy of the DOS diskette into the A drive and start your system.

2. Type the current date and press ⌷Enter⌸.

3. Type the date and press ⌷Enter⌸.
   After DOS has been loaded, the disk drive will be silent and its red lights will be off. You should then see the following symbol, called the *A prompt,* on your screen:

   A>

   You are now ready to start WordPerfect. Please be aware, though, that if you learn to start the program from drive B, it will greatly simplify the tasks of saving and retrieving your files. Here's how you do it.

1. Put the data disk in drive B.

2. Type **B:** and press ⌷Enter⌸. You should see the B prompt on the screen:

   B>

3. Remove the DOS disk.

4. Place the disk labeled WordPerfect 1 into drive A.

5. Type **A:WP** and press ⌷Enter⌸.

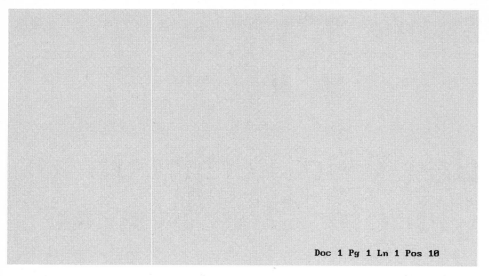

Doc 1 Pg 1 Ln 1 Pos 10

FIGURE B.I
*The WordPerfect edit
screen.*

After your computer whirs for a time, you will see this message at
the bottom of your screen:

`Insert diskette labeled WordPerfect 2 and press
any key`

6. Remove the WordPerfect 1 disk and replace it with WordPerfect 2,
and press any key. You should see the screen shown in Figure B.1
and are now ready to begin Chapter 1.

C

Starting WordPerfect on a Hard Disk

If your computer system has a hard disk, it probably has been set up so that you can load DOS just by turning on the computer.

1. Turn on your system.

   What happens next depends on how your computer system has been set up. If you see a menu on your screen, you will have to follow its instructions to start WordPerfect. If you do not see a menu, the following prompt should appear on your screen:

   C>

2. Type **WP** and then press ⎡Enter⎤.

   If you see the screen shown in Figure C.1, you have succeeded in starting WordPerfect. Congratulations! You are now ready to start Chapter 1. If you see a message like "Invalid directory" or "Bad command or filename," WordPerfect is probably located in a different directory from the one you are in—or the program is not yet on your hard disk.

3. Type **CD** and press ⎡Enter⎤.

4. Type **DIR** *. and press ⎡Enter⎤.

   RESULT: You will see a listing on your screen of all the files and directories in your root directory. See if you can find a directory that has either WP <DIR>, WP5 <DIR>, or WORD <DIR> in its name. If you do not find one, then contact your instructor, or the person who set up your system. If you do find one, then enter the appropriate command listed in the following table.

FIGURE C.I
The WordPerfect edit screen.

Doc 1 Pg 1 Ln 1 Pos 10

Look For	**Then**
A. WP <DIR>	1. Type **CD\WP** and press Enter. 2. Type **WP** and press Enter.
B. WP5 <DIR>	1. Type **CD\WP5** and press Enter. 2. Type **WP** and press Enter.
C. WORD <DIR>	1. Type **CD\WORD** and press Enter. 2. Type **WP** and press Enter.

You should see the screen shown in Figure C.1 and are now ready to begin Chapter 1.

D

WordPerfect 5.1 Command Summary

`Shift`-`F8`, 3, 5	Create a Document Summary
`Alt`-`F7`, 1, 3	Define a Column
`Alt`-`F7`, 1, 1	Turn Columns On
`Alt`-`F7`, 1, 2	Turn Columns Off
`Ctrl`-`Home`, `→`	Move cursor one column to the right
`Ctrl`-`Enter`	Create a new column
`Shift`-`F1`, 3, 8	Set Measurements Units
`F5`, `Enter`, 5, 2	Show Long Display
`Shift`-`F1`, 3, 4, 1	Make a document summary mandatory
`Shift`-`F8`, 2, 7, 1	Create a landscape format
`Alt`-`F7`, 2, 1	Define a table
`Alt`-`F7`	Edit a table
`Alt`-`F7`, `Ctrl`-`←`	Make table columns narrower
`Alt`-`F7`, `Ctrl`-`→`	Make table columns wider
`Alt`-`F8`, 3, 2, 1	Create a paired style
`Alt`-`F8`, 1	Apply a style sheet
`Alt`-`F8`, 3, 2, 2	Create an open style
`Alt`-`F8`, 4	Edit a style sheet
`Ctrl`-`F7`, 1, 1	Create footnotes
`Alt`-`F8`, 6	Save a style
`Alt`-`F8`, 7	Retrieve a style

Shift - F9 , 1	Enter Field codes
F9	End Field code
Shift - F9 , 2	End Record code
Ctrl - F9 , 1	Merge primary and secondary files
Shift - F9 , 1, ?	Skip line if field is blank
Shift - F9 , 3	Enter information from the keyboard during merge
Ctrl - F9 , 1, F9	Merge letters that contain an Input code
Shift - F8 , 2, 7, 1	Change form to envelope
Shift - F7 , 2	Print envelopes one at a time
Shift - F7 , 1	Print envelopes all at once
Ctrl - F10 , envelope Enter , desc, Enter , Ctrl - F9 , file Enter , file Enter	Create a macro that merges an envelope file
Alt - F10 ENVELOPE	Start the Envelope macro
Ctrl - F10 ENVELOPE, 2	Edit the Envelope macro
Shift - F9 , 3	Enter Input code
Alt - F7 , 2, 1	Create a table
Alt - F7 , 2, 2, 3	Justify a column
Alt - F7 , Ctrl - ↑ or →	Change column width
Alt - F7 , 5, 4	Enter a subtotal code
Alt - F7 , 5, 5	Enter a total code
Alt - F7 , 3, 7, 1	Eliminate all lines in a table
Alt - F7 , 3, 4, 2	Enter a subtotal line
Alt - F7 , 3, 4, 3	Enter a double underline
Alt - F7 , 5, 1	Perform calculations
Shift - F5 , 4, 1	Turn Outline On
Enter F4	Enter first-level section
Tab	Go one level deeper
Enter Tab F4	Enter second-level section
Enter Tab Tab F4	Enter third-level section
Shift - Tab	Back up a level
Shift - F5 , 4, 2	Turn Outline Off

[Ctrl]-[F9], 3, a, [Enter], [Enter], [F7], 1   Sort alphanumerics

[Ctrl]-[F9], 3, n, [Enter], [Enter], [F7], 1   Sort numbers

[Ctrl]-[F9], 6, 1, 1   Sort in ascending order

[Ctrl]-[F9], 6, 2, 1   Sort in descending order

[Alt]-[F4], [Alt]-[F5], 1, 1   Mark first-level heading in table of contents

[Alt]-[F4], [Alt]-[F5], 1, 2   Mark second-level heading in table of contents

[Alt]-[F5], 5, 1   Define a table of contents

[Alt]-[F5], 5, 3   Define an index

[Alt]-[F5], 6, 5, Y   Generate an index or table of contents

E

Cursor Position on a Page with 1 Inch Margins
10 Pitch Font

Line Position		Space Position	
Line — Inches	Line — Inches	Space — Inches	Space — Inches
1 — 1"	28 — 5.5"	10 — 1"	43 — 4.3"
2 — 1.17"	29 — 5.67"	11 — 1.1"	44 — 4.4"
3 — 1.33"	30 — 5.83"	12 — 1.2"	45 — 4.5"
4 — 1.5"	31 — 6"	13 — 1.3"	46 — 4.6"
5 — 1.67"	32 — 6.17"	14 — 1.4"	47 — 4.7"
6 — 1.83"	33 — 5.33"	15 — 1.5"	48 — 4.8"
7 — 2"	34 — 6.5"	16 — 1.6"	49 — 4.9"
8 — 2.17"	35 — 6.67"	17 — 1.7"	50 — 5.0"
9 — 2.33"	36 — 6.83"	18 — 1.8"	51 — 5.1"
10 — 2.5"	37 — 7"	19 — 1.9"	52 — 5.2"
11 — 2.67"	38 — 7.17"	20 — 2"	53 — 5.3"
12 — 2.83"	39 — 7.33"	21 — 2.1"	54 — 5.4"
13 — 3"	40 — 7.5"	22 — 2.2"	55 — 5.5"
14 — 3.17"	41 — 7.67"	23 — 2.3"	56 — 5.6"
15 — 3.33"	42 — 7.83"	24 — 2.4"	57 — 5.7"
16 — 3.5"	43 — 8"	25 — 2.5"	58 — 5.8"
17 — 3.67"	44 — 8.17"	26 — 2.6"	59 — 5.9"
18 — 3.83"	45 — 8.33"	27 — 2.7"	60 — 6.0"
19 — 4"	46 — 8.5"	28 — 2.8"	61 — 6.1"
20 — 4.17"	47 — 8.67"	29 — 2.9"	62 — 6.2"
21 — 4.33"	48 — 8.83"	30 — 3.0"	63 — 6.3"
22 — 4.5"	49 — 9"	31 — 3.1"	64 — 6.4"
23 — 4.67"	50 — 9.17"	32 — 3.2"	65 — 6.5"
24 — 4.83"	51 — 9.33"	33 — 3.3"	66 — 6.6"
25 — 5"	52 — 9.5"	34 — 3.4"	67 — 6.7"
26 — 5.17"	53 — 9.67"	35 — 3.5"	68 — 6.8"
27 — 5.33"	54 — 9.83"	36 — 3.6"	69 — 6.9"
		37 — 3.7"	70 — 7.0"
		38 — 3.8"	71 — 7.1"
		39 — 3.9"	72 — 7.2"
		40 — 4.0"	73 — 7.3"
		41 — 4.1"	74 — 7.4"
		42 — 4.2"	75 — 7.5"

References

Kelly,S., *Mastering WordPerfect 5.0,* Sybex, San Francisco, 1988

Laing, J., Consulting Editor, *Do-It-Yourself Graphic Design,* Swallow Publishing Limited, 1984.

Neal, Arminta, *Exhibits for the Small Museum: A Handbook,* American Association for State and Local History, Nashville, 1976.

Robbins, J., *WordPerfect Step by Step,* Sams/MacMillan Co., Carmel, IN., 1990.

Simpson, A., *Mastering WordPerfect 5.1,* Sybex, San Francisco, 1990.

Thomason, A., *Learning WordPerfect 5.0,* Houghton Mifflin Company, Boston, 1989.

Warren, Jefferson, *Exhibit Methods,* Sterling Publishing Co., New York, 1972.

Index

Site Volume Pricing Agreement

WordPerfect Corporation's site volume Pricing Agreement is designed to enable virtually any state-accredited or federally-accredited educational institution, elementary through university, to purchase WPCorp software at prices that correspond with school budgets. Any state- or federally-accredited educational institution needing more than 10 copies of a WPCorp micro computer software product qualifies as a Site.

What is a Site?

A site is considered to be any group of computers that is administrated by one person. A Site can be one classroom, one school, several schools or more. Any changes made to the Site (e.g., adding a minimum of 10 stations, purchasing manuals, updating to a new revision) must be directed through the Site Administrator.

Under the SVPA, the site pays for the initial Master diskettes or Master tape, and an additional price per station (a minimum of 10) which covers the cost of the template, Quick Reference card, and license fee for each station. The site has the option to purchase additional manuals as explained under Additional Manuals.

The Master will be accompanied by a title page stamped with a Grant of Rights. *This title page is the Site's contract with WPCorp and a complete record of the Site purchase.*

Any time changes are made to the Site, this title page needs to accompany the order sent to WPCorp.

Grant of Rights

The accredited educational institution purchasing this package from WordPerfect Corporation may make up to _____ copies of the enclosed master disks for use on institutionally owned or controlled computer workstations only. Copies of these disks may not be taken off the institutional Site for any reason by any person. The educational institution may purchase _____ sets of documentation, of which _____ have already been purchased. To update your Site stations (when future revisions are released), add more stations to your Site, or purchase additional manuals, this title page <u>MUST</u> be returned with the order.

Each time the Site places an order, a new title page with updated information will be returned to the Site.

What are the Prices?

Master Pricing

Includes manual, template, Quick Reference card (if applicable), and software.

	U.S.	Canada†
PC Master*	$75.09	$97.00

*Includes MS/DOS PC machines, Apple IIc/IIe/IIGS, Macintosh, Amiga, and Atari ST. This amount is charged for the first set of Masters and software updates.

†Canadian prices quoted in Canadian dollars. For other Canadian pricing information, call J.B. Marketing at (613) 938-3333 or the WPCorp Orders Department at (800) 321-4566.

Note: Master Prices are quoted for U.S. English versions only. Master Prices for international versions are quoted upon request.

Prices are subject to change without notice or cause.

Per-station software Pricing

Includes license fee, template, and Quick Reference card (if applicable), and software.

Purchase Order Quantity (Not Cumulative)	Price/Station WordPerfect Plan Perfect DataPerfect DrawPerfect WP Office	Price/Station WP-Mac WP-Amiga WP-Atari WP-Executive	Price/Station WP Library WP-Apple IIe/c or IIGS WP Language Modules	Price/Station Int'l Versions
	US/Canada†	US/Canada†	US/Canada†	US/Canada†
10+	$40/$52	$38/$49	$28/$36	$47/$61
20+	$29/$38	$26/$34	$18/$23	$33/$43
30+	$25/$33	$22/$28	$14/$18	$29/$37
100+	$23/$30	$21/$27	$13/$17	$28/$36
500+	$22/$28	$19/$25	$12/$15	$27/$35
1000+	$20/$26	$17/$22	$11/$14	$25/$35
5000+	$19/$25	$16/$21	$10/$13	$24/$31
10000+	$18/$23	$15/$19	$9/$11	$23/$30

†Canadian prices quoted in Canadian dollars. For other Canadian pricing information, call J.B. Marketing at (613) 938-3333 or the WPCorp Orders Department at (800) 321-4566

Prices are subject to change without notice or cause.

Existing Site Updates

A school may update its SVPA Master package for $75. The cost to update its station licenses is $5.00 per station, which includes a newly revised keyboard template and Quick Reference card (if applicable) for each updated station license. Product revisions and updates for VAX, DG, or UNIX products may be obtained by paying an annual subscription fee based upon the type of host machine being used. Contact WPCorp Information Services at (801) 225-5000 for more information.

Individual school-owned packages of WPCorp Software products may be transferred to Site at the time the product is being updated or when additional stations are ordered. Converted stations are under the same restrictions and covenants as any other SVPA station. Contact WPCorp Information Services for further details.

WordPerfect Corporation
1555 N. Technology Way
Orem, Utah 84057
(801) 222-2300
Educational Accounts (801) 222-2300